Computer System
Reliability

WILEY SERIES IN COMPUTING

Consulting Editor
Professor D. W. Barron, *Department of Mathematics, Southampton University*

Numerical Control—Mathematics and Applications
P. Bezier

Communication Networks for Computers
D. W. Davies and D. L. A. Barber

Macro Processors and Techniques for Portable Software
P. J. Brown

A Practical Guide to Algol 68
Frank G. Pagan

Programs and Machines
Richard Bird

The Codasyl Approach to Data Base Management
T. William Olle

Computer Networks and their Protocols
D. W. Davies, D. L. A. Barber, W. L. Price and C. M. Solomonides

Algorithms: Their Complexity and Efficiency
Lydia Kronsjö

Data Structures and Operating Systems
Teodor Rus

Writing Interactive Compilers and Interpreters
P. J. Brown

A Relational Data Base Management System
A. T. F. Hutt

G.P.S.S. Simulation made Simple
Thomas M. O'Donovan

Computer System Reliability
Roy Longbottom

Computer System Reliability

Roy Longbottom
Head of Large Scientific Systems Branch
Central Computer Agency

A Wiley–Interscience Publication

JOHN WILEY & SONS
Chichester · New York · Brisbane · Toronto

British Library Cataloguing in Publication Data:

Longbottom, Roy
  Computer system reliability.—(Wiley series in computing).
  1. Computers—Reliability
  I. Title
  001.6′4   QA76.5   79-40649

  ISBN 0 471 27634 0

Typeset by Preface Limited, Salisbury, Wiltshire
Printed in Great Britain by Page Bros (Norwich) Ltd., Norwich

Contents

Acknowledgements   **xix**

Introduction   **xxi**

Chapter 1   Failures   **1**
  Introduction   1
    The bathtub curve   1
  Theoretical reliability prediction   2
    Processor modules   2
    Overall processor   2
    Peripherals and system   5
    Software   5
    Problems in defining failures   5
  Failures seen by the user   7
    Failure pattern   7
  Probability of failure   9
    Exponential distribution   9
    Poisson distribution   10

Chapter 2   Reliability variations with time   **13**
  Reliability stabilization   13
    Early failures   13
    Population of processors   16
    First production models   17
    Commissioning   19
    Disturbance failures   20
  Wear out failures and lifetime expectancy   20
    General electronics   20
    Computers   21
    Spares   22
    Peripherals   23
    Maintenance support   23

Maintenance costs 24
Enhancements and change of workload 24
Accommodation 25

Chapter 3   Quality considerations **26**
Design 26
Procedure 26
Resulting reliability 27
Quality of design 27
Utilization effects 28
New technology 30
Modifications 30
Large processor 32
Mini computer 33
Best case 34
Quality assurance 35
Organization 35
Design qualification 35
Component selection 37
Goods inwards quality control 38
Module testing 39
Unit testing 39
System testing 40
Packaging and delivery 41
Feedback and fault analysis 41
Neglected areas 42

Chapter 4   Environmental aspects **44**
Air conditioning 44
Effects of environment 44
Room conditions for medium/large systems 45
Room conditions for small and mini systems 46
Design conditions 46
Design specifications for medium/large processors 47
Design specifications for small computers, mini and micro
processors 47
Design specifications for large system peripherals 52
Design specifications for mini and micro computer peripherals 53
Heat dissipation and space requirements 56
Processors 56
Reliability and heat dissipation 58
Peripheral controllers and main stores 59
Mainframe peripherals 60
Overall mainframe systems 60
Small and mini computer system heat dissipation and space
requirements 60

Microprocessor system heat dissipation and space requirements 61
The need for air conditioning 62
Maximum permissible temperature and heat dissipation 62
Minimum relative humidity 64
Maximum relative humidity 64
Dust 65
Cost of air conditioning 66
Mains power supplies 66
Specifications 66
Protection 68
Reliability effects of switching off and on 68
Electromagnetic radiation 69
Specifications 69
Earthing requirements 69
Shock and vibration 70

Chapter 5   Software reliability **71**
Comparison with hardware 71
Failure mechanisms 71
Error rate 72
Corrections 72
Early life 73
Software error classifications 73
Problems seen by users 74
Error reports submitted by users 74
Error reports accepted by the manufacturer 76
Problems identified and corrected 77
Overall error rate 78
Software quality assurance 78
Configurations 78
Content of tests 78
Duration of tests 78
Criteria of success 79
Testing organizations 79
Effectiveness of testing 79
Software service 80
Backlogs 80
Response time 80
Priorities 80
Serviceability, down time and system failures 81
Reliability variations with time 83
Average long term effects 83
Average short term effects 84
Individual system short term effects 86
Reliability variation compared with hardware 87

Variations from one supplier to another   87
Long term variations   87
Variations on computers of the same type   89
Short term variations   89
Specification of software reliability   90

Chapter 6   Fault symptoms   **92**
Consequences of failures   92
Undetected errors   92
  Processors   92
  Peripheral equipment   95
  Manufacturers' specifications   97
  Overall system   97
User recorded fault symptoms   98
  Processors   99
  Peripheral equipment   99
Software fault symptoms   102
  Controlling operating system   102
  Compilers and assembler   103

Chapter 7   Down time and maintenance time   **105**
Down time definitions   105
  Matched down time and failure classifications   107
Investigation time   107
  Small computer   107
  Mini computer   110
  Large computer   110
  Peripheral equipment   112
User observed down time   112
  Distribution   113
  Maintainability effects   113
  System down time   115
Peripheral equipment down time   116
Scheduled maintenance time   117
Supplementary maintenance time   117

Chapter 8   Serviceability and availability ratios   **119**
Definitions   119
History   121
  Early systems   121
  Multiprogramming   121
  Weighting factors   121
Variation in results   123
  Varying measurement method   123
  Range of serviceability ratios   123

Varying reliability effects   126
Varying period effects   127
Varying down time distribution effects   128
Worst case effects   129

Chapter 9   Maintainability and fault tolerance features   133
Definitions   133
Fault diagnosis   133
Test programs   134
   Diagnostic test programs   135
   Functional test programs   135
   Exerciser test programs   136
   Interaction test programs   138
   On-line test programs   139
   Timing test programs   140
   Compatibility test programs   141
Hardware testers   141
   Exercisers   141
   Maintenance processors   142
Module testers   142
Constructional and functional modularity   144
   Constructional modularity   144
   Functional modularity   144
   Large scale integration   147
Margins   148
   Voltage margins   149
   Timing margins   149
   Temperature margins   149
   Other forms of margins   149
Error detection and correction   150
   Parity checking   150
   Error correction   151
Fault recording   152
   History recording   152
   Error logs   152
   Console and display facilities   153
Redundancy and reconfiguration   153
Recoverability   155
Maintenance organization   155
   Maintenance charges   155
   Resources required   156
Effects of maintainability and fault tolerance features   157
   Measurement   157
   Short term effects   157

Chapter 10 Acceptance trials   **160**
  The need for trials   160
    Reliability trials   161
    Facilities testing and performance measurement   164
    Support services   164
  Practical acceptance trials   165
  CCA's standard procedures   166
    Demonstrations   167
    Cyclic testing   169
    Supervisor's role   171
    Records   172
    Test schedules   172
    Trials' results   172
    Advantages and disadvantages of CCA's type of trials   176
    Previous standard CCA trials   177
  GSA procedures   177

Chapter 11 Practical reliability calculations   **179**
  Electronics   179
    General   179
    Central processing units   180
    Main stores   183
    Architectural considerations   185
    Peripheral controllers   187
    Examples of relative reliability   187
    Investigation times   188
    Incidents and down time as seen by the user   189
  Peripherals   193
    Exchangeable disks   193
    Factors affecting reliability   196
    Magnetic tape units   197
    Peripheral summary   197
  Examples of predictions   200
  Software reliability predictions   204
  Examples of software and hardware predictions   208
  Quality of service from a user's point of view   209

Chapter 12 Practical reliability and serviceability calculations for
             complex systems   **211**
  Units in parallel and series   211
    Units in parallel   211
    Units in series   212
    Recovery factor   213
    Complex areas   214
  Total system calculations   215

Medium sized system	216
Serviceability and reliability over short periods	223
Spoilt work time	223
Weighting factor serviceability calculations	224
Scheduled maintenance	225
Multi processor systems	225
Message switching system	227
Multi-mini system	227
Communications subsystems	229
Line reliability	229
Modems	232
Terminals	233
Appendix 1 Exerciser test programs written in FORTRAN	**238**
FOPR00 Processor test	239
FOPR01 Processor and store test	241
FOPR02 Processor test	245
FOPR03 Processor test	247
FOPR04 Processor test	249
FODK00 Random disk test	254
FODK01 Disk test or FOMT01 Magnetic tape unit test	259
FODK02 Disk test or FOMT00 Magnetic tape unit test	268
FODK03 Disk test or FOMT02 Magnetic tape unit test	270
FOLP00 Line printer test	275
FOCP00 Card punch test	283
FOCR00 Card reader test	286
FOTP00 Paper tape punch test	291
FOTR00 Paper tape reader test	293
Appendix 2 Serviceability calculations for complex systems using a programmable calculator	**297**
Appendix 3 Estimating processor speed	**305**
Index	**307**

List of Figures

1.1 Bathtub curve
1.2 Failures occurring over a period

2.1 Early failures on one type of large processor
2.2 Early failures on a second type of large processor
2.3 Early failures on a third type of large processor
2.4 Range of early failures on large processors
2.5 Reliability stabilization of 2 different populations of processors
2.6 Reliability stabilization as fig. 2.5 but showing system failures

3.1 System failures caused by processor faults vs. CPU utilization
3.2 System failures per 1000 hours due to mainframe faults
3.3 Modifications on a medium/large mainframe
3.4 Modifications on a mini processor

4.1 Temperature and RH conditions for medium/large systems
4.2 Temperature and RH conditions for small/mini systems
4.3 Reliability vs. heat dissipation of medium/large mainframes
4.4 Times of excessive heat for computer

5.1 Software errors reported by users
5.2 Error reports received and problems identified
5.3 Accepted and resolved error reports
5.4 Correction activity on an operating system
5.5 Response times for software correction
5.6 Trend in system failures caused by software faults from first delivery of a large operating system
5.7 System failures on a population of computer systems
5.8 Apparent early failures caused by software faults
5.9 System failures caused by software faults from handover to user
5.10 Software caused system failures before and after new releases

6.1 Undetected errors on mainframes per 1000 hours
6.2 Undetected errors on mainframes per 10^{12} instructions

7.1 Investigation time on small processor A
7.2 Investigation time on small processor B
7.3 Investigation time on a mini computer C
7.4 Investigation time on a large processor D
7.5 Investigation time on a large processor E

8.1 Serviceability ratios obtained according to mean reliability and down time
8.2 Serviceability ratios, fixed down time distribution, fixed hours variable reliability
8.3 Serviceability ratio distribution over different periods
8.4 Serviceability ratio distribution, fixed reliability, fixed hours variable down time
8.5 90 per cent confidence limits of serviceability
8.6 99 per cent confidence limits of serviceability

9.1 Modularity
9.2 90 per cent confidence limits of number of incidents or investigations
9.3 99 per cent confidence limits of number of incidents or investigations

10.1 Reliability as recorded during acceptance trials
10.2 Intermittent faults as recorded during acceptance trials

11.1 Central processing unit (less store) investigation rates vs. processor speed for established populations
11.2 Main store investigation rates vs. store cycle time
11.3 Architectural considerations
11.4 Reliability predictor for processors (less store) and peripheral controllers
11.5 Reliability predictor for main stores

12.1 Serviceability of units in series
12.2 Serviceability of units in parallel
12.3 Calculations where units can be cross coupled
12.4 Unserviceability of general purpose computer systems
12.5 Fairly simple medium sized configuration
12.6 Equivalent chains for configuration in Figure 12.5
12.7 Multi-processor system
12.8 Message switching system
12.9 Multi–mini system

12.10 Remote batch terminal
12.11 Remote batch terminal, better configuration
12.12 Transaction/enquiry terminal
12.13 Time sharing terminal

List of Tables

1.1 Failure rate predictions for a mini computer
1.2 Overall failure rate and mtbf of a mini computer
1.3 Reliability predictions for complete systems
1.4 Practical reliability of a central processor
1.5 Probability of success
1.6 Number of failures per month

4.1 Heat dissipation and space requirements
4.2 Number of integrated circuits, speed and heat dissipation of medium/large mainframes less store
4.3 Mains supply specifications for medium/large systems

5.1 System failures and unserviceability on a number of computers supplied by various manufacturers
5.2 System failures and unserviceability on eight computers of the same type

6.1 Faults giving undetected errors
6.2 Recoverable, irrecoverable, detected and undetected error rates claimed by manufacturers

7.1 Down time and failure classifications
7.2 Investigation time range of various processors
7.3 Typical down time on various processors
7.4 Typical down time on various systems
7.5 Examples of scheduled/preventative maintenance for various mainframe peripherals

8.1 Serviceability ratios for a processor
8.2 Weighting factors and standard recovery times for a simple system
8.3 Serviceability ratios for a system

9.1   Characteristics of systems with good and bad maintainability
9.2   Measurement of maintainability

10.1 Duration of a reliability trial based on confidence limits of the Poisson distribution, with user's and contractor's risks
10.2 Duration of a reliability trial based on confidence limits of incident distribution with user's and contractor's risks

11.1 Reliability of exchangeable disk units
11.2 Reliability of magnetic tape units
11.3 Reliability predictor for peripheral equipment
11.4 Reliability prediction for a basic mini computer system environment to be determined
11.5 Mini vs. small mainframe comparison—good environment
11.6 Reliability predictor for controlling software
11.7 Unit availability including preventative maintenance

12.1 Calculations for a complete medium-sized computer system
12.2 Prediction of serviceability using weighting factors
12.3 Calculations for multi–mini system

Acknowledgements

The author gratefully acknowledges the assistance he has been given, in compiling the information used in this book, by his many colleagues in the Central Computer Agency, especially Ian Thomson for his work on computer system maintainability and Trevor Jones for advice on environmental aspects. Thanks are also due to those computer suppliers who freely discuss reliability and maintainability of their systems and provide detailed field reliability statistics. Acknowledgement is also given to the Civil Service Department for giving permission for this book to be published.

Figures 2.1, 2.2, 3.3, 4.1, 4.2, 4.4, 5.5, 5.10, 8.5 and 8.6 in Chapters 2, 3, 4, 5 and 8, and Tables 4.1, 4.2, 5.1 and 5.2 in Chapters 4 and 5 are Crown Copyright and have been reproduced with the permission from the Controller of HMSO.

The views expressed by the author in this book are not necessarily those of the Central Computer Agency.

Introduction

This book has been written to explain the complications of reliability assessment of computer systems and is mainly based on the author's experiences, over 18 years, in analysing reliability statistics, evaluating new computer systems, appraising maintainability techniques, specifying and supervising acceptance trials, and providing comparative assessments for projects requiring computer systems, varying from small mini computers, to the largest commercially available systems.

The book is intended to provide an explanation of and standards for all practical aspects of reliability, availability, serviceability and maintainability, to enlighten anyone interested in the design, manufacture, maintenance and use of computers; also, to a limited extent, to pinpoint areas, where further research is required, in order to understand what makes a reliable system.

The book begins by explaining the misinterpretations that can be made of the standard reliability term of mean time between failures or mtbf, and why the reliability seen by the computer user is unlikely to be the same as predicted by manufacturer, when the accepted standard reliability prediction techniques are used. The next chapter shows how reliability varies with time, particularly emphasizing differences from the theoretical bathtub reliability stabilization and wear out curve, where the 'burn-in' time may be as high as 10,000 hours and wear out mainly dependent on the availability of spares and maintenance manpower.

Chapter 3 covers quality, including design and quality control considerations, showing that the quality control should match the design, a poorer design requiring much more extensive quality control to achieve a reasonable reliability level. It is also shown that reliability of the electronics can vary considerably, according to utilization, and that, when considering a number of computers of equivalent speeds, those using *the most* components may well give the best reliability. Details of the likely frequency of design changes and the range of quality assurance and control techniques, currently being used, are given.

The next chapter is concerned with environmental aspects, discussing the effects on reliability of temperature, relative humidity, dust and mains supplies, with the range of manufactures' specifications being given for most types of equipment. The need for air conditioning is also discussed, with particular reference to mini computers. It is also shown that reliability is, perhaps, more dependent on heat dissipation than one would think.

Chapter 5 examines software reliability, showing differences from and similarities to hardware reliability. Various illustrations of software reliability characteristics are shown with particular emphasis on software errors which give rise to overall system failures. The following chapter examines hardware and software fault symptoms as observed by the user, also answering the question—how frequently do computers make undetected mistakes?

Chapter 7 gives a detailed analysis of down time characteristics and the various interpretations that can be placed on the second major reliability term, mean time to repair or mttr. The chapter illustrates that systems which are highly maintainable may have the *longest* mean down times.

The following chapter gives various methods of measuring system serviceability and availability or percentage up-time. The effects of varying down time and reliability characteristics are shown along with likely short term variations, invaluable for incorporation in a reliability sizing exercise.

Maintainability and fault tolerance features of current systems are considered in Chapter 9, including an analysis of the many forms of engineering test programs, constructional techniques, spares requirements, error detection, correction and logging facilities. It is indicated that, perhaps, resources are being wasted in providing facilities for diagnosing faults and more emphasis should be placed on reproducing faults of an intermittent or transient nature. Methods of measuring maintainability and fault tolerance are also given along with the likely short term reliability effects on user operations and engineering resource requirements.

Chapter 10 provides a detailed assessment of computer system acceptance trials, indicating the risks involved in attempting to measure reliability. The advantages and disadvantages of various forms of acceptance trials are considered, including the standard CCA procedures, which have been used in more than 1500 trials.

The last two chapters provide practical methods of predicting reliability and serviceability (or availability) of mainframe processors, mini computers, microprocessors, communications subsystems, peripherals, software and systems, including the many variables introduced in other chapters of the book. Examples are given of the range of reliability statistics obtained in practice and in the use of the suggested techniques.

The appendices give details of a wide range of programs, which can be used as the basis of effective computer system acceptance trials. A further program is given, for use on a programmable calculator, to provide a simple means of using the serviceability prediction method detailed in Chapter 12. Finally, in a number of places in the book, reliability figures are given relative to processor speed, so the last appendix gives a means of estimating the speed, where this is not known.

Because of the scope of the subject, it is unlikely that many people will wish to study every chapter in detail. A computer user or consultant may wish to study the chapters covering basic hardware and software failures, fault symptoms, availability measurement, acceptance trials and practical reliability predictions. On the other hand, an engineer involved in designing or maintaining computers may wish to concentrate on the chapters covering design quality considerations, environmental aspects, maintainability and down time characteristics.

Chapter 1

Failures

INTRODUCTION

Since computers were first invented, reliability has been one of the major considerations and, over the years, with announcements of new ultra reliable technologies, one would have expected that a user would not need to worry about this area. In practice, many users are far from happy about the reliability of their system and feel that the computer supplier has mislead them with claims of high reliability and availability. Some reasons for the continuing unreliability are fairly obvious, such as the more complex and larger systems, but one of the main reasons is that reliability is not fully understood. The first area of misunderstanding is the term failure.

The Bathtub Curve

During training engineers are taught that reliability follows the bathtub curve, as shown in Figure 1.1, indicating how the failure rate varies with time. The initial period of high failure rate is known as burn-in on the electronics or bedding-in on mechanical items and is due to manufacturing and assembly defects: this is followed by a constant failure rate during the useful life and, finally, the wear-out period when reliability rapidly deteriorates.

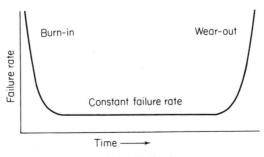

Figure 1.1   Bathtub curve

1

The bathtub curve does not completely apply to most computer equipment; the constant failure rate may not be achieved for some years, due to problems associated with the initial design not being completely correct or due to an unexpectedly long burn-in period; after this initial period, the reliability may be far from constant, with variations being caused by different utilizations or other disturbance factors; general purpose computer systems usually only have a required lifetime of 5 to 10 years, so wearout is not often a problem.

THEORETICAL RELIABILITY PREDICTION

Processor Modules

When a computer system is first designed, the manufacturer usually calculates the ultimate steady state reliability of replaceable modules, units and overall system, the calculations being used as an aid to sorting out the initial problems or for resource allocations. An example of failure rate calculations for a typical mini computer processor is shown in Table 1.1. The calculations use the component count of each module and component failure rate, which usually takes into account stress factors, according to design parameters on ambient temperature, voltage and power ratings: other factors may also be taken into account, according to the environment in which the equipment will work. More refined reliability prediction methods, such as given in the MIL Handbook 217B, may be carried out on an individual component basis, rather than total components on a module, and take into account complexity factors, such as the number of gates in an integrated circuit.

The predictions given in Table 1.1 reflect one of the primary problems governing the use to the predictions, that is, all failures shown require engineering attention for repair but all do not lead to system failure; for example, on the control panel, most of the expected failures are due to lamps, which are unlikely to cause the processor to stop.

Overall processor

The overall failure rate of the complete processor is calculated by adding the individual module failure rates, as shown in Table 1.2 for a processor with two sizes of main store. The standard reliability term meantime between failures (mtbf) is then determined as the reciprocal of the failure rate ($\times 10^6$), giving mtbfs of 9267 and 5446 hours for the two different sizes of processor.

Table 1.1 Failure rate predictions for a mini computer (failure rates in failures per million hours)

Component	Failure rate	Central processor		4K words core store		Control panel		Power supply and cabinet	
		Qty	Failure rate	Qty	Failure rate	Qty	Failure rate	Qty	Failure rate
Integrated circuits	0.1	190	19.00	70	7.00	20	2.00	10	1.0
Diodes	0.02	6	0.12	150	3.00				
Diodes	0.5							10	5.0
Transistors	0.05			60	3.00				
Transistors	0.3							9	2.7
Capacitors	0.002	120	0.24	150	0.30			15	0.03
Capacitors	0.04							3	0.12
Resistors	0.01	160	1.60	300	3.00	80	0.80	100	1.00
Resistors	0.1							2	0.20
Transformers	0.1	1	0.10	40	4.0				
Transformers	0.2							3	0.60
Solder joints	0.0001	4000	0.40	3000	0.30	400	0.04	200	0.02
Connectors	3.5	4	14.00	2	4.00				
Connectors	2.0								
Cores	0.00001			64K	0.64				
Switches	0.2					25	5.00		
Lamps	0.5					50	25.00		
Fuses	0.1							2	0.20
Circuit breaker	0.5							1	0.50
Fan	3.0							1	3.00
Total			35.46		25.24		32.84		14.37

Table 1.2 Overall failure rate and mtbf of a mini processor

| | 4K word system | | 16K word system | |
	No of units	Failure rate per million hours	No of units	Failure rate per million hours
CPU	1	35.46	1	35.46
Core store	1	25.24	4	100.96
Control panel	1	32.84	1	32.84
Power supply	1	14.37	1	14.37
Total		107.91		183.63
Mtbf hours		9267		5446

Table 1.3 Reliability predictions for complete systems

SYSTEM A

	Failures/10^6 hours
Processor with 4KW store	107.91
Typewriter controller	10.20
Typewriter	1000.00
Total	1118.11

System mtbf 894 hours

SYSTEM B

Processor with 16KW store	183.63
Extra 48KW store	302.88
Typewriter controller	10.20
Typewriter	1000.00
Disk controller	15.40
Disk	256.00
Magnetic tape controller	14.30
Magnetic tape unit	345.00
Paper tape reader controller	10.50
Paper tape reader	250.00
Line printer controller	13.20
Line printer	428.00
Extra power supply/cabinet	14.37
Total	2843.48

System mtbf 352 hours

Peripherals and System

Failure rates of the peripheral equipment and associated controllers can be calculated in the same manner as Table 1.1 and similarly, total system reliabilities can be estimated. Table 1.3 shows the predictions for two processors with various peripherals; system A represents the smallest configuration which can be used as a computer system, indicating that the overall mtbf can be expected to reduce considerably to 894 hours due to the inclusion of a typewriter; System B with additional core store, power supplies and peripherals gives a further reduction in estimated mtbf to 352 hours. These reliability predictions represent average values and it is fairly obvious that the manner of utilization and activity on the electromechanical peripherals could have some influence; for example, on the larger system, the typewriter is likely to be only used for operator/machine communications but, on the basic configuration, it may well be used for continuous input/output, leading to a much lower reliability. Reliability of the electronics can also vary according to the manner of utilization, especially where design faults have not been identified and rectified.

Software

Currently, there is no equivalent standard method of predicting software reliability, even though software problems often give rise to more concern than the hardware. However, software faults are almost entirely classified as design errors and, even for hardware, it is extremely difficult to predict meaningful failure rates for the design stabilization period.

Problems in Defining Failures

The next snag is that the reliability predictions are only as good as the basic failure rates used. For any component a multitude of failure rates can be found from various sources, for example anything from 0.01 to 0.4 per million hours for integrated circuits. The reasons for the wide variations in failure rates lie between the method of measurement and the definition—what is a failure?

It must be appreciated that, when considering processor components with such a low failure rate, many millions of device hours must be clocked up to provide the true figure; on initial manufacture of a new component, the failure rate in the field may not be available for a long time after equipment has been designed using it. So the component supplier may provide an initial estimate based on experience of components produced by the same manufacturing techniques.

A more usual method of providing the initial estimates of failure rates is for the component supplier to carry out tests of a large batch of components for a fairly long period at extremes of temperature and other design limits. Any component failing during the test will be removed from test and analysed to find out what went wrong and may not be counted as a failure if, for instance, it is found that a slight change to manufacturing processes will overcome the problem. After the test, failure rates can be estimated statistically using well proven techniques.

This method of testing a batch of components and immediately removing any which are indicated as faulty leads to the first concept of a failure; that is a faulty component can only give one failure before it is replaced.

The failure rates derived from the component batch testing can be realistic but they are dependent, firstly, on whether the component suffers from some hidden failure mode which was not revealed by the particular method of testing; secondly they assume that the components will always be used within the design specification; and thirdly, that the components will be correctly screened during quality control tests to weed out any which have been incorrectly manufactured.

For military or space type computer applications with generous budgets, allowing extra special care to be taken, the lowest component failure rates may be achieved.

On general purpose computer systems with limited budgets and necessary mass production lines, it is unlikely that the lowest failure rates will be obtained in practice. Also, the initial design is likely to be far from perfect and time not money will be available to bring the reliability within specification. (The effects of design failures are considered in Chapters 2 and 3.) So for these systems the manufacturers are likely to adopt more conservative failure rates.

The next method of assessing component or system failure rates, which has been adopted by a number of small computer manufacturers, is to run a number of systems for a year or so, again examining every failure in detail and making assumptions about changes in procedures or design to overcome the problem, and thereby producing the magic figure. Depending on assumptions made and testing techniques used, a wide variety of results can be obtained.

A few years ago a mini computer processor with about 300 integrated circuits was produced with an initial design mtbf of about 4000 hours, according to calculations based on the component count and fairly low failure rates. Later, based on a life test of a number of systems, the mtbf claims were increased to 10,000 hours. Later, when feedback was obtained from systems working in the field, it was found that, from a user's point of view, mtbfs varied between 100 and 2000 hours with an average of about 300 hours. At the same time feedback to the manufacturers indicated an average mtbf of more than 600 hours. The wide variation between different installations was found to be due to design deficiencies, and are considered later, but why the difference between the average figures seen by the users and the manufacturer?

FAILURES SEEN BY THE USER

Failure Pattern

The concept of a failure mentioned earlier was that one faulty component can only give one failure but, in practice, this is not true, as 50% or more of component faults are of an intermittent or transient nature; these faults tend not to be readily reproducible by standard test techniques and the user may not bother to call the engineer every time. This leads to a typical failure pattern as indicated in Table 1.4, where 50 faulty components can lead to 100 engineering investigations where parts are changed which are not really faulty. On top of this are 50 abortive investigations by the engineer where 'no fault found' is indicated by the test programs and 200 further incidents where the user does not call the engineer or prefers to restart and carry on working without incurring long periods of investigation time. In this case, assuming that 50% of the faults are intermittent, the 25 solid faults will give rise to 25 system failures, which must be repaired before operation can continue. On the other hand the 25 intermittents give rise to 325 incidents or 93% of system failures are due to intermittent faults.

The above indicates the reasons for different mtbf figures being provided according to the source of the information, so it is necessary to define failures more precisely; also each of these mtbfs has its own use.

Table 1.4   Practical reliability of a central processor

Class of failures	Number of failures in 10,000 hours	Mtbf hours	Proper definition of mtbf
Failures seen by the user	350	28.6	Mean time between system failures (mtbsf) or mean time between system interruptions (mtbsi)
Investigations by the engineer	150	66.7	Mean time between engineering investigations or service calls
Parts replaced or repaired in situ	100	100	Mean time between repair attempts
Parts replaced and actually found to be faulty plus genuine repairs in	50	200	Mean time between component failures or component mtbf

1. Component failures—this first concept can be used to define failures, where one faulty component gives one failure. The figures are used for predicting inherent reliability by the design authority and, when faulty components are identified, for establishing that the design reliability has been achieved; or to identify components which are not meeting the design criteria.
2. Repair attempts—for replaceable items, these failures are used to determine spares holdings and resources required for the testing and repair depot.
3. Engineering investigations or service calls—these failures are usually the ones provided by manufacturers when indicating reliability of equipment in the field; they are the ones most easily derived as the manufacturers usually have some fault reporting procedure for every investigation. The figures are used for planning maintenance manpower resources.

   The ratio Engineering investigations divided by component failures (Investigations per fault) is a useful measure of how easy it is for the engineer to reproduce and rectify faults. (Maintainability and diagnosibility are considered further in Chapter 9.) For the system shown in Table 1.4 the features are not very good, leading to 3.0 investigations per fault.
4. Incidents—to avoid confusion with the other types of failure, it is better to define those seen by the user as incidents or, where the whole computer stops, as system interruptions or system failures. (These different definitions are required to cover the consequences of a failure—see examples in Chapter 12). Another useful measure is the ratio incidents per fault, this time also reflecting fault tolerance or resilience features of a system. The incidents per fault ratio for the system shown in Table 1.4 is 7.0 which is again not too good, although figures of greater than 10.0 have been recorded. At the other extreme it is possible to achieve less than 1.0 incidents per fault where the fault tolerance features keep the system going until scheduled maintenance periods, when the faults are investigated and cleared.

   The number of incidents per fault is also dependent on the nature of the problems and user attitudes; some users opt to attempt to restart for almost every incident but others will insist that the engineer investigates every time, reducing the overall number of incidents but increasing investigation times.

With all these various types of failure, the term mean time between failures or mtbf becomes ambiguous and needs clarifying, otherwise, as indicated in Table 1.4, the mtbf of a system could be correctly given as 200 hours or 28.6 hours, where the former really indicates mean time between component failures (component mtbf) and the latter mean time between system failures seen by a user (mtbsf or mtbsi).

PROBABILITY OF FAILURE

It is not the purpose of this book to go into theoretical statistics in detail; however, it is useful to examine some of the simpler formulae used in reliability predictions and to consider their limitations when applied to general purpose computer equipment.

Exponential Distribution

It is usually assumed that complex equipment will suffer from a constant failure rate (1/mtbf or $1/m$) and the probability of success (P_S), or probability of failure free operation, for a period t is:

$$P_S = e^{-a}$$

where a is the expected failures or t/m. Conversely the probability of failure P_F is:

$$P_F = 1 - e^{-a}$$

An example of these probability calculations is indicated in Table 1.5 for equipment with a component mtbf of 1000 hours running for a period of T hours. So the probability of success of a short run compared with the mtbf is quite high, but at a run duration equal to the mtbf, the probability of success has dropped to 0.368 and at 5 times the mtbf there is not much chance that the period will be failure free.

This Exponential Distribution described above relies on the assumption that the failure rate is constant and failures random, so the equipment must be free from burn-in and design failures; also the distribution ignores the effects of intermittent faults. If it could be considered that Figure 1.2A represented random component failures over time T, then Figure 1.2B could represent the effects of intermittent faults, which tend to be bunched immediately following a component failure. If a run was started when one could be absolutely sure that no intermittent faults were present, then the Exponential Distribution could apply; but if a run was started, such as at point × in Figure 1.2B, then the chances of success are pretty remote.

Table 1.5   Probability of success (mtbf of 1000 hours)

Running time T hours	Probability of success P_s	Probability of failure P_f
100	0.905	0.095
500	0.607	0.393
1000	0.368	0.632
5000	0.007	0.993

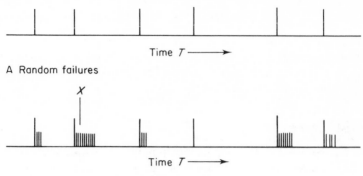

Time $T \longrightarrow$

A Random failures

Time $T \longrightarrow$

B Random failures + intermittent repeat incidents

Figure 1.2   Failures occurring over a period

The Exponential Distribution is used quite successfully in military or space type projects when calculating reliability of one-shot devices where the design and testing techniques may be adequate. On general purpose computers, because of the effects of intermittent faults and other non-constant failure mechanisms, it is not recommended that this formula is used for predicting the probability of computing payroll on a Thursday afternoon.

Poisson Distribution

On equipment which is used for long periods compared with the component mtbf, it is necessary to repair them sometimes, and the number of failures expected in a period is of more use than the probability of failure; in this case, for convenience when dealing with random events occurring in a period of time, the Poisson Distribution could be used, where the probability of no failures in time t is again e^{-a}, and full probabilities:

Probability of 0 failures $\quad e^{-a}$

Probability of 1 failure $\quad ae^{-a}$

Probability of 2 failures $\quad \dfrac{a^2}{2!} e^{-a}$

Probability of 3 failures $\quad \dfrac{a^3}{3!} e^{-a}$

Probability of n failures $\quad \dfrac{a^n}{n!} e^{-a}$

When considering the number of months or weeks with 0, 1, 2, 3 etc failures, the above are multiplied by the total number of periods T.

Table 1.6 Number of failures per month

	Class of failure	Number of months T	Number of failures	Mean failures per month a	Number of failures						
					0	1	2	3	4	5	6
a	System failures recorded by user	34	46	1.352	17	5	4	3	2	2	1
b	Predictions using Poisson distribution	34	46	1.352	8.8	11.9	8.0	3.6	1.2	0.3	0.1
c	Predictions using Poisson distribution for component failures	34	23	0.676	17.3	11.7	4.0	0.9	0.1		

The Poisson Distribution suffers from the same problems as the Exponential Distribution, in that the design must be stable and failures random, such as when assessing component failures on an established system.

An example of the Poisson Distribution is shown in Table 1.6 for a period of 34 months on an established system with an incident per fault ratio of 2.0. Table 1.6a represents the distribution of incidents seen by the user, where for 17 of the months 0 incidents were recorded and for 5 months 1 incident occurred etc. Table 1.6b indicates predictions using the Poisson Distribution with the same expected mean failures per month of 1.352: the differences between the predictions and actual results are quite clear, there being twice as many periods recorded for 0 incidents and at the other extreme the recorded figures for 4, 5 or 6 incidents in a month being in excess of the predictions. Table 1.6c represents a Poisson prediction where an average of 0.676 component failures (1.352 incidents at 2 incidents per fault) are expected per month and comparing this with the actual recorded incidents indicates the effects of intermittent faults; during the 17 months where 0 component failures are expected 0 incidents were recorded but during the other months some of the faults gave rise to more than one incident; for example of the 11.7 months with 1 fault, 5 were rectified at the first investigation but others gave 2, 3, 4, 5 or 6 incidents. (For detailed analysis of this effect see 'Analysis of computer System Reliability and Maintainability', R. Longbottom, *The Radio and Electronic Engineer*, **42**, No. 12, December 1972.)

On systems with very poor maintainability and fault tolerance facilities the differences between recorded incidents and Poisson predictions becomes even greater, such that there may be a high and equal probability of 0 and 50 incidents occurring in a period.

With all the foregoing problems in defining, predicting and measuring failures it is of little wonder that some contractors are reluctant to release reliability information and, for those who do, it would be equally amazing if the system behaved exactly as predicted. However, in order for a user to choose the best configuration from the best contractor and to be able to make contingency plans for times of trouble, it is important that he understands the sort of failure pattern expected and the effects of any maintainability, diagnosability, fault tolerance or resilience features offered. Failure patterns showing the effects of design, early and disturbance failures, on both hardware and software reliability, are given in Chapters 2, 3 and 5.

Chapter 2
Reliability Variations with Time

RELIABILITY STABILIZATION

Early Failures

When complex hardware is first constructed it is almost certain that it will not work due to wiring errors, wrong assembly or faulty components and the components themselves are likely to be faulty due to imperfect construction. Quality control checks are carried out at various stages of manufacture to weed out the faulty components and to correct the other manufacturing defects. These checks normally ensure that solid faults are corrected but certain intermittent faults may not be; besides intermittents, a number of components may have inherent weaknesses which fail within a short time, for example, following a period of temperature cycling, due to switching on and off. When the equipment is delivered, a series of tests are normally carried out during commissioning but, like those carried out in the factory, do not check every mode of utilization and almost certainly not in every possible combination and sequence with every data pattern. Hence, even after hand over to the user, early failures, as reflected in the bathtub curve in Figure 1.1, may still be apparent but the time for reliability to stabilize depends on the characteristics of the particular device.

Figure 2.1 shows the burn-in characteristics of one type of large processor, derived from over 500 faults, and shows the number of faults found after power on. The initial 5 weeks, or 800 hour period, comprised the main commissioning period, when engineering test programs were run: after this, as the software and user programs were run, the fault rate increased for a period. On the systems the reliability slowly improved to give a replacement rate of 0.2% of modules per week, after a year (of 8000 hours) but some of the improvement was due to the incorporation of newly designed modules.

Figure 2.2 shows the burn-in characteristics of another type of large processor, derived from over 100 faults repaired on a number of systems

13

14

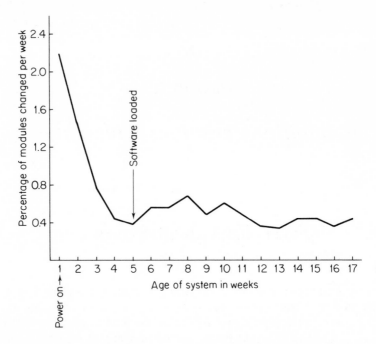

Figure 2.1   Early failures on one type of large processor showing
the percentage of modules changed each week

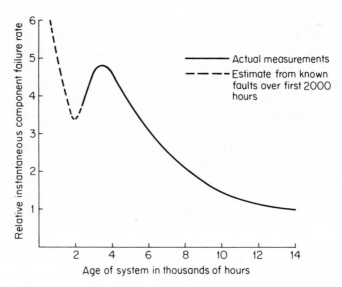

Figure 2.2   Early failures on a second type of large processor
after hand-over to the user

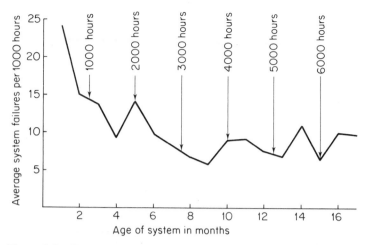

Figure 2.3 Early failures on a third type of large processor showing monthly system failures caused by all hardware faults, after hand-over to the users

but, this time, after hand over to the user. This type of processor is also sensitive to user activity, with the reliability deteriorating over 2000 to 3000 hour period (6 to 9 months for this system) corresponding to the build-up of user work. Also, the overall change in reliability is 5 or 6 to 1, compared with just over 3 to 1, after handover to the user, for the system shown in Figure 2.1.

Figure 2.3 shows early failures on large systems supplied by a third manufacturer. This time the figures are for system failures caused by all hardware faults and are derived from monthly figures for 30 different systems. This time, because we are dealing with incidents as observed by the user, the short term changes are much greater than before but the average improvements would appear to be about 3 to 1 and reliability stabilization period about 3000 hours: also, although more difficult to prove in this case, there could be a deterioration in reliability during the first 2000 hours (5 months).

Taking the above examples, smoothing the curves and putting them on a common scale, gives the range of burn-in characteristics, after handover to the customer, shown as A and C in Figure 2.4: these curves indicate that the time for reliability to stabilize is, surprisingly, as high as between 3000 and 12000 hours. In the case of the processor with 12000 hours burn-in time, the manufacturer has shown that the improvement happens automatically, without any particular actions to improve the design or maintenance arrangements and is caused by marginal or imperfectly processed devices. However, as shown later, it is also a question of design and quality control: with a marginal design and average/poor quality control any marginal components included in the machine may not be

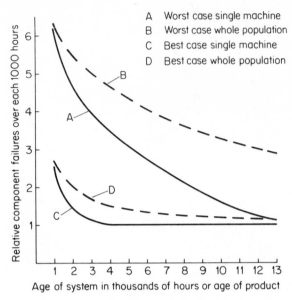

Figure 2.4   Early failures on large processors after hand-over to users

weeded out prior to delivery and may give rise to intermittent user program dependent failures. Thus the 12000 hours burn-in period is required for the computer to gradually collect a set of components which work within the particular design tolerances and reduction of the burn-in time may be achieved by:

1. Improving the design to make it less marginal.
2. Incorporating maintainability features which allow equipment characteristics to be varied, in order to reproduce faults caused by marginal components.
3. Improving quality control so that the control matches the design: this may mean special selection of components with mid point characteristics which suit the particular marginal areas.

Population of Processors

The early life characteristics considered so far are derived from populations of processors but a common installation date is assumed to reflect the failure rate encountered on any average system. When one considers the reliability of the whole population at a particular point in time, with systems of varying ages, the picture is somewhat different. Curves B and D in Figure 2.4 have been derived from the other curves to reflect the total number of faults recorded over each 1000 hour period, by assuming a constant production rate where as time progresses, the proportion of new systems reduces and reliability of the population slowly improves. These new curves represent the average processor reliability as observed by the field service organisation and, although the end reliability of the individual processors of the two different types is the same, the average of all systems is completely different; in fact, over the 12000 hours (typically 2 to 3 years) shown, the spares and maintenance manpower requirements are three times greater on one of the types of system: that is the price of poor quality.

First Production Models

In practice, when considering the overall failure rate of a populations of machines, the reliability of the first production models is worse than the later deliveries, due to the initial machine or component design being less perfected and, as shown later, numerous design improvements may be incorporated. Figure 2.5 shows actual reliability stabilization of two different populations of processors of about the same speed, over the first five years of life (showing 6 monthly averages each of about 2000 hours). Considering only early failures (as in Figure 2.4 but over ten 2000 hour periods) reliability improvements of the overall population varies between 2.0 and 2.6 times and of a single machine between 1.7 and 5.2 times. From Figure 2.5, including design failures, the improvement in population

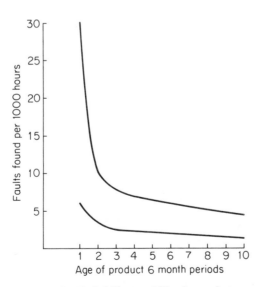

Figure 2.5   Reliability stabilization of two different populations of processors from first delivery of a new type of system

18

reliability is:

Best case average improvements: 4 to 1
Worst case average improvements: 6.8 to 1

Thus, on a 2000 hour/6 monthly basis, reliability of the population improves by a further 2 to 2.6 times due to design changes. Similarly, it can be shown that reliability of the first machines delivered improves by between 2 and 3 times on the same basis. It should be noted that, for the systems shown, the majority of these design improvements take place during the first six months of operation. Although, in other cases, manufacturers continue design improvements over a longer timescale, these are often to overcome problems found on particular sites and may not affect the total population reliability too much.

Figure 2.6 shows reliability stabilization of the same two systems as Figure 2.5 but, this time, in terms of system failures per 1000 hours: also, for the worst case system, besides the total population, an indication is given of the first system delivered. This type of processor has poor maintainability features with an incident per fault ratio of about 10, against just over 3 incidents per fault for the better system.

The better processor is well designed and has good quality control and pre-first delivery design quality assurance, but the introduction to live user work reveals a number of new design problems. The worst case system has

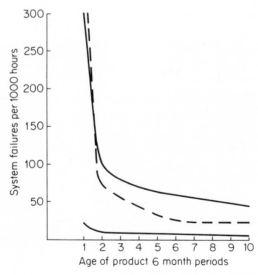

Figure 2.6 Reliability stabilization of same processors as Figure 2.5 but showing system failures per 1000 hours (average over 6 months). – – – – first system delivered, ———— total population

a more marginal design and, although the quality control and design qualification tests are reasonable, they do not match the design and poorer maintainability features. Between the 2 and 5 year period, reliability improvements are similar to those for the overall populations in Figure 2.4, but the difference in end reliability of the two systems is much greater, indicating that the individual processors do not have the same end reliability.

Commissioning

A further indication of the differences in quality between the two systems shown in Figure 2.5 can be seen by looking at statistics for an average system during the commissioning period, for systems delivered one year after the first delivery:

	SYSTEM A	SYSTEM B
Commissioning time	100 hours	1000 hours
Integrated circuit faults	4	52
Other processor faults	5	42
Main store faults	6	21
Total faults/mainframe	15	115
Faults/1000 hours during commissioning	150	115
Relative fault rate during commissioning to population average afterwards	100:1	25:1
Thousands of ICs in mainframe	25	13
Percentage of ICs changed during commissioning	0.016%	0.4%

Overall, the analysis of reliability stabilization characteristics is very complex and has the following complications:

1. The characteristics appear to be different when looking at the behaviour of a single system against looking at the whole population.
2. Burn-in failures caused by incorrect construction, and initially imperfect components occur as expected, but the number of failures is variable between system types and the burn-in period may be longer than expected, e.g. up to 10000 hours or more: the major problem is product quality, including both quality control and design aspects.

3. Also of significance on early production models is the correctness of the design of either the components or the complete system.

Disturbance Failures

Whenever engineering activity is required, there is a chance that a mistake will be made, which leads to more component failures. Modifications may not be correctly pre-tested or may be incorporated wrongly, thus causing further problems, possibly in a different area. Similarly, when a faulty module is replaced, contacts may be bent or the new module may suffer from early failures (these are not usually pre-burnt in). Also, as reliability of all equipment is dependent on utilization, changes in workload, operational hours or new software releases can cause higher or lower component failure rates.

Other disturbance failures are caused by mistakes in preventative maintenance (on one system, store failures can be almost guaranteed if a particular test program is run too long), by new engineers or changes in procedures. Further ones may be as a result of changes in the system's environment, such as temperature or relative humidity variations, mains supply variations, transients or disconnections. Overall, these disturbance failures make the steady state reliability, indicated in the theoretical bathtub curve, difficult to achieve in practice.

WEAR OUT FAILURES AND LIFETIME EXPECTANCY

General Electronics

Wear out can occur on electronic equipment in the form of an ever increasing deterioration in reliability, when a large number of components of the same type develop faults at about the same time and it is either not possible or not economic to replace them. These effects can be caused by:

1. High temperatures—causing wiring to become brittle, insulation and solder joints to crack;
2. High humidity—causing corrosion or leakage—one old valve type computer died due to silver migration, which is humidity dependent;
3. Contaminated atmospheres—e.g. dust, salt, sulphur dioxide cause corrosion and contact problems;
4. Choice of components—some components, e.g. resistors and capacitors drift in tolerance with time and, even so called high stability ones, can drift way out of specification after a number of years;
5. Shock and vibration—can cause wiring to weaken, including bonding wires within components;
6. Thermal shocks (due to switching on and off)—these can cause components to deteriorate;

7. Quality control—during initial manufacture of components or systems, some contamination may be introduced or weak connections made, which are not detected at the time and, rather than giving early failures, give rise to decreasing reliability after a time;

8. New technologies—these can develop new wear out failure modes, which are not found in quality control, as unknown factors cannot be catered for. Plastic encapsulated integrated circuits, the major component in most computers, are still avoided in the military field, due to various factors which can lead to corrosion or thermomechanical failures;

9. Maintenance or operational disturbance—after a period of changing or repairing items numerous times, plugs and sockets, wiring and connections can be damaged beyond repair. Also switches can wear out with heavy use, and may not be easily replaceable.

Maintenance disturbance in conjunction with the combination of other wear-out failures can cause the end of life, e.g. attempting to change worn-out contacts where wiring is also brittle.

Military equipment, which is specifically designed to cope with some of the above effects, has a required lifetime of up to 20 years, but this may be working in adverse environments and stored for periods without being used. The British Post Office works on a 30 year life for telecommunications equipment but, generally, the equipment is unlike computers by being more modular with more redundancy.

Computers

As far as computers are concerned, there are various factors which affect the wear-out failure modes:

1. Environment—medium/large computers are installed in air conditioned environments so excessive temperatures and humidities are not usually encountered over long periods; also contamination is kept to a minimum, due to the filtration in the air conditioning system. Shock and vibration is usually quite small but electronics in peripherals could suffer from this effect. Computers are usually switched on for long periods so, unless the system is subject to frequent external power disconnections, thermal shock effects, compared with military equipment, should be minimal.

2. Components and quality control—components used in computers are not exactly the high stability and expensive military types, but careful choice is usually made, within an economic range, to ensure that they are not subject to wide variations with life, but design margins adopted sometimes absorb the tolerances. Quality control is not up to military standards for commercial computers and is very variable between different manufacturers; hence; there is a reasonable

probability that contaminated components or weak connections will be incorporated; this is especially the case as the latest technologies tend to be used on computers.

3. Method of construction—fortunately most modern computers use large replaceable modules, which are produced over a period of at least 5 years, and between 50–100% are likely to be replaced during the lifetime of a particular system, so it is likely that components will be from a different vintage and different environment. Hence, even if some quality control problems were encountered at one point in time or the particular environment is bad, it is unlikely that a complete degradation in reliability would occur. However, reliability could be severely degraded for a period until the faulty modules are sorted out. There are certain exceptions to this rule, that is where modules are repaired on site, returned to the original site from the repair depot or where the modules are very small; in the latter case 90% or more of the original modules may remain in a system after 10 years.

Machines with fixed backplanes and contacts are most susceptible to wear-out problems but those with easily removeable backplanes (e.g. plugable multilayer printed circuit backplanes) or removeable contacts should be all right, providing spares are available.

Core stacks on some existing machines could be in danger of wear-out problems as they contain numerous crimped and soldered connections, fragile cores and some other components (e.g. sense diodes) all within a large module; they may also be subject to wide temperature swings and, as they are quite expensive, there could be a spares shortage. The stores may be replaceable by ones using a more modern technology but a new set of problems may be introduced (see *Enhancements and Change of Workload*).

4. Disturbance—fixed backplane connectors are particularly vulnerable to wear-out, caused by frequent module replacement and, on an old machine, classic wear-out could occur by disturbing the back wiring in attempts to replace the connectors. When module production has ceased, all modules will be subject to disturbance on repair and there may come the time when spares cannot be trusted. A source may be found for manufacturing new modules but this could present a problem on complex ones.

Overall most computer mainframes should be able to achieve a mean life of 20 years or more, but this does not mean that all machines will last for this period. Due to the various problems mentioned, a small number of systems could be expected to develop wear-out symptoms after a much shorter period—the problem is to identify which ones.

Spares

The availability of spares may well limit the economic life of computer systems. For many, cannibalization from old systems may keep them going for a period, but ultimately new spares will be required. Certain spares e.g. complex modules may only be able to be produced at prohibitive prices. The supply of certain components required for repair will dry up after a time and the manufacturing process may no longer be available to produce new ones (e.g. ICs of unusual construction).

In certain cases alternative components may be available but, in order to incorporate these, some design changes may be required to other parts of circuits and the expertise may not be available to carry out the design work. It is also likely that the design rules will be no longer available from the original supplier.

The storage of spares and components is also a contributory factor which could affect the life of systems. It is a known fact that certain components can become irreversably damaged by storing, without use, for long periods. The shelf life is also affected by the environmental conditions of the store and during transit.

Peripherals

All peripherals have some electronics within them and the wear-out problems may be more severe, due to vibration and the presence of oil and dust from the media.

On the mechanical side, providing *all* parts are replaceable there is no limit to the life, subject to spares availability. However, because of the method of construction and testing facilities, it is most unusual for all parts to be checked and changed if they show signs of wear. So, at some point in time, lots of different parts become worn and, in order to extend the life, a major overhaul is required, which may require the units to be shipped back to the factory.

At some point in time it is inevitable that peripherals will require overhaul (or replacement) and one major drawback is the prohibitive charges by manufacturers.

Maintenance Support

Perhaps the most significant contributor to the limit of life is the lack of support, either due to a manufacturer refusing to renew the maintenance contract or due to the shortage of experienced personnel.

It is possible that third party maintenance organizations will be able to take over some systems in place of the supplier, but there are some systems which the other maintenance bodies will not have the expertise nor the desire to carry out the maintenance.

On any system, there are different levels of support required. It is relatively easy to obtain engineers and train them to the normal field service level but the specialist area is a different question. The requirement to consult designers on old machines should be minimal except on the most complex systems, although design errors have been found on all types of systems, even after 10 years.

Most maintenance engineers prefer to move on to newer ranges of systems and, if attempts are made to keep them on old systems, they will probably leave and work for another company. With key support engineers leaving, the life expectancy of many systems could be very limited.

Maintenance Costs

The price/performance of some of the older systems is not very good when compared with modern systems and, with inflation, maintenance charges have increased over the years, such that they may be 10% pa or more, based on the original capital cost. Hence, for certain applications, it may be economically possible (and desirable) to extend the life of an application by providing a new or refurbished modern system giving equivalent power and facilities to the original. For example, a small system, original cost £50K, current maintenance charges £5K pa, may be replaceable by a modern mini at £5K pa rental (subject, of course, to the cost of program conversion).

The above is especially the case where manufacturers significantly increase maintenance charges for old systems.

Enhancements and Change of Workload

In certain cases, the workload on an old system could change or increase significantly; this may require the system to be enhanced. Alternatively, peripherals or stores may be replaced because they are worn out. These enhancements or changes may be of a different type to those previously used. The foregoing could lead to new problems on the main system which could cause a cessation of useful operation:

1. On old systems it is unlikely that information on the modification state of machines will be available and the manufacturer's modification documentation may have been disposed of. If the newer devices have different characteristics, the system may not work at the given mod state. If design expertise is not available, the life of the system may have to be terminated. (The problem of mod states could also affect cannibalization of modules or units from other sites.)
2. Connecting replacements or enhancements which require existing equipment to work at a faster rate can reveal wearout type problems in the old equipment.
3. Any significant increase or change in workload (or times worked) can degrade hardware reliability and in conjunction with spares and support areas could reduce the life of a system.
4. The disturbance on existing equipment when installing enhancements could be a life limiting factor.

5. When installing an item of new technology on an old processor (with relatively heavy currents) there is a fair chance that electrical interference problems will be met. To overcome these, design changes may be required to the old equipment.

Accommodation

The air conditioning plant and power supply equipment have the same wear-out problems as computer equipment, and in many cases it may only be possible to carry out overhauls, to extend the life or to replace equipment, at a high cost and with severe disruption to computer operations. Other problems may be caused by old building materials starting to create excessive dust in the computer rooms.

Chapter 3

Quality Considerations

DESIGN

Procedure

Chapter 2 showed that the average reliability of a poor quality processor can improve naturally by five times over five years, and by a further three times due to design improvements. All equipment undergoes this design improvement, to a greater or lesser extent, depending on the newness of the technology, techniques used, architecture, basic design rules employed, thoroughness of pre-first delivery design qualification tests, manufacturing/quality control tests used and the environment in which the equipment works. All these various aspects are interdependent: for example, the quality control should match the design; a poorer design needs a better level of quality control to specially select components to suit the requirements of particular areas: another example is that a poor design may work well in a good environment. Looking at the design in isolation, it is useful to consider how the design failures are introduced.

Computer equipment is quite complicated and it is almost impossible to produce an initial design specification which is logically complete and correct. Initial tests carried out can ensure that there are no gross logical errors, but it is impossible to specify or test for all combinations and sequences of functions and data patterns through all areas of a system; hence, it is almost certain that logical errors will come to light as systems are used in different ways and, from a user's point of view, these often have the same sort of symptoms as any other reliability problem, that is many of an intermittent like nature.

When the basic technology is decided upon, design guides will be available or will be evolved to indicate such factors as loading, ambient temperature limits, constructional manufacturing and timing constraints. At other times the facilities and speed of operation are decided upon; also the basic module sizes and interconnection techniques to be adopted. The design then becomes a compromise; the highest reliability is likely to be achieved with the lightest loading on the components, working at the

26

lowest temperature and with the widest allowances for timing margins; but this is likely to mean a large slow and expensive system. So, to achieve the required speed, using the minimum number of components, some areas will be designed to the limits of the specifications.

Resulting Reliability

As indicated later, components of the same age, of equal complexity, working in similar environments can have a 5 to 1 difference in reliability due to quality, including design and other quality considerations. At unit level, reliability of different units comes closer together because the most reliable components are used in greater quantities. For example, medium/large mainframes, less store, from different manufacturers who have offered them for the same job, have the following characteristics:

	Thousands of integrated circuits	Faults found per 1000 hours
Processor A	10	0.77
Processor B	26	0.56
Processor C	38	0.27

or the most reliable processor is the one with the *largest* number of integrated circuits. The above are derived from large populations of machines at about four years after first delivery so, as indicated in Chapter 2, reliability of individual machines of the same age could have different characteristics.

Quality of Design

In order to compare the quality of the design, a reliability index can be calculated as:

$$\text{Reliability index} = \frac{\text{Faults found}/1000 \text{ hours}}{1000\text{s of ICs}}$$

representing faults per 10^6 hours per IC but including faults outside the IC area. The reliability indices of the above processors which, as a matter of fact use integrated circuits of about the same complexity in terms of gates per IC, are:

	Reliability index
Processor A	0.077
Processor B	0.022
Processor C	0.007

showing that the integrated circuits are significantly more reliable on the systems using the largest quantities. (Note that these figures are population averages so, on the older processors, the difference between best and worst may be 5 : 1.)

The above figures are for medium/large systems. Larger systems using faster technology but of similar complexity appear to have reliability indices in the range of 0.05 to 0.25. As indicated below, mini computers are much worse than the medium/large processors at the component level and not much better at unit level. Part of the difference is due to using integrated circuits of greater complexity and part due to the average environment being worse but, equally, the design quality plays an important part.

Accurate information on microprocessor system reliability is difficult to come by, but the following example gives some figures for microprocessors, this time including a small amount of main storage besides power supplies and basic input/output channels: again, the reliability index is much larger than on mainframes.

	Faults found per 1000 hours range	1000s of ICs range	Reliability index range
Minicomputers	0.1 –0.6	0.2 –1.1	0.2–1.0
Microprocessor systems	0.05–0.2	0.02–0.06	0.8–3.3

Utilization Effects

One of the major reasons for the worse reliability indices of both the larger processors and minis/micros is the question of utilization. The larger computers are designed so that more operations are overlapped, maximizing utilization. Mini computers tend to be designed using the minimum number of components, with little redundant hardware for maintenance, checking or monitoring purposes, hence, the few components that are provided are fully utilized.

On even larger processors, multiple functional units may be provided, necessitating far more components but utilization of the units may be relatively low, so the reliability index can again be low.

Another general point regarding utilization and design is that, the worse the design, the bigger the reliability variation between equipment of the same type. These arguments are usually accepted for the electromechanical peripheral equipment but not for the electronics: some evidence follows regarding variations in reliability with utilization and, although the evidence may not be taken as conclusive, the main intention is to promote more research in this area.

Figure 3.1 shows the relationship between system failures and CPU utilization for a number of processors of the same type, each system being used for about the same number of hours per month. The results indicate a worsening of reliability as processor utilization increases. Besides average

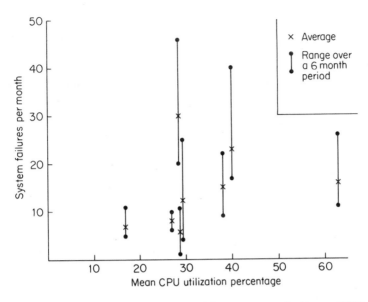

Figure 3.1   System failures caused by processor faults vs. CPU utilization

values, Figure 3.1 also shows the range over 6 monthly periods, indicating that the average values are representative and can be consistently good or consistently bad.

Core stores have been notoriously utilization dependent; for instance continuous accessing of one location is deprecated on some systems and, on others, the access time is deliberately slowed down to prevent overheating. Continuous accessing of each location in turn for a time and worst case noise patterns represent standard test routines on many manufacturer's test systems for core stores. On the relatively recently introduced MOS memories a lot of emphasis has been placed on pattern sensitivity and variability in timing according to utilization. These utilization effects, like processors, generally give rise to intermittent faults with transient failure modes, varying from installation to installation according to the workload.

There are two specific areas where utilization can be seen to affect reliability. If one considered that all the electronics are subject to transient failures, from time to time, where all circuits are fully utilized continuously, all these failures would affect system reliability, leading to more investigations, more parts changed and, apparently, more faults. On the other hand, where the electronics have a low utilization, only those which affect the active circuits would be apparent. The other area is the question of junction temperature in the integrated circuits, which affects reliability and where, for certain technology types, the heat dissipation is dependent on the frequency of operation or, in other cases, the ambient temperature may be varied. The heat problems are further compounded by the particular construction and air cooling arrangements (e.g. aerodynamic effects), timing constraints and associated limitations in component testing arrangements. The effects of heat, which along with timing is possibly the most significant common quality factor, are considered further in Chapter 4.

Sometimes of even more significance than processors are the peripheral equipment channels, controllers or data buses, which with fewer components, are sometimes less reliable than the central processor and, besides the usual utilization problems, the almost infinite variety of peripheral equipment adds fuel to the fire. With peripheral controllers connected to different models of processors, reliability can come out worse on the faster processors, which maintain a higher throughput rate. An example of engineering investigation rates of controllers on medium and high speed computers is:

	Medium speed computer	High speed computer	
Communications processors	1.36	2.03	} investigations
Exchangeable disk controllers	1.26	2.97	} per 1000 hours

New Technology

As should be expected, once the newer techniques or technologies become stabilized, the overall reliability shows improvements over earlier systems: this is reflected in Figure 3.2 showing best case system failures per 1000 hours versus processor speed for medium/large mainframes using different technologies and techniques. (Figure 3.2 is idealized but the graphs are mainly derived from data given in Chapter 11.) The graph shows significant improvements on going from transistor machines to integrated circuit ones and, similarly, from incorporating error correction to the core stores or using a higher level of integration for the processor, including MOS memories with error correction. It should be noted that a new technology, in isolation, may not give an improvement, for the dynamic MOS stores without error correction are subject to more frequent transient failures than the equivalent core stores. (See Neglected Areas later.)

MODIFICATIONS

Chapter 2 indicated that reliability improvements due to early failures can occur automatically as a system gradually collects a set of good components. On the other hand reliability improvements to overcome design problems require fundamental change to the hardware.

Once design failures have been identified, eventually, depending on the

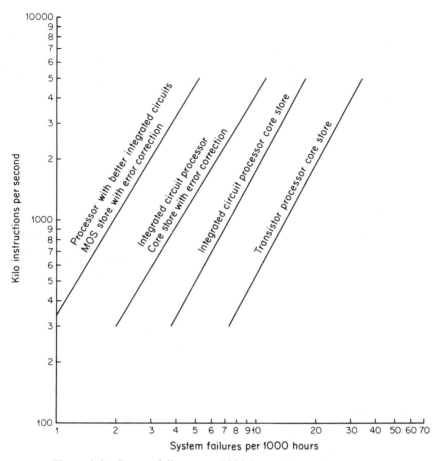

Figure 3.2   System failures per 1000 hours due to mainframe faults

nature of the problem and efficiency of the particular manufacturer, engineering changes (modifications) will become available. When these changes are issued to the field for fitment they are often known as Field Change Orders (FCOs). Besides providing modifications to overcome design reliability failures (including logical errors), FCOs may also be issued for safety purposes, to bring facilities and speeds within specification, to provide new maintainability features, or may be in conjunction with changes to the software. It should be noted that there are a number of processors, from different manufacturers, working on the field that never achieved the design specification on speed of operation and, rather than redesign large parts of them, the specifications were changed.

The number of logic changes required during the first year of operation of a new type of system has been found to be up to one per 50 integrated circuits (one per 100–200 gates) or about 400 FCOs on a fairly large processor with 20,000 ICs; the number of changes can vary considerably, depending on the novelty of the architecture and newness of the technology, and most manufacturers avoid the combination of both to minimize design stabilization problems. The procedures for fitting the changes depends very much on the particular manufacturer, some will be mandatory on all systems and others may be fitted if the particular design problem is encountered on a site. Along with logic change FCOs, there are usually minor mechanical changes to cabinets and other Engineering Change Orders (ECOs) which only apply to manufacturing. The latter may be due to changes in the availability or design of particular components used in making the system.

Large Processor

Figure 3.3 gives an example of logic change FCOs, from first delivery, on a system with somewhat more than 10,000 integrated circuits and represents about one change per 80 integrated circuits, during the first year. The high initial peak represents changes evolved between the time that the design was frozen (to enable factory commissioning tests to be completed) through delivery and installation. The changes then build up to a second peak after five months, the modifications being required to overcome utilization sensitive problems revealed by the new user work. The next peak at

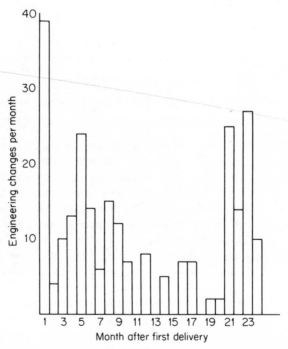

Figure 3.3   Modifications   on   a   medium/large
mainframe

21 months is due to the introduction of a new model but, of course, most of these will not be required to be fitted to the earlier model.

Mini Computer

Figure 3.4 represents all engineering changes on a mini computer with about 800 integrated circuits.

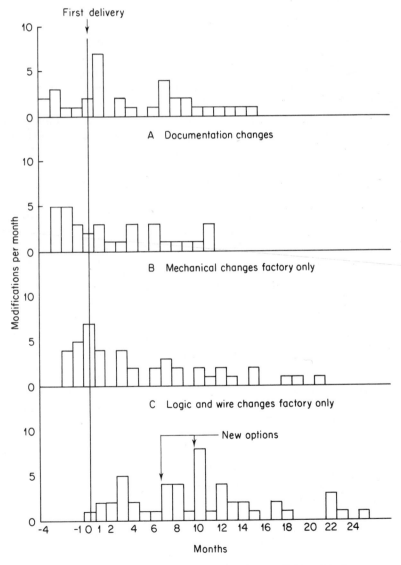

Figure 3.4   Modifications on a mini processor

1. Documentation changes—these are changes to the engineering drawings, over about an 18 month cycle, with a peak shortly after first delivery and a second peak following the introduction of new options to the field.
2. Mechanical changes—these are mechanical changes to allow easier assembly, changes to brackets, hole dimensions and so on. The figure indicates that the mechanical design is stabilized within 12 months of the first delivery, with a major emphasis prior to this.
3. Logic and wire changes factory only—these comprise reworking printed circuit boards to reduce external wiring, changes in components, **either** as a **cost reduction or where** the **old ones are no** longer available. The production cycle for mini computers is only a matter of a few weeks so, even for the first delivery, it is usual to incorporate all changes prior to delivery, this being indicated by the peak at week 0.
4. Logic and wire changes factory and field—besides including changes to overcome reliability problems, there are one or two included to overcome safety hazards and others to bring the speed/performance within specification. A peak of FCOs occurs three months after first delivery and further significant ones with the introduction of new options, which require certain changes to be made to existing modules. During the year after first delivery, the number of modifications required is about one per 25 integrated circuits but, excluding those due to new options this becomes approximately one per 40 ICs. During the second year the ratio of modifications/integrated circuit improves to one per 50, but this again is influenced by further problems due to the inclusion of new options.

Best Case

The above examples of modification rates represent the worst case situation. At the other extreme the rate may be as low as one per 1000 gates or better. For the latter, it is often found that extensive design automation and simulation techniques and thorough manual design checks have been employed to ensure that the design is logically correct and to establish confidence that the circuits are electrically within the required tolerance. Also lower modification rates can be expected where a different technology is used to build a system with well established architecture. A low modification rate, by itself, does not necessarily indicate good quality, the only way this can be determined is by evaluating the reliability of the end product. Finally, in considering the number of modifications in a period, or the rate of improvement, it is necessary to take into account exposure, in terms of number of installations and variety of utilization, in conjunction with procedures for showing that design deficiencies exist.

QUALITY ASSURANCE

Organization

On visiting almost any computer manufacturer, one of the standard presentations and tours around the factory concerns quality assurance and quality control. The standard presentation normally covers policy, reporting structures, documentation, procedures and relevant national, international or military standards employed. The tour of the factory, with its automated manufacturing and computer controlled testing, serves to amplify an apparent high quality product. Unfortunately, most quality control procedures are based on statistics and sampling plans designed for high volume production or methods of testing for equipment designed and costed for military use. It is difficult to question the procedures on theoretical grounds and, on practical grounds, it is necessary to compare the procedures with those on competing systems and to relate these to field reliability figures obtained, to provide an assessment of overall quality.

As indicated earlier, the quality control should match the design; a good design with minimum testing may give a similar field reliability as a poor design with outstandingly good testing. Similarly, if the product is of high quality, the results are more predictable and the quality organization can be weaker: it is generally accepted that the QA organization should not report to the production manager but, with a high quality system, it may not matter: on a system of poorer quality, the apparently powerful QA organizations can still be overruled.

In practice, the two extremes are met where a company may produce a system with marginal design and also have lax QA, criteria of success being altered as tests proceed or results ignored: the other extreme may be a well designed system with testing periods and criteria of success far beyond what one would expect. When comparing the procedures used on mainframes and minis, the latter often appear to have more onerous testing, but they probably need it because of their lower inherent quality.

The following sections give the range of tests, duration and criteria of success for the various quality control or assurance stages employed in the design and manufacture of a computer system. Where appropriate, the differences in techniques between minis and mainframes are highlighted.

Design Qualification

The QA organization will have responsibilities for ensuring that a product is designed with due regard being paid to quality in the form of ease of production, reliability, etc. They will be also responsible for drawing up plans for testing design or production prototypes for ensuring that specifications are achieved.

Initial qualification

Initial qualification is normally of the form of various levels of paper appraisal and component or unit evaluation as they become available. Concerning total systems, the amount and validity of the testing depends very much on availability of software—with hardware developed before software, eventually when the two come together a new set of hardware design problems is inevitable; so, even for environmental tests, software should be included-with appropriate user programs.

Environmental Tests

Each significant stage is likely to have tests which show that the environmental specifications are met (see Chapter 4) on:

Temperature and relative humidity
Electromagnetic interference
Vibration and shock
Sensitivity to atmospheric pollution
Mains supply voltage, frequency, disconnections and transients.

At the final production stage, it is likely that transportation to sites will be simulated.

Not all suppliers have facilities for carrying out these environmental checks, e.g. some do not have environmental chambers large enough for complete systems but may transport the equipment to an external testing organization or use a plastic tent with limited testing. Other suppliers go to the other extreme and test each of the above areas for 2–3 weeks continuously, even to the extent of running programs under software control, whilst being vibrated on a shaker table.

Other Tests

Also, at the early stages, facilities are checked by running engineering tests and user software. Performance (speed) is also checked by engineering means and by including user benchmarks and other specially written timing programs. It is not normally possible to measure reliability accurately (see Chapter 10) because this would possibly need thousands of hours of operation, but margins are checked by varying voltages and clock frequencies: also various peripheral configurations may be tried out. In lieu of attempting to measure reliability, extended running periods may be required with criteria of success of a limited number of system failures during the period.

The larger systems being tested at this stage are still likely to be undergoing significant numbers of design changes, so one main criterion is to produce a sufficiently stable design to provide meaningful results, as it is so easy to write off incidents to known design deficiencies.

Extent of Testing

After the initial tests have proved reasonably successful, the system is likely to be announced and design qualification tests continued until well after delivery to the first customers. The design stability of the first systems is likely to be highly dependent on the size of system and finance available for development. Even on larger systems, manufacturers have been known to produce 10 production prototypes for in-house use within the company and to run them for up to a year before the first customer shipment. These systems are used for software development, running potential user's benchmarks, developing user application programs and in-house production work. The more successful developments are achieved by ensuring detailed analysis of all problems, for identifying new design weaknesses, and by ensuring that all systems include all the latest hardware and software design changes, irrespective of the effects on the work being run.

In the case of mini computers, besides the in-house systems, the larger manufacturers are likely to give away a number of production prototypes to selected users, to identify design deficiencies in a user environment.

Individual items of peripheral equipment undergo similar design qualification tests as units and then through system integration, where the whole range of system tests may be rerun.

Component Selection

All manufacturers give convincing presentations on how they proceed in evaluating components, for use in the systems, and also on appraisal of the component suppliers and their quality control techniques. The end result is often the choice of commercially available components which can be multi-sourced from a number of suppliers—this can ensure adequate supplies, also extensive feedback from multiple users for revealing component design and inspection weaknesses, but restricts the computer system design. An extension of this is to choose a new technology, which is likely to become a market standard but the first user may have all the problems in sorting out the component design deficiencies, on top of the ones introduced by the new system.

In certain cases, advanced technologies are chosen, but the danger of advanced technology and advanced computer architecture can magnify design problems many fold.

Some computer manufacturers design their own components, probably within the scope of a known technology and then select a company (possibly themselves) to produce the new components. This technique may be adopted to achieve the best cost/performance but again amplifies the problems in sorting out the design.

For the occasional system, manufacturers justify single sourcing of components on the basis that multiple suppliers produce multiple and different component design, production and testing deficiencies: with the single supplier a more watertight contract can be entered in to and the supplier is more inclined to help in identifying problems. This method is, of course, fraught with potential delays in the event of a component production problem developing but can be overcome, to some extent, by over purchase.

Goods Inwards Quality Control

Quality control of incoming components is invariably carried out according to some well established standard, defining sampling plans, and testing techniques; for example, on integrated circuits, a combination of the following tests may be carried out:

DC tests
AC tests
Parametric characteristic measurements
Marking
Solderability
Vibration and shock
Lead strength
Thermal shock and thermal intermittents
Moisture resistance
Decapitation and checks that devices conform to specified internal dimensions and plating

Many manufacturers go further than the specified sampling plans and carry 100% tests for one or more of the first three tests mentioned, but criteria vary from rejecting the whole batch if more than a predefined percentage fail, to sorting and only rejecting failing components. For all the tests, variables are introduced by the testing equipment, be it manual, semi-automatic or fully automatic, and by the duration and repetition frequency of the tests. In certain cases, the manufacturer tests to a tighter specification than that provided by the component supplier, especially to suit characteristics of certain areas of the equipment.

Where sampling plans are adopted, sample sizes and acceptable quality levels (AQLs) are dictated by the appropriate standard, manufacturers sometimes using the higher level military standards for certain tests or introducing new test methods for newly discovered failure modes.

The above variables can lead to rejection rates, for the same fairly simple integrated circuits, of 0.1% to 5% or more of individual components, on 100% testing, and 5 to 25% of batches.

On integrated circuits employing higher levels of integration, including memory and micro processor chips, besides the other tests, it has been found necessary to carry out 100% burn-in, in an oven up to 50°C for 8 to 24 hours, with the devices being functionally exercised, some at worst case voltage and timing margins. This results in rejection rates of 5% to 25% on an individual component basis or a mean of up to 50% of batches. There are some manufacturers, however, who do not carry out these burn-in tests.

Similar variations in procedures are found on all other components at the goods inward stage and on quality control checks following in-house production of components, such as printed circuit boards and backplanes.

Module Testing

Inspection stages following component insertion and flow soldering can indicate that 20% of modules need touching up, or more if the soldering process quality checks have not been carried out properly. At this stage, a number of modules are rejected completely but the yield figure may be rather meaningless as a limited number of defects per board are likely to be allowable.

Because of the infinite variety of populated circuit boards across the market place, module testers are generally purpose designed and built. Tests can vary from less than a second on a simple comparator to a several minute functional test with varying margins and vibration. Mini computer boards are often tested in a known working processor and, occasionally, a manufacturer can be found who runs the tests for several hours at elevated temperatures. Besides burn-in tests at component level, MOS memory boards may also be tested in an oven for several minutes. Similarly, on micro-processor boards, even with very large production rates, it is not unknown for tests to be carried out for 24 hours on every one, at up to 50°C. At the module test stage, up to 50% may fail and require attention. The higher reject rates do not necessarily indicate a poor manufacturing process but, more likely, a good functional testing stage or poor goods inwards testing. Similarly, a high yield does not confirm that the manufacturing process is good, but may indicate inadequate testing at this stage. The main benefit of measuring the yield is to detect a deterioration in production quality.

Modules used for construction of new units and systems generally have further extensive tests, but those for use as spares, by the field engineering organization, are normally shipped following these limited tests. This may result in 4–20% of modules being found 'dead on arrival' and others causing disturbance failures, due to intermittent faults, when inserted in systems in the field.

Unit Testing

The electronic units for the larger systems may or may not be assembled in a separate unit build area but, whichever procedure is adopted, testing is quite similar. The duration of tests for a processor, store or controller can vary from two hours for one manufacturer's products, to 10 days for another's. Even during the two hours, faults may be allowed. For the 10 day test, criteria of up to 24 hours failure free operation may apply. On one medium/large system, the CPU is put into a heat chamber and temperature cycled for 24 hours, followed by a test, requiring eight hours failure free operation: similarly, other manufacturers carry out heat cycling of completed semiconductor stores. Mini computer CPUs, stores and major options often have more severe tests than their mainframe counterparts, including vibration and temperature cycling of each unit for two days continuously. On others, the unit may only have 15 minutes testing, if the test programs run failure free on the first pass.

At the peripheral assembly area, in certain cases, the units may only have two hours testing and then be shipped directly to sites. The testing may assure 95% confidence that the units have been correctly assembled, but this could mean that 1 in 20 units delivered may be faulty. In other cases, peripherals can be tested for 2 or 3 days and then passed to a system build area, where further testing takes place.

The length of time in unit build and test depends very much on the number of faults found per unit; this can be as low as less than one fault per unit, even for large mainframe units with extensive testing, to a requirement to replace 10% of modules and to correct numerous wiring errors.

System Testing

In certain cases, system testing may only be carried out on a sample of systems, the remainder being shipped directly to users following unit test as separate stores, processors, channels and peripherals.

The procedure in the system build and test area normally comprises a series of tests, including margins, by the production staff, followed by updating to the latest modification state, then inspection and acceptance testing by the QA organization. Variables introduced are:

1. Configurations—these vary from using simulators or the bare minimum peripherals required to run engineering tests, through using standard factory peripherals (and perhaps overconfiguring), to fully configuring the system as ordered, including cables. Full configurations of the user's system is more prevalent on mini computers.

2. Tests Run—varying from stand alone engineering tests, through engineering system interaction and exerciser programs, to extensive testing under the operating system to be delivered with the system.

3. Environment—most systems have voltage margins and timing varied but generally only at normal temperatures. Other systems have part of the testing carried out at elevated temperatures. On certain mini systems the whole configurations, including all user peripherals, are heat cycled for a day or more.

4. Duration—on larger systems, the duration of testing, including QA acceptance, varies from 2 or 3 days to several weeks. On mini computers, all assembly and test work may be carried out in less than 2 days, including a requirement to run tests for only 4 or 5 hours. At the extreme, certain mini systems may be in the area for 3 weeks or more with, perhaps, a minimum of 50 hours testing, depending on the configurations.

5. Criteria of Success—these vary, virtually, from one clear pass of each engineering test, which may only take a few minutes, through more extensive testing with a number of failures allowed, to many hours of failure free operation.

Packaging and Delivery

When computer systems are delivered, in spite of extensive factory testing, quite often items are faulty or missing, test programs, software and documentation wrong, and equipment damaged. Most of the missing or wrong types of items are brought about in disassembly and packaging of the system (e.g. often 10 to 20% of cables are misplaced): other deficiencies are introduced by leaving the system on the factory floor after final QA, where the tendency is for someone to 'borrow' known working parts: further wrong items are introduced when peripherals, software and documentation are sent by different sources, to meet up on site, with the various items being at different and incompatible modification levels. One manufacturer attempts to get over these problems by ensuring that all items are tested in the factory, including actual program and software tapes to be delivered: after touch up, disassembly and packaging, all items are removed from boxes and rechecked.

Often major damage is caused on delivery and it would appear that almost every large system, which is delivered by air, has at least one unit severely damaged. Various different packaging methods are employed but they do not appear to make much difference. Usually, in these circumstances, new items are delivered very quickly, but it is likely that these have not been tested to the same standards as the earlier damaged ones.

Feedback and Fault Analysis

Perhaps the most neglected area in the overall quality control cycle is feedback of fault information and analysis. Generally the fault records are kept but these are often of different form to suit a specific requirement, for example in the following areas:

1. Design qualification—to validate the design and to provide initial modifications. There may be an inadequate review of subsequent modifications to determine how they could have been revealed at the earlier stage.

2. Manufacturing stage—to show that the quality of a particular process is maintained. There may be insufficient comparison with other processes or with subsequent field reliability.
3. Field figures—to determine manpower and field service training requirements. There is often insufficient site to site comparisons, action on a particular installation often only being initiated following user complaints. Also, these figures do not generally indicate incident rates observed by the user.
4. Module repair depot—to determine spares holdings and, initially, to provide comparisons with theoretical module failure rates. The latter may be in conjunction with unit reliability derived from field figures but, for certain manufacturers, the comparisons are carried out with the view to improving component selection and manufacturing quality whereas others also attempt to identify design related reliability problems.
5. Error logs—the information in a system's error log is used (or should be used) for determining preventative maintenance requirements and for providing diagnostic information for a particular site. Generally, manufacturers do not carry out global comparisons with error logs and other field reliability statistics. For certain types of system, independent companies provide an error log analysis service, giving detailed unit by unit comparisons with large population averages.
6. Software—software fault reporting procedures are generally completely different and divorced from those on hardware, even though, for many types of failure, it is difficult to tell the difference between hardware and software causes (see Chapter 5).

Neglected Areas

Most manufacturers achieve the objectives in some of the above specific areas and in coordinating the figures to identify design and manufacturing weaknesses at component, module or unit level. However, as analysis is generally carried out on total populations of items, certain weaknesses may be missed: this is especially the case where the figures are used to ensure that predetermined objectives are met, rather than to achieve the best possible reliability. Where maintainability is particularly poor, giving large numbers of investigations or incidents per fault, the only way to improve user observed reliability may be to carry out sufficient analysis to identify and provide corrections for many more weaknesses. Areas where particular attention can be given are:

1. Incident rates, investigation rates and fault rates of systems, units, modules and components—analysis by application, utilization, environment, daily switched on hours, time of day, day of week, production batch or age. For the latter area, modules require the inclusion of serial numbers at the final assembly stage with records

kept of component batches used and the location of each module. Only a limited number of manufacturers keep such records.

2. Replacement rates or fault rates on modules and components—analysis by physical location and functional area. A recent CCA investigation, on one type of processor, showed that particular types of modules were replaced more frequently in input/output areas and at the bottom of the processor, these also being the hottest areas. A further example is that one manufacturer initiates a design investigation if integrated circuits are replaced in the same physical location on two processors out of a small population. It should be noted that the probability of this happening, with purely random failures, can be very low.

The greatest success obtained in this area is where a centralized quality organization has been responsible for the collection and analysis of all the different forms of fault statistics mentioned, with feedback to the various departments to suit their specific requirements; also, where the same organization has teams of hardware and system engineers who are responsible for, firstly, carrying out the design qualification tests, then quality audits and high level support to the field, for both hardware and software. The alternative of independent collection of statistics, with centralized coordination, does not appear to be as successful.

The basic problem in attempting to improve product quality, by detailed analysis of all statistics, is the cost and effort required. However, as indicated in Chapter 2, the price of poor quality can be a threefold increase in spares and maintenance manpower requirements over that required for a good quality product.

With technology advancing into the large scale integration area, quality assurance and failure analysis are becoming more complex, as is the design for implementing the technology. The QA for successful LSI implementations is tending to place the emphasis on timing and retiming of components, modules, units and systems. Failure analysis has to consider that the limitations of the technology are being reached, with transient failures being caused by alpha particle bombardment from small amounts of radioactivity naturally present in the packaging materials: this has been found to be the cause of the transient failures in MOS memories, which were mentioned earlier (see 'Dynamic memories racked by radiation', *Electronics International*, June 8 1978). Some of the testing procedures described in this chapter were introduced to overcome a failure mode which was not understood at the time.

Chapter 4

Environmental Aspects

AIR CONDITIONING

Effects of Environment

Reliability of electronics generally deteriorates as temperature rises; for example, reliability of integrated circuits (ICs) is dependent on internal junction temperatures which, in turn, are dependent on ambient temperature, IC thermal characteristics, type, complexity and mode of utilization. ICs are designed to be used in a wide range of ambient temperatures, e.g. 0 to 80°C but, as shown in calculations based on the MIL Handbook 217B and, over the range of temperatures likely to be encountered inside the computer cabinets, reliability variations of 1.5 to 1 can be expected within the range. Other less well defined thermal effects, for example due to switching on and off, due to rapid variations or due to internal air turbulence can give further reliability degradation. The latter is especially the case when combined with marginal quality components which together give rise to numerous intermittent or transient type faults. On the electromechanical peripheral equipment, temperature variations can decrease tolerances and cause adjustments to wander.

At low relative humidity, static electricity discharges can occur between the equipment and personnel or furniture and can cause data corruptions or, occasionally, destruction of electronic components. At high relative humidity moisture can enter imperfectly sealed components and internal or external corrosion can be encouraged. On the peripheral equipment, media problems are also likely.

Dust can cause filters and cooling airways to be blocked and degrade reliability due to higher operating temperatures. Air pollution, for example, sulphur dioxide causes corrosion and, hence, worse reliability and reduced life. Certain peripherals, for example magnetic devices, are particularly sensitive to dust which can lead to data corruptions or can physically damage the media.

With all the above problems caused by varying air conditions, it is little wonder that manufacturers insist that full air conditioning is provided for the larger systems. However, detailed examination of environmental specifications and recommendations indicates that some manufacturers have much more stringent requirements than others and, hence, have probably encountered environmental related design problems at some point in time.

Room Conditions for Medium/Large Systems

Temperature and Relative Humidity

Suppliers of medium/large systems provide fairly tight figures for limits of temperature and relative humidity within a computer room: these are generally in the following range:

	Temperature °C	Relative humidity %
Worst	21 ± 1	50 ± 5
Best	21 ± 3	50 ± 5

These stringent requirements are sometimes given to provide the basis of the air conditioning control design, based on the assumption that this will ensure that computer design limits are not exceeded. In other cases the computer equipment really requires the limits to be maintained for reliability purposes and the small print may indicate that they are contractual requirements, rather than recommendations.

Rate of Change

Besides the above specifications/recommendations, other figures are often given for rate of change of conditions and sometimes for maximum temperature differences across the room:

	Maximum rate of change		Maximum temperature
	Temperature °C per hour	Relative humidity % per hour	difference °C
From	3	10	3
To	11	20	8

Switched Off Conditions

All the major manufacturers specify switched off conditions but these can vary from 0–40°C and 10–90% RH to normal equipment switched on design specifications, including the defined rate of change figures.

Air Filtration

For air filtration standards, most suppliers of the larger systems specify 95% efficiency at Test Dust 2 or 5 microns: however, this is not really good enough as the dust level in the room depends on external conditions and a filter of higher efficiency is required in areas with heavy pollution. To overcome this problem, there is only one real way to specify the requirements, that is by indicating the maximum permissible dust levels within the room: one manufacturer specifies three separate ranges, according to the sensitivity of different types of equipment:

Particle size	Particles per cubic metre of air		
microns	Range A	Range B	Range C
0.5–1	1×10^6	4×10^6	4×10^7
1–5	1×10^5	4×10^5	4×10^6
5+	1×10^4	2.5×10^4	4×10^5

Room Conditions for Small and Mini Systems

Mini computer suppliers do not normally recommend air conditioning and usually specify either a normal office environment or refer to the equipment design specifications. However, normal office conditions really means acceptable to people and, to achieve this, some form of cooling is often required. Also, some of the design specifications cannot be met without the provision of air conditioning plant. As shown later, there is nothing magic about mini computer systems; reliability degrades with varying environments but, because of the low component counts, the degradation can often be tolerated; the need for air conditioning is also governed by the amount of time that a user is prepared to lose because the room conditions are intolerable for the people or the computer.

The most diverse recommendations/specifications apply to the small systems supplied by the mainframe manufacturers. On one hand, some state 'normal office conditions' as on mini computers and others require conditions equivalent to the most stringent on large systems.

Design Conditions

Design specifications for temperature and relative humidity are generally available and normally represent much wider limits than those given for room conditions. Usually, separate specifications are given for each type of device but one or two manufacturers give an overall specification. Examination of the specifications often indicates where manufacturers have had environment sensitive design reliability problems.

Figure 4.1 shows design limits in bar chart form for the central processing unit and peripherals supplied by a number of mainframe manufacturers, the room conditions also being shown for comparison purposes. Similarly, Figure 4.2 shows specifications for a number of small systems and mini computers.

Design Specifications for Medium/large Processors

On the medium/large processors, the temperature specifications vary from 10 to 38°C to 17 to 23°C. It is interesting to note that the system with the widest specification has proved to be one of the most reliable CPUs and the one with the narrow specifications, the least reliable. The latter is because of the sheer volume of components and, it is also interesting to note that the larger processors in a range (see Figure 4.1), generally being the least reliable, have the tightest temperature specifications. Some of these figures may be rather surprising as it has been suggested that machines with built in cooling, supplied directly by chilled water, should be able to cope with wide room conditions, but this is not the case.

One of the manufacturers represented in Figure 4.1 has design limits of certain processors of 40–60% relative humidity but this is more of a self protectionist attitude. Of the other processors, one has a lower limit of 40% RH and it is known that an earlier processor from the same manufacturer suffered from static electricity problems, which caused system stoppages. Another of the processors has an upper RH specification of 60% and, at one time, this machine had moisture related diode problems. In general it appears that tighter design limits are specified in two cases:

1. As a precaution, especially on the larger processors, which are the least reliable anyway;
2. Where environmental design/reliability problems have been met on current or earlier processors. In the latter case, the problems should really be designed out of new equipment and conditions relaxed.

Design Specifications for Small Computers, Mini and Micro Processors

Specifications for small computers and mini processors are usually in the following ranges:

	Temperature °C		Relative humidity %	
	Best	Worst	Best	Worst
Small computers	10–35	15–32	8–80	20–80
Mini processors	0–55	4–38	0–95	20–80

Providing the heat dissipation is not excessive, the above can be met most of the time without the provision of air conditioning. However, certain small processors can be found with lower RH specifications of 40% which will certainly require the provision of humidification.

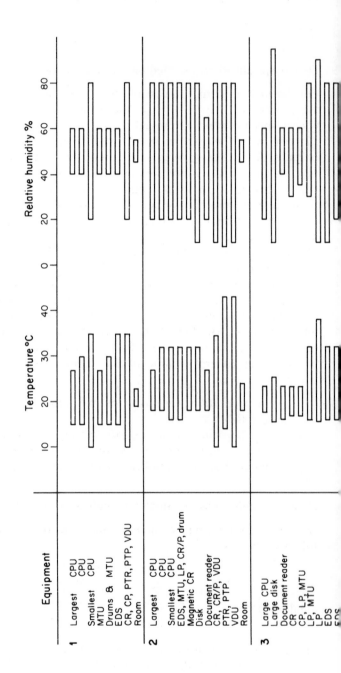

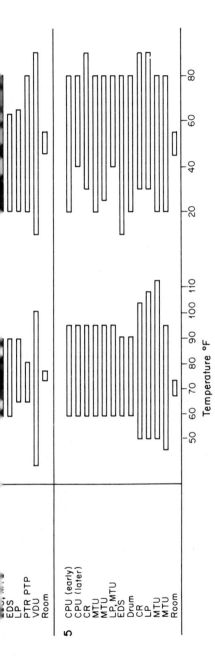

Figure 4.1 Temperature and RH conditions for medium/large systems

50

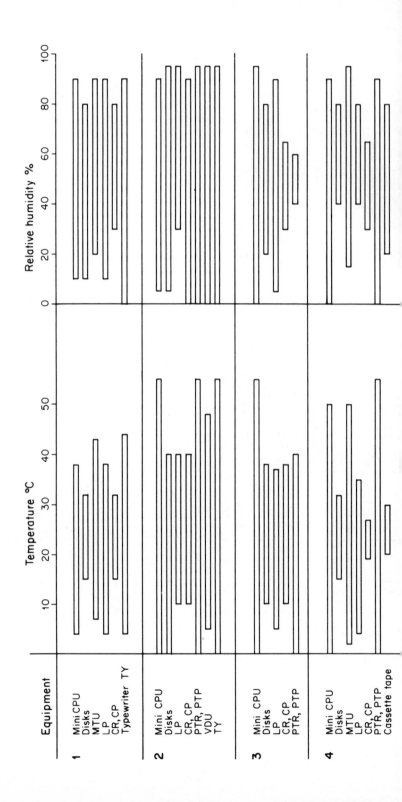

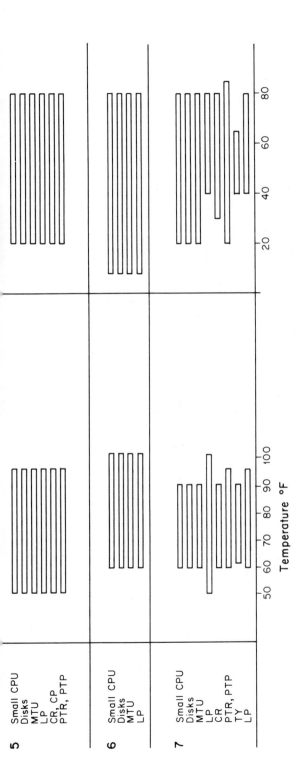

Figure 4.2 Temperature and RH conditions for small/mini systems

Typical specifications for microprocessor systems are similar to the best minis above but, sometimes the upper limits are 40°C and 90% RH.

Design Specifications for Large System Peripherals

Exchangeable Disks (EDS)

As indicated in Figure 4.1, on the larger systems, exchangeable disk units have design specifications of at least 15–32°C but there is some variation on RH conditions with 20–80% RH quite common. Certain of the systems shown have disk units supplied from the same source but different specifications are given by the system supplier.

Switched off design conditions for the units vary from 15–32°C, 5–95% RH and 10–44°C, 8–80% RH to −40 to 60 °C, 0–95% RH, in each case with no condensation.

On filtration, the units generally are fitted with a 0.3 micron two stage absolute filtration system, so the main requirement is to prevent the packs being contaminated during loading or storage. The disk packs have a built-in course filter at the base of the pack, through which the air flows when loaded and running. The filter should be regularly checked by the users.

It is sometimes stated that the conditions for the equipment is dictated by the media. In the case of disk packs, this does not appear to be the case, with the operational specifications for temperature and humidity being typically 15–48°C and 8–80% RH. Storage requirements for packs are typically −40°C to 65°C, 8–80% RH, no condensation (for up to five years). For reconditioning after storage it is sometimes stated that this should be equivalent to the time out of operating conditions with a maximum reconditioning period of 2 hours.

Magnetic Tape Units (MTU)

Design temperature and RH conditions for magnetic tape units are more variable than disks, the widest limits for high-speed high density decks being 15–32°C and 20–80% RH. One supplier who has in the past had reliability problems on tape units, has the most stringent limits of about 17–23°C and 35–60% RH for one type of unit. Other suppliers, who may or may not have had problems, also have RH specifications of either 40 or 60% or both.

It is generally accepted that tape units are severely affected by dust (although the units may be susceptible to creating their own dust problems by scraping oxide from the tapes), so it is important that the appropriate precautions are taken and, often, the recommended room filtration standards are governed by the tape units.

There are also wide variations in the recommendations for tape storage, the following specifications being available.

Specification	Temperature °C		RH %
A	4.5–32	20–80	10 °C and 10% per hour max rate of change
B	4–32	20–80	
C	10–32	20–80	long term storage
D	16–25	35–60	
E	15–27	40–60	
F	5–32	30–80	for transit purposes
G	4–32	20–80	
H	4–49	20–80	unrecorded
I	4–32	20–80	recorded
J	0–50	10–80	

The reconditioning recommendation after storage is usually 6 hours, but one supplier says 4–16 hours and another equal to storage time, with a maximum of 24 hours.

The tape manufacturers' design specifications for use of the media appears to vary between 4–32°C and 15–32°C for temperature and 20–80% and 30–80% for RH. However, these conditions are generally somewhat tighter than those for storage. Again some of the tight specifications for magnetic tape units are not justified by the media.

Cassette tape units have much wider specifications with typical figures being 10–40°C and 20–80% RH for use and −30 to 70°C and 10–90% RH when switched off.

Printers (LP), Card (CR and CP) and Paper Tape Equipment (PTR and PTP)

For each of these devices, examples can be found where specifications are fairly tight, especially on relative humidity (see Figure 4.1).

In the case of these items, the overall requirements can be dictated by the media and, in fact, the specifications for punched cards or paper tape could be said to be the dictating factor for air conditioning requirements. The specifications for these items are generally 18–24°C and 40–60% RH.

Design Specifications for Mini and Micro Computer Peripherals

Mini Computers

As for the larger systems, the environmental requirement design specifications for mini computer peripherals reflect the problems that a particular manufacturer has encountered on the particular device. Sometimes the same unit used by different system suppliers have vastly different specifications, but often the specifications are the same as the peripheral supplier's. Examples of temperature and RH specifications

Table 4.1 Heat dissipation and space requirements

Processor size kilo instructions per sec (KIPS)	No.	CPU, store channels controllers console	6 EDS	4 MTU	CR & LP	Total	Total air flow m³/sec	Approx. min. room size m²
						Heat dissipation KW		
Extra large 4000–8000	1	40 to air 41 to water	6.3	7.6	6.2	60.1 air 101.1 total	7.0	190
	2	40 air 100 water	8.4	14.8	7.0	70.2 air 170.2 total		160
	3	34.6	6.3	7.6	6.2	54.7		130
Large 1500–4000	1	27.3 air 27.5 water	6.3	7.6	6.2	47.4 air 74.9 total	5.07	170
	2	44	8.4	16.0	6.2	74.6	7.16	170
	3	47.8	9.1	6.0	4.9	67.8	7.75	180

2	27.1	6.3	7.6	6.2	47.2	4.17	120
3	18.7 air* 58.8 water	8.1	6.0	4.6	37.4 air 82.7 total	3.63	180
4	5.5 air 10.4 water	8.4	14.8	7.0	35.7 air 46.1 total		120
5	10.9	8.4	5.2	5.0	29.5		120
6	16.9	9.1	6.0	4.9	36.9	5.0	120
7	15.2	6.2	5.0	2.8	29.2		100
Medium 250–600							
1	20.0	8.0	6.0	3.3	37.3		120
2	12.5	6.2	5.0	2.8	26.5		100
3	14.7	8.4	6.3	6.2	35.6	4.0	120
4	11.7	8.1	6.0	4.6	30.4	4.38	120
5	24.0	6.3	7.6	6.2	44.1	3.9	120

*includes heat to air when doors open

for peripherals on the small/mini systems are shown in Figure 4.2 and have the following range, with the best figures being similar to the processors:

	Temperature °C		Relative humidity %	
	Best	Worst	Best	Worst
Disk units	0–40	15–32	0–95	40–70
Magnetic tape units	2–50	10–30	6–95	40–70
Card equipment	0–50	19–26	0–90	30–60
Paper tape equipment	0–55	10–35	0–95	40–60
Printers	4–38	16–32	3–90	40–80

Hence, it appears that various manufacturers have had problems with each type of peripheral, especially on relative humidity and, in these cases, air conditioning would be required to ensure that the design conditions are not exceeded.

Micro Computers

Microprocessor systems may have built-in peripherals such as cassette tape units, diskettes or visual display units with overall specifications similar to the best ones above. Others may use identical external peripherals to mini computers.

HEAT DISSIPATION AND SPACE REQUIREMENTS

Information on heat dissipations and space requirements of ranges of medium/large mainframes and peripherals from various manufacturers are given in Table 4.1, systems in each of the ranges shown having competed with each other.

Processors

There is a great diversity in heat dissipations of comparable electronics; for example processors of the same speed capabilities can have a 5:1 difference in heat dissipation, reasons for the diversity being:

1. Technology—processors with similar features and speeds could be constructed from different technologies, e.g. ECL or TTL with 50% more TTL Integrated Circuits (ICs) but the ECL heat dissipation per IC may be 4 times greater. Table 4.2 shows the technology/heat/speed characteristics of various processors, some being ECL, some TTL and some a mixture of both. The table also shows the heat dissipation per IC as calculated for a particular processor but including the heat from other components, fans and power supplies etc; also a typical average expected heat dissipation

Table 4.2   Number of integrated circuits, speed and heat dissipation of medium/
large mainframes less store

Processor	Thousands of ICs	Speed KIPS	Heat KW	Watts per IC	Technology spec watts per IC average
1	44.0	5000	37.1	0.84	0.35
2	2.0 LSI	4000	19.0	9.5	2.0
3	24.0	2500	21.8	0.91	0.17
4	5.0	1200	9.0	1.8	0.15
5	14.0	1200	9.0	0.64	0.18
6	13.0	1000	31.0	2.38	0.50
7	26.4	900	4.8	0.18	0.04
8	11.6	800	9.4	0.81	0.15
9	37.8	600	15.6	0.41	0.10
10	18.0	450	12.2	0.67	0.10
11	10.0	350	3.0	0.30	0.04
12	8.0	200	2.2	0.27	0.04

from the ICs themselves. In most cases it appears that only about one fifth of the heat is dissipated by the ICs. The scale of integration of the ICs used can have a considerable effect as the heat dissipation does not necessarily rise in proportion to the IC complexity. Processor 2 (see Table 4.2), using Large Scale Integration, reflects the latter, where the heat dissipation per IC is by far the highest but the total heat for a given speed is fairly low.

When designing a computer, options may be available for alternatives with differing heat dissipation, e.g. Processor 5, an ECL machine, is designed to have less than a given heat dissipation and design rules employed recommend the use of a low heat option when possible: this is no doubt one reason why the heat dissipation obtained per IC is lower for this machine when compared with others using the same sort of technology, e.g. Processors 3, 4, 5 and 8 use a large proportion of the same type of ECL.

2. Architecture—all computers of the same speed do not have equivalent hardware features, in some cases much is carried out by software, reducing total throughput but not necessarily raw processor power, also between 10% and 40% of the total components provided are for maintainability purposes.

3. Cooling and power supplies—the cooling fans and arrangements and power supplies can easily account for two thirds of the heat dissipation, e.g. Processor 6 logic, power supplies and cooling about 10 KW each. In some cases the figure may be greater, e.g. Processor

4 has series regulators in the power supplies which pushes up the heat dissipation considerably. It should be noted from Table 4.1 that many of the faster processors have built in water cooling arrangements, which ease air handling problems but may introduce addition costs. The LSI Processor (2 in Table 4.2) is of special interest as it gives an indication of the likely future requirements of other manufacturers, the heat dissipation over the area of the processor being 5 KW per m^2, that is nearly twice as high as the next nearest air cooled machine of high dissipation.

Reliability and Heat Dissipation

Figure 4.3 gives an overall indication of reliability versus heat dissipation for a number of medium/large processors and also gives details of processor speed. The graph again reflects wide divergencies in heat dissipation on processors of the same speed and that, generally, the fault rate increases with heat dissipation.

Looking at heat dissipation versus reliability further, the following gives comparisons between dissipation per integrated circuit (systems from Table 4.2), for air cooled processors, and the reliability index (see Chapter 3), but this time in terms of faults and incidents:

Faults/1000 hrs per 1000 ICs	Reliability index Incidents/1000 hrs per 1000 ICs	Watts per IC
0.21	2.8	2.38
0.10	1.35	0.67
0.077	0.67	0.30
0.026	0.11	0.27
0.022	0.05	0.18
0.007	0.05	0.41

With one notable exception, the fault rate increases with heat dissipation: although this trend is expected, taking into account the airflow and technology characteristics of the different processors, such wide variations would not be predicted. The incident rates have an even wider variation and, although these are affected by other maintainability considerations, the incident per fault ratio increases with heat, even for the system which does not follow the other trends. Thus, besides a decrease in reliability, the effects of increased heat seem to alter the failure mode, making it more of an intermittent nature.

On computers where liquid coolant is piped directly to the modules, to provide more direct cooling, there appears to be an improvement of 4 to 1 or more in the reliability index for a given heat dissipation per IC for a particular technology type and an improvement in the incident per fault ratio for particular maintainability features.

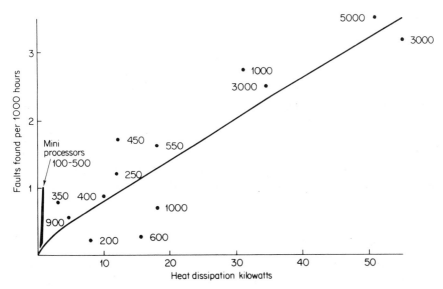

Figure 4.3   Reliability vs. heat dissipation of medium/large mainframes including I/O channels but excluding store. Also shown is processing power in kilo instructions per second (KIPS)

At the other extreme, on mini computers, the reliability index appears to be at least 4 times worse for a given dissipation per IC, with most mini processors giving an overall figure of 0.5 to 1.0 watts per IC and reliability index between 0.2 and 1.0 faults/1000 hours/1000 ICs. The reliability heat dissipation and speed characteristics for certain mini computer processors are shown in Figure 4.3, indicating a fairly constant overall heat dissipation. However, the wide variations in reliability generally increase in line with the watts per IC ratio. Again, predictions based on the technology and airflow characteristics would not indicate such wide variations.

An indication of potential difficulties in adequate cooling of mini computers, which tend to be packaged in small cabinets, is the overall heat dissipation by cabinet volume. On minis the figure is normally between 3 and 15 KW/m^3 compared with 0.5 to 5 KW/m^3 on most air cooled mainframes.

Peripheral Controllers and Main Stores

Similar variations in heat dissipations to those mentioned at the beginning of this section can be found on peripheral controllers and main stores. Heat dissipations for core stores are at least twice the figure for equivalent MOS stores but the MOS stores occupy less space. On MOS stores using the same ICs, heat dissipations can vary by 3 to 1 (e.g. for 128 Kbytes 0.28 KW to 0.97 KW) one of the factors being how hard the stores are driven.

Mainframe Peripherals

For the small configurations shown in Table 4.1, the overall heat dissipation of peripherals mainly varies between 0.3 and 0.6 of the total but with wide variations on individual types of peripheral. On magnetic tape units of the same speed, those from one supplier can give twice the heat dissipation of another. The figures in the table represent running conditions and are generally somewhat less idling. Over the area of the tape units, if all are assumed to be running simultaneously, the heat dissipation is about 8 KW per m² for one type of unit, that is much higher than the LSI processor mentioned earlier. Exchangeable disks generally have less heat dissipation than tape units but again devices of the same capacity and speed can have vastly different dissipations.

Overall Mainframe Systems

From the figures given in Table 4.1, the overall heat dissipation to room air varies between 0.20 and 0.44 KW per m². The peripheral equipment in Table 4.1 occupies about 70 m² giving the same overall range as the total systems, of 0.20 to 0.44 KW per m². The electronics give a much wider variation of 0.11 to 0.57 KW per m², with the lower figures being achieved by certain of the water cooled processors.

One of the major problems in designing air conditioning plant to give an even temperature throughout the room is the volume and velocity of air being blown through the computer equipment - this leads to higher than normal ceiling heights. Table 4.1 shows the air flow in m³/second for the systems where the figure is generally available, indicating wide variations and the systems with the higher figures may suffer from more reliability problems in the presence of a poorly designed air conditioning system or room.

Small and Mini Computer System Heat Dissipation and Space Requirements

Typical heat dissipations for mini computer and small mainframe equipment are as follows:

	Small systems KW	Mini systems KW
Processors	2.0–5.0	0.5–2.5
Disks	0.3–1.5	0.3–1.5
Magnetic tape units	0.6–1.8	0.2–1.3
Card readers	0.5–2.5	0.2–2.0
Line printers	0.7–4.0	0.3–2.0
Paper tape reader/punches	0.5–2.0	0.2–1.0
Typewriters/consoles	0.1–1.0	0.1–0.3

There are also a number of mini processors with heat dissipations as low as 150 watts and certain small processors with heat dissipations over 10 KW. Heat dissipation and space requirements of mini and small systems are normally in the following ranges:

	Equipment	Heat dissipation KW	Minimum space m^2
Basic mini	CPU, paper tape reader/punch type-writer	1–3	7.5
More typical basic mini	As above plus a disk	1.5–4	9.0
Larger mini	As above plus a magnetic tape unit, card reader and printer	3–6	20.0
Basic small system	CPU, card reader printer, disk, console	3–8	25.0
Typical small system	As above but 2 larger disks and 2 magnetic tape units	6–15	36.0

The heat dissipation of the minis and small mainframes is quite similar at 0.13 to 0.44 KW per m^2 for the minis and 0.12 to 0.42 for the small systems. The lower heat dissipations represent about half those on the larger systems but the higher figures are comparable and, hence, air conditioning design problems may be no different.

Microprocessor System Heat Dissipation and Space Requirements

Heat dissipation for microprocessor boards is, typically, in the range 10 to 50 watts but, on completed processors, it may rise to 50–250 watts, with the inclusion of power supplies, fans, extra memory and input/output controllers. A small desktop personal microprocessor system with built in visual display unit, cassette reader and keyboard, may give a minimum heat dissipation of 150 watts. With a number of these in a room, the minimum space requirements is about $2m^2$, giving an overall dissipation of 0.075 KW per m^2. At the other extreme, using the same peripherals as the mini computers, the figure can rise to over 0.3 KW per m^2.

THE NEED FOR AIR CONDITIONING

When it comes to determining the need for air conditioning, there is nothing magic about mini computers and even microprocessors, the main considerations for all types of computers being the amount of time a user is prepared to lose due to:

1. Lower reliability.
2. Switching off the equipment because the environment is unacceptable for people or outside the equipment design specifications.

Reliability deteriorates in conjunction with adverse environments but on small or mini computers, with small configurations, the lower reliability may still be acceptable; for example, on the typical basic mini configuration mentioned above, in a good environment, there may be less than two faults per year and in a poor environment the number may not be much worse than one per two months. On the larger systems with, perhaps, more than one major fault per month, air conditioning is likely to be required to keep the user happy.

Without any form of air conditioning, the temperature and relative humidity within a room are dependent on the outside conditions, building construction, location and orientation, room size and heat dissipation of contents etc. When it is decided to consider air conditioning, it is usual to base calculations on worst case summer conditions with maximum solar gain, making it relatively easy to show that air conditioning is necessary. Other calculations can be carried out on average outside conditions and may show that air conditioning is not required. The truth is often somewhere in between and, in any room with electrical equipment installed, it is almost certain that sometimes it will be too hot, either for the equipment or the people working in the room and it will be necessary to switch off some equipment; also, without air conditioning, it may be necessary to switch off because it is too dry or too dirty.

Maximum Permissible Temperature and Heat Dissipation

For any room, it should be possible to calculate the expected range of temperature variations throughout the year or to plot a curve of the percentage of time that a particular temperature is exceeded for various heat dissipations: for example, Figure 4.4 shows such a curve for a north facing room, in a modern lightweight office block in the London district, different curves being shown for various means of controlling the environment that is with windows closed or open, by using sun blinds and by the provision of mechanical ventilation by fans: for the sun blinds, the lines drawn represent the best case protection with external louvres, that is a facility for which it may not be possible to obtain planning permission: the mechanical ventilation figures are calculated for 30 air changes per

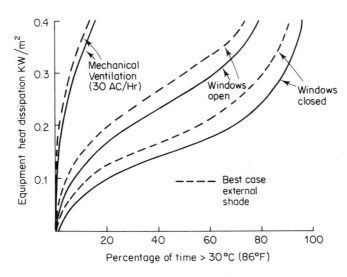

Figure 4.4 Times of excessive heat for a computer in a modern lightweight building with no air conditioning—north facing room

hour, a typical maximum rate giving acceptable levels of complaints about draughts and noise.

Figure 4.4 is drawn for a temperature of 30°C, a typical maximum design temperature; other curves could be drawn for 27°C, which is sometimes accepted as the maximum temperature for staff comfort.

Although Figure 4.4 cannot be taken as typical, if one accepted that the equipment could be switched off for 5% of the time due to the equipment temperature design specification being exceeded, the following would apply:

Means of controlling temperature	Maximum permissible heat dissipation/square metre
None (windows closed)	0.05 KW/m²
Open windows when required	0.1 KW/m²
Mechanical ventilation	0.25 KW/m²

So with the range of heat dissipation on small/mini machines and larger systems of 0.12 to 0.44 KW/m² and 0.20 to 0.44 KW/m² respectively, most would need at least mechanical ventilation to maintain the required limits. On the south side of the building or at a lower temperature, the situation would be worse but, in a heavy weight building, the situation may be much better. Above 0.25 KW/m² air cooling is required but, if it is only necessary to control temperature, the requirement may be met by the provision of a relatively inexpensive cooling unit. It should be noted that the above calculations are for minimum room sizes, where the equipment heat dissipation governs the environment. At the other extreme a single low heat dissipation system e.g. a simple microprocessor system, in a reasonably sized room, will have little effect on the overall environment.

Minimum Relative Humidity

In a non air conditioned room in the UK, providing the room is populated by a small number of staff with low activity, at an internal temperature of 21°C, relative humidity can be expected to be below 30% RH for about 25% of the time and below 20% RH for about 6% of the time, these periods generally being between December and March. When cooling plant is provided, moisture is removed from the air, thus reducing the RH even further: also, of course, when the temperature is above 21°C, the RH is lower.

On the larger systems (see Figure 4.1) all manufacturers specify lower design limits of at least 20% RH and there is no doubt that humidification of the air is necessary in order to meet the specification: similarly, humidification is necessary to meet the lower RH specifications of 20–40% for the media. Failure to provide the humidification can result in the following:

1. Data corruptions or physical destruction of electronic components caused by static electricity discharges—it may be possible to treat the floors or furniture to minimize this problem: the floor resistance to earth should be less than 2×10^{10} ohms. The resistance should also be greater than 5×10^5 ohms, for safety reasons.
2. Curling of the media due to lack of moisture or media sticking to other materials, due to static electricity—both of these problems can cause media misfeeding or misreading and, sometimes, damage to the equipment.

On the small and mini systems (see Figure 4.2), lower RH specifications of 20% or above can often be found for certain pieces of equipment so, if one does not want to become liable for any damage caused by working outside the specification, it may be necessary to switch the equipment off sometimes; also, even if the equipment is switched off when environmental specifications are not met, the optimum reliability and serviceability levels are unlikely to be met without air humidification. If the requirements of the particular project warrant it, the problems may be overcome by the provision of a room humidifier, which may not be too expensive.

Maximum Relative Humidity

In the non air conditioned room at 21°C in the UK, relative humidities of greater than 60, 70 or 80% RH can be expected for about 11%, 3% and

1% of the time respectively, mainly in the June to October period. When cooling is provided, as this will almost certainly be used during the periods of high RH, sufficient moisture is likely to be removed from the air to keep the RH below 60% for most of the time: also, if air conditioning is not provided, with the hotter summer room conditions, the RH should be less than 70% for most of the time.

Mainframe and mini computer manufacturers generally specify an upper RH design limit of at least 80% for most types of equipment but there are some exceptions where 60% is the upper design limit; for the latter, dehumidification of the air is necessary in order to meet the specification; similarly dehumidification is required to meet the upper RH specifications on certain types of media, particularly the paper varieties.

Reliability and lifetime expectancy do get worse as the RH increases above 50% but, within the range encountered in the UK, the effects are not as significant as those caused by low RH or high temperature. Providing that the RH is less than 70% for most of the time, it should be possible to design out problems on equipment caused by RH changes in the 50–70% area; for media handling problems, closer attention to acclimatization may be required.

Dehumidification

In order to achieve dehumidification, it is usual to decrease the temperature of all or part of the air until the desired dew point is reached (for 21°C and 50% RH, dew point is 10.5°C) and then to reheat the air to give the desired room input conditions. With the nominal recommended air conditioning plant design limits of 50 ± 5% RH, the cost of extra cooling plant and running costs to provide dehumidification can be significant. For small and mini computers it is considered that in only exceptional cases should dehumidification facilities be provided. For the larger systems, manufacturers should be encouraged to increase the recommended upper room limit to 70% RH and to ensure that all devices are capable of operation at 80% RH or more.

The most likely time that excessively high relative humidity will be encountered is when the equipment is switched off and the temperature drops to cause condensation. This condensation is more likely in normally air conditioned environments or in lightweight buildings and can usually be overcome by the provision of background heaters.

Dust

With a small computer, working in an office with the windows closed, dust may not give rise to problems but, when windows are opened, mechanical ventilations or cooling units provided, the likelihood of problems increases. For the mechanical ventilation or cooling units, the plastic foam filter normally available will give adequate filtration, providing the atmosphere is not excessively dirty. Where dust problems are encountered when windows are opened for cooling purposes, the only solution may be to switch off the equipment.

Cost of Air Conditioning

One major misconception is that air conditioning plant costs more than computer equipment. With the high rate of inflation over the recent years, the cost of the computer building has increased considerably including air conditioning plant, but current costs are **approximately (in the UK):**

1. Small/mini computers, room units for cooling, humidification and filtration—1.5% to 20% of capital cost of computer. The higher figure is for a small mini, with high heat dissipation, a requirement for continuous availability and working in an area with high solar gain.
2. Medium/large computers, full air conditioning using room units—1% to 5% of computer system capital cost.
3. Medium/large computers, full air conditioning using central plant and ducted air—2% to 7% of computer system capital cost.

In many cases, the cost of providing the air conditioning would seem well worthwhile, as out of specification temperatures could easily be encountered for a significant proportion of the time. In south facing rooms with high heat dissipation equipment, it may be necessary to switch the computer off for more than 20% of the time, this being the case where the cost of air conditioning may be 20% of the computer capital cost.

MAINS POWER SUPPLIES

Specifications

Computer system power units are designed to withstand certain variations in the supplies and, when these are exceeded, are usually arranged to switch the system off. On the magnetic peripheral equipment, the devices may work at varying frequencies but reading difficulties may be encountered if the writing took place at a different mains frequency. In the UK, the Supply Authority undertakes, in normal circumstances, to maintain the voltage within ± 6% and also states that the mains frequency is normally within ± ½% of the nominal. In times of load shedding, due to excessive demands or industrial disputes, these variations can be exceeded, so it may be wise to buy equipment which can tolerate wider excursions. The power units can also tolerate a certain amount of distortion of the mains waveshape, short term disconnections of the supplies or high voltage short term transients superimposed on the supplies. All mains supplies are subject to these spikes and, when the design specifications are exceeded, the result may be data corruptions or destruction of components.

Table 4.3   Mains supply specifications for medium/large systems

Voltage tolerances	Frequency tolerances	Other requirements
+10%–8%	±1%	—
±10%	±1%	Momentary line voltage outages not exceed 100 μsecs. Spikes not to exceed 100 volts or a duration of 10 μsecs.
±10%	±1%	Total harmonic distortion not to exceed 5%. For 100% load change nominal voltage to be recovered within 310 m secs. Transients to be within ±10% of voltage. (These are specifications for output of alternator set.)
+7%–7½%	+1%–2%	Greater than ½ cycle not to be lost in 10 consecutive cycles. Transients not to exceed 10 volts at 1 KHz varying to 400 volts at 4 MHz (filter characteristics).
±7%	±1%	System can withstand 1 kV spikes for 2 μsecs duration.
±10%	±5% (CPU) ±1% (peripherals)	Total harmonic distortion not to exceed 10% of fundamental. Interruptions not to exceed 600 μsecs. Surges to be limited to 1 kV.
±5% ±2% for 1 sec	±1%	Total harmonic distortion not greater than 5%. Alternators required.
+6%–10%	±2%	Transients not to exceed: 0.7 nominal line voltage for ½ sec 2.5x nominal line voltage for 10 m secs 5.0x nominal line voltage for 5 m secs.

Table 4.3 gives details of mains supply requirements for various systems from the mainframe suppliers. It can be seen that there are wide variations in voltage and frequency requirements and even more so for total harmonic distortion, mains disconnections and transients; as for the air conditioning requirements, those with the tightest tolerances can indicate design weaknesses.

Small, mini and micro computer suppliers give specifications, usually of ± 10% for voltage and between ± 1% and ± 10% for frequency. In many cases, no specifications are given for transients, disconnections or distortions but, on others, they are just as varied as the mainframes. Many of the mini processors have power fail safe facilities, which ensure that contents of registers can be placed in a non-volitile store, when the supply is disconnected, and to restart automatically when the mains are reconnected: this is all very well for real time applications dependent only on the processor but input/output transfers to peripheral equipment are likely to be lost.

Protection

When mains voltages are subject to wider variations, disconnections or distortions than the specification, certain protection may be available by the provision of motor alternator sets (e.g. up to 1 sec. disconnection) and the effects of frequency variations can be minimized by the provision of an AC/DC/AC converter. Protection against mains transients can also be made by providing motor alternator sets and, often, by the provision of RF filters or isolation transformers.

Large systems provided from the USA suppliers are sometimes designed to work only on 60 Hz supplies, so alternator sets have to be provided. Similarly, many of the large processors have 400 Hz power supplies, for which alternators are required, thus giving more protection.

Where the systems are subject to long term mains supply disconnections or variations, which cannot be isolated as above, it may be necessary to provide a standby diesel generator which, with additional provisions, can be arranged to give no break supplies for critical applications. However, these are expensive and cannot be justified for most applications.

Reliability Effects of Switching Off and On

Whenever power is disconnected/reconnected to a computer system, the components undergo a thermal shock, which may eventually give rise to a component failure, depending, of course, on the quality of the particular components or products. On one very large system it was found that early models of the system only worked on 50% of occasions when the power was reconnected. The manufacturer gave the following expectations for unscheduled mains failures:

Duration of break in supplies	System likely to be available in	Extra down time likely over next 15 days
<5 mins	3 hours	3 hours
5–30 mins	4 hours	3 hours
>30 mins	6 hours	3 hours

The above indicates that, the longer the break, as the machine cooled down more, the thermal shock of switching on was greater and more down time could be expected on reconnection of the supplies. Also on switch on, further troubles could be expected over the following 15 days, due to more intermittent faults.

A more recent CCA study of morning sickness on a modern processor indicated that power-on did not introduce solid faults (which require immediate repair) but transient incidents, where the incident rate gradually declined from 12 times the long term mean at 1 hour after switch-on, to 1.5 times the mean after 15 hours, without any engineering intervention. The foregoing was after a weekend switch-off and little effects were evident following switch-off periods of less than 12 hours.

Other effects noted are that, whenever the operational periods are changed, reliability may deteriorate. When a processor is switched off and on, on a daily basis, eventually the marginal components which are affected by this mode of operation are weeded out. If the system is then left switched on continuously other component weaknesses may be induced and reliability may deteriorate again until the newly found marginal components are changed. These effects are more apparent on the larger systems and, when a supplier insists that the processor be left on overnight, even though it is not being used, this should be taken as a possible sign of a poor quality product, which is delivered with marginal components included.

ELECTROMAGNETIC RADIATION

Specifications

Computer systems are susceptible to data corruptions due to radiated interference and, where specifications are given, they are usually in the range:

Not to exceed 100 mv/metre over the range 15 KHz–9 GHz, to

Not more than 1 volt/metre over the range 15 KHz–9 GHz, and sometimes

Up to 14 volts/metre over the range 15 KHz–35 MHz

To avoid field strengths in the above ranges, it may be necessary to site the computer 1 mile or more from powerful radar or radio transmitters. Alternatively, protection may be obtained by installing the computer in a screened room, or where the limits are marginally exceeded, by the careful siting of equipment, cable runs and mains supplies to lighting and power points.

Earthing Requirements

To avoid interference problems, including any generated by the computer system itself, most of the major system suppliers specify a signal earth, isolated from the protection earth, and going back to the building earth on to earth spikes or plates, from one central point in the computer room. Variations can be found in earth resistance specifications, normally from 1 ohm to 5 ohms: in the former case, the specification is likely to be for the cable resistance only. One manufacturer specifies 2' × 2' mesh of copper wire beneath the false floor, attached to the building earth.

When systems are first installed, great care is taken to avoid earth loops but, in practice, it has been found that, when systems are enhanced with additional equipment, earth loops/misconnections may be introduced; to overcome this problem it is useful to have facilities to easily disconnect the signal earth system for testing purposes.

SHOCK AND VIBRATION

Sometimes manufacturers specify equipment tolerances for shock and vibration, these are typically:

Maximum shock   5 g for 10 ms 5 seconds between shocks
to 30 g for 11 ms $\frac{1}{2}$ sine wave from 3 axes

The above is mainly of importance as the equipment is being transported.

Maximum vibration   ±0.0015" maximum displacement at 10–31 Hz
0.15 g at 31–100 Hz

or   0.02" maximum displacement at 5–10 Hz
0.25 g at 10–100 Hz

or   0.012" peak to peak displacement at 10–55 Hz
1 g at 44 Hz

Chapter 5

Software Reliability

COMPARISON WITH HARDWARE

Failure Mechanisms

Given precisely identical circumstances, software always behaves in a consistent manner and, once it is correct, it could be said to be totally reliable. Unfortunately, the question of correctness may be open to dispute if the software does not behave in the way a user expects, even though it may appear to conform to some broad specification. Compared with the hardware failure mechanisms, there are some similarities and some differences.

HARDWARE	SOFTWARE
A Design logically incorrect or incomplete	Design logically incorrect or incomplete
B Constructed incorrectly	Coded incorrectly, assembled incorrectly
C Inherent unreliability	
D Wear out (increasing unreliability)	

When the software is first written and assembled, as for hardware, it usually undergoes a series of design quality assurance tests to ensure that the specification is met on facilities, performance and on physical resource requirements. It is again fairly easy to check out the broad facilities provided but impossible to forecast and test for all possible modes of operation, combinations and sequences. One difference with the hardware is that, the writing of comprehensive tests for the software is often regarded as an overhead, whereas for hardware, comprehensive tests are written as a natural process for identifying constructional defects on all new equipment and for overcoming long term reliability problems. So, when software is first delivered, it is almost certain that the design will not be quite correct or some coding errors will be present.

D

It is arguable as to whether software is more complex than hardware but, on amount provided and variety, software is generally far more excessive. For most main range systems, the total software comprises at least 500,000 instructions or data words. If the gate count on the processor could be related to the instruction count, the amount of software could be regarded as being at least 3 to 10 times the hardware for a typical range of systems, although on the super computers, available from one or two suppliers, the hardware becomes excessive.

Because of the size of the software, it is likely that all required facilities will not be provided initially and plans will be made for these to be included in future releases. Unlike hardware, it is almost impossible to determine the speed of operation of the software at the design stage so, inevitably, more areas of the software will be found to be slow when tested, and further software releases will be planned for the incorporation of performance improvements. Closely associated with performance are the hardware resources required by the software and these are also inevitably excessive initially, requiring major rewrites of parts of the software. On top of these are changes in conjunction with hardware modifications and for initially unplanned major changes/enhancements. The net result of all these new release requirements and corrections of user observed problems, is that the software is continuously changing, giving a similar effect to that which would be obtained if large parts of the hardware were replaced by newly designed parts at regular intervals.

Error Rate

For the software, manufacturers can calculate an error rate to represent the number of design/coding errors relative to total instructions. Figures quoted are usually in the range of $\frac{1}{4}$/1000 instructions to 10/1000 instructions, so initially, on new software of 500,000 instructions, between 125 and 5000 errors could be expected. The pre-delivery QA usually gets rid of the simple problems and, although a peak of errors can be expected immediately following first delivery, the rate of new errors being reported is often fairly constant due to the software being introduced to different users over a period and the more obscure errors requiring a long and wide variety of work to reproduce them. When a new release of the software comes along (this may be anything from a few weeks to a year) there are likely to be faults still present in the old release, even in code that has been changed to fix other problems; hence, it is little wonder that manufacturers usually require all customers to make use of new releases after a fairly short period of time.

Corrections

When a software error is reported and eventually a cure is found, this is likely to be initially of a temporary, not properly tested variety and, although all users are generally informed via some software error publication, only those who have encountered the error are encouraged to include the revised code; there are, of course, exceptions to the foregoing for particular classes of problems but they may only represent a small proportion of the problems (e.g. in the case of one manufacturer 10% of the corrections were such that they should be incorporated by all users). The corrections are then gathered together and incorporated in a future release, which may be a separate maintenance release or in conjunction with planned enhancements.

Early Life

The software errors above include those due to the design being incorrect or incomplete and those due to being coded incorrectly. Constructional problems of a particular customers software are not the same as hardware, as a good copy of software (at least an identical copy) can be generated and verified. Problems are encountered when the controlling software for a particular user is assembled from standard modules; this may be due to incorrect assembly or to the uniqueness of the configuration, when the software may not have been pre-tested in that particular form.

Overall, on a system comprising newly designed hardware and software, software problems are likely to be predominant initially, mainly because:

1. There is more of the software to go wrong;
2. The software is continuously being changed (redesigned).

There have been exceptions to the above on some of the super computers, where hardware problems have always been predominant. As the systems get older, software becomes more correct and users become used to software restrictions, then hardware failures come to the fore, due to the built in failure mechanisms.

SOFTWARE ERROR CLASSIFICATIONS

In collecting statistics on software correctness/reliability, comparisons between software supplied by different manufacturers can be difficult. An example of this is the definition of software errors, which could be any of the following:

1. All instances of problems seen by users;
2. Error reports submitted to the manufacturer;
3. Error reports accepted by the manufacturer;
4. Problems identified;
5. Problems for which corrections are devised;
6. Problems for which corrections are devised and sent to users.

Problems seen by Users

There are no statistics available on the overall frequency of fault incidents as observed by users or programmers; some of the faults give similar symptoms to system hardware faults (such as causing the whole system to halt) where each incident may be reported (not necessarily to the software department) but others, not observable from a central point, may only be reported occasionally. It should be noted that certain hardware problems (such as a device making undetected mistakes) are similar to the latter, where one fault report is given to the contractor for many incidents affecting individual programs. An indication of types of software faults encountered is given in Chapter 6.

Error Reports Submitted by Users

Figures 5.1 and 5.2 show the number of error reports per month submitted by users on software from two different manufacturers (both have been around for a few years). Figure 5.1 shows details of both operating system and other software fault reports: in the operating system area, an average of 92 reports per month were submitted, with the maximum of 134 being influenced by a new software release: in the other software area, the reporting rate averages at 103 per month. Figure 5.2 shows operating system error reports over a period covering three releases, with the

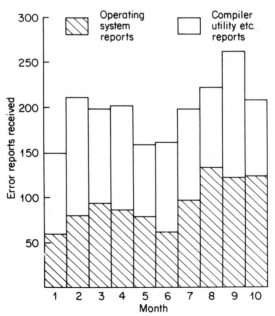

Figure 5.1 Errors reported by users, manufacturer A

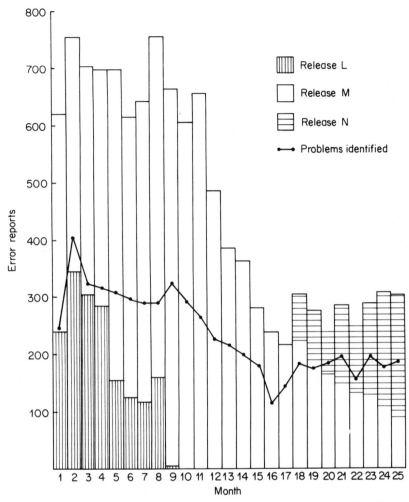

Figure 5.2   Error reports received and problems identified over 3 software
releases of an operating system, manufacturer B

reporting rate fairly constant over the first 11 months, at 605 to 758 per
month, and again over the last 11 months, at 217 to 308 per month.

In comparing the software between the two manufacturers, it should be
noted that the second operating system is both larger in terms of the
number of instructions and has nearly twice as many users. Overall useful
figures calculated for both, including short term monthly variations are
approximately:

Reports/month/1000 instructions	0.4–2.0
Reports/month/reporting installation	0.5–4.2
Reports/month/1000 instructions/100 installations	0.3–1.0

These figures do not take into account factors such as number of changes made, basic design concepts, quality of programming staff, pre-delivery QA and feedback to users on known problems. However, for a particular manufacturer's software they should provide the basis for planning support—in the case of one manufacturer, a forecast is made of the number of systems and support staffing recruited on the basis that there will be 12 reports/year/installation.

Error Reports Accepted by the Manufacturer

In the case of manufacturer A (as Figure 5.1), approximately 25% of the error reports submitted contain insufficient information to be considered or contain suggestions, and a further 25% are found to be user or documentation errors, leaving about half of the reports as indicating real software problems.

For a second manufacturer (B) (as Figure 5.2) 5–10% of reports are classified as no error, 5–17% insufficient evidence, 5–10% problems in other areas, e.g. hardware, and up to 5% documentation errors. These figures are somewhat less than the first case, probably because users are encouraged not to send in a report unless a problem has been seen at least twice.

For a third manufacturer (C), on an established operating system, somewhat less in size than the second one above but with twice as many installations, accepted software errors for a particular release are shown in Figure 5.3, giving an average of 171 accepted errors per month.

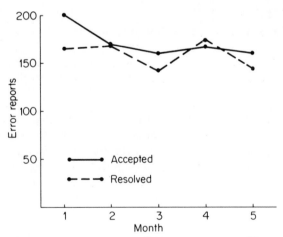

Figure 5.3 Accepted and resolved error reports on one release (R) of an operating system, manufacturer C

Problems Identified and Corrected

For manufacturer A's software, it was claimed that, about 25% of error reports are for new problems, and 25% are further reports of previously accepted problems. From Figure 5.1 this indicates that new problems revealed per month were about 23 on the operating system and 26 on compilers etc. For one particular 6 month period the following figures applied:

Number of times reported	Number of problems with correction given
1	172
2	48
3	25
4	5
5	5

Or 388 reports for 255 problems giving an average of 1.52 reports per problem. The foregoing problems are ones for which corrections are sent to users with a further 10 reports classified as new restrictions and a further 16 as problems to be fixed in later releases, representing 2% and 4% of accepted error reports respectively.

For manufacturer B, discovered, but not necessarily corrected, problems

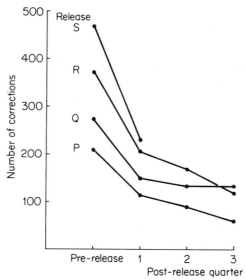

Figure 5.4 Correction activity on an operating system, manufacturer C (various releases shown—P, Q, R, S)

are also shown in Figure 5.2. The ratio of errors reported to problems identified is 2.18 for year 1 and 1.6 for year 2. However, these figures apply to all types of error reports and problem classifications.

In the case of manufacturer C, correction activity is shown in Figure 5.4 for four different releases (issued in the order P, Q, R, S) on a quarterly basis. For release R, after release, the ratio of accepted errors (Figure 5.3) to corrections sent out is about 2.8 over a period.

Overall Error Rate

The diversity of software problems is reflected in the above range of between 1.5 and 2.8 reports/problem, which indicates that different users experience different problems and software errors have high applications dependency; this, of course, affects the overall error rate. Of the information available, details are not known of how many of the correctable problems are in the old code nor how much of the code was changed, but if one assumed that the whole code was rewritten once per two years, then the error rate for the three manufacturers' software is in the range 2.3 to 4.5 errors per 1000 instructions.

SOFTWARE QUALITY ASSURANCE

There are widely varying standards on testing of software prior to release, on test contents, configurations used for test, criteria of success and duration of tests; some examples of these follow.

Configurations

For in-house testing of operating systems, configurations vary from a single mid-range system, through a maximum configuration top of the range system, to a variety of systems. Most manufacturers also provide for a pre-release field test, which may be overlapped with the in-house testing, with the number of systems varying from one or two to 15 or more, including mandatory use by all the manufacturer's in-house production systems.

Content of Tests

These can vary from running a number of tests obtained from users to specially designed tests to check facilities, measure performance, etc.

Duration of Tests

These are of course dependent on configurations used and content of tests but typical duration of tests, including field testing, can vary from a month to 6 months or more for an operating system: one manufacturer reported 40,000 hours of testing prior to release.

Criteria of Success

Examples of these for operating systems are:

1. Best endeavours—in one case where this was employed, besides new problems, 50% of old problems were carried forward from one release to the next;
2. No more than eight known problems in each of the major software packages;
3. No more than one system crash per 12 hours during last week of in-house testing: no release to be supplied to the field with more than 50 patches for corrections: no more than five uncorrected known uncritical problems and no known system crash problems and other critical errors;
4. Small amount of lost work: better than one system crash per week with no more than 10 minutes recovery: no more than 10 known faults (including those submitted from field testing).

For some of the more stringent criteria, it is known that the criteria have not always been achieved prior to release but they have usually ensured that the particular software gave rise to fewer problems than the average.

Testing Organizations

The in-house testing organization can vary from testing by the programmers who wrote the software to a full blown independent QA organization. One manufacturer reverted to programmer testing on the basis that the QA organization was ineffective.

Effectiveness of Testing

From the figures given earlier, it is quite clear that, because of the diversity of problems, it is quite impossible to expect the pre-release testing to rid of software of all errors but at least it should lead to corrections of common problems which affect a large number of users.

An indication of QA effectiveness and support requirements is given in Figure 5.4 where, for the first three releases shown, it appears that the corrections prior to release remained fairly constant at about 40%. Bearing in mind that the number of installations more than doubled over the period covered, problems had to be reproduced and corrected at an ever increasing rate prior to release.

SOFTWARE SERVICE

Backlogs

Over any particular monthly period, a manufacturer should have sufficient resources available to resolve an equal number of reports to the new ones received but, due to the time required to resolve the first problems received and subsequent difficult ones, inevitably a backlog of errors builds up. For the three manufacturers considered earlier, this backlog is equivalent to 8 to 39 days worth of new reports; in other cases, backlogs of up to 6 months have been recorded.

Response Time

Response time can be defined as the period between a manufacturer receiving an error report to sending out a response to the user. In comparing response times there is the same difficulty as the definition of an error, that is, the quality of the response can vary: in one case, measured average response time was 14 days but 40% of the responses were 'under investigation'; in another case, the average response time was in the range 35 to 56 days, over different periods, but the responses provided corrections for most of the problems. Figure 5.5 shows the distribution of response times for a number of error reports on the latter system but, this time, the response time is from date received to the date when a general publication is issued to all users, giving a mean response time of 82 days.

Overall, given constant resources, the average response time is likely to be at least as long as the backlog mentioned earlier.

Response times for specific users can, of course, be improved by having suitably qualified and experienced on site support and, experience has shown that this can lead to a large proportion of errors being found and corrected in the same day as reported.

Priorities

Most manufacturers have a priority system for user error reports but these can vary from a simple low/medium/high system to a comprehensive list of priorities against particular fault symptoms, e.g. priority 1—no work runable; priority 2—vital job not runable, etc. When fault reports are submitted with the highest priority, one would expect the response time to be shorter. On one type of system, with a comprehensive priority scheme (system above with 14 days mean response time), the response time for priority 1 reports was 3 days. On another system, using the simpler priority scheme (as above with response time 35–56 days), there appeared to be no difference in response times for high, medium and low priorities, although operating system problems had a response time less than other software.

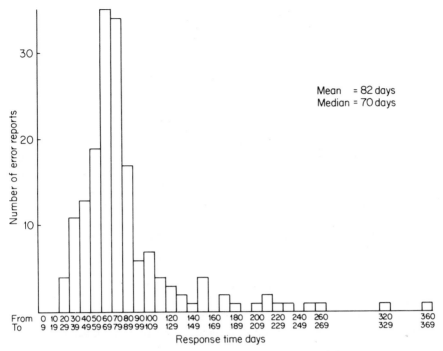

Figure 5.5   Response time for software correction from receiving report to general publication of conditions

Serviceability, Down Time and System Failures

Chapters 8 and 7 cover serviceability (availability during scheduled hours) and down time respectively but, essentially, the serviceability ratio is:

$$\frac{\text{Up time}}{\text{Up time} + \text{Down time}}$$

Similarly, the unserviceability ratio is:

$$\frac{\text{Down time}}{\text{Up time} + \text{Down time}}$$

For a computer system, the unserviceability ratio can be broken down into its constitutional parts to represent the effects of the various hardware and software elements, e.g.:

$$\frac{\text{Mainframe down time}}{\text{Up time} + \text{Total down time}}$$

$$+ \frac{\text{System down time due to peripheral equipment faults}}{\text{Up time} + \text{Total down time}}$$

$$+ \frac{\text{System down time due to software faults}}{\text{Up time} + \text{Total down time}}$$

A serviceability ratio could also be calculated for software to take into account its completeness, correctness and time to actually correct certain classes or errors. However, it is considered that such a single figure would be rather meaningless for application across the board. On the other hand, as for hardware, a system serviceability ratio is most useful, where only down time directly affecting the whole system is taken into account.

As far as the operating system is concerned, at varying intervals the whole computer system stops due to software error being encountered and down time may be incurred due to:

1. Time wasted in taking a dump of the main store;
2. Recovery time;
3. On-line investigation time—some systems are being provided with facilities for remote on-line interrogation for diagnosing software problems;
4. Waiting time for service—in exceptional cases the user may declare the system unusable until a particular problem is corrected, e.g. in the case of random breaches of security or data corruptions: this attitude may be taken, just as it may be for similar problems caused by hardware faults;
5. Time to install and test software corrections, either in conjunction with 4 or when other corrections have to be installed during normal operational time;
6. Time spent by the engineer in examining the system to determine whether the system failure is caused by hardware or software. This is a real problem as it is often impossible to tell the difference without detailed examination, which could take hours. (In one case, 60% of system stoppages reported as software problems on a number of systems were eventually found to be hardware.)

In most cases only 1, 2 and 6 will apply and, often only recovery time.

As indicated in 6, the engineer may have trouble in determining whether an incident is due to a hardware or software fault. In other cases there is difficulty in apportioning the blame, e.g. for a fault in error recovery software, a hardware fault, which should normally be recoverable, leads to a system stoppage; or a software fault does not allow on-line engineering test programs to be run, so the whole system has to be taken over to enable a peripheral to be tested.

RELIABILITY VARIATIONS WITH TIME

Average Long Term Effects

As indicated earlier, because of initial incorrect and incomplete design and incorrect coding, when software is first delivered, numerous software faults can be expected. An example of the trend in improvement in system failures, caused by software faults, is shown in Figure 5.6 for an operating system from first delivery. The graph represents average failure rates on medium and large processors, ignoring the short term effects of new releases, which caused average degradations of up to 10 times. The overall improvement, based on 6 monthly averages, is 60 times over 5 years, that

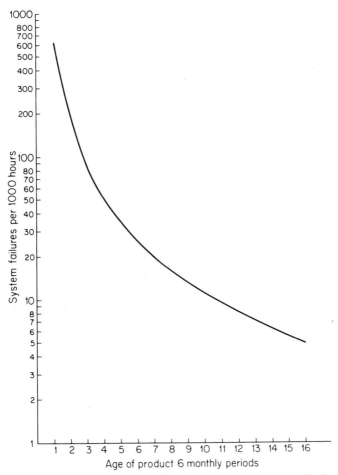

Figure 5.6   Trend in system failures caused by software faults from first delivery of a large operating system

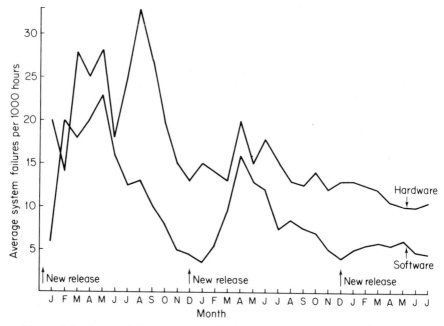

Figure 5.7   System failures on a population of established computer systems

is much greater than the worst case processor, shown in Chapter 2; the shape of the curve is different, and reliability continues to improve, giving a 120 times improvement after 8 years. Providing errors are still corrected, this improvement should continue until the software is perfect and a zero failure rate is recorded; however, it can be seen that this would take many years and is never really achieved in practice. The initial failure rate in terms of mean time between system failures is about 1½ hours, so it can be seen that the system would not be capable of producing much work.

Average Short Term Effects

New Releases

Figure 5.7 shows the characteristics of another operating system over 2½ years, but not from first delivery and reflects the average system failure rate. With the introduction of new releases the average degradation is 3 to 4 times. This increase in failure rate would be more severe, of course, if all users brought the new releases into use at the same time. Following the high failure rates, improvement is at a somewhat slower rate, as corrections are included.

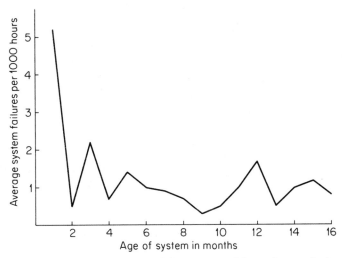

Figure 5.8   Apparent early failures caused by software faults
on an established operating system (good sites)

Early Failures

Considerable site to site variations can be expected on systems of the same
type, examples being shown in Figures 5.8 and 5.9, which are for the same
type of system over the same period. Figure 5.8 has been drawn from the
results on 28 systems, delivered over a one year period, to reflect a
common hand over date and represents early failures on the average good

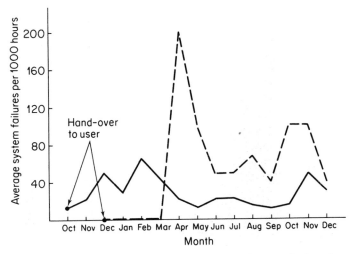

Figure 5.9   System failures caused by software faults from
hand-over to user (2 bad sites)

system. (Systems shown in Figure 5.9 were excluded as they distorted the pattern.) In the first month, the failure rate is 10 times greater than the second month. The other peaks are probably caused by average effects of new releases and, in the third month, by the build up of user work.

The best system reported no system failures, caused by software, over the 16 month period, obviously a simple application for which the software was adequately pre-tested.

Individual System Short Term Effects

Of the worst systems shown in Figure 5.9, one is consistently bad, that is an average of 20 times worse than the average good system; however, this system is a manufacturer's bureau machine, with widely varying applications and is also used for some software testing. The initial degradation is thought to be by the build up of work and the later ones by the introduction of new releases.

The second bad system reported no system failures caused by software, over the first four months, then collapsed. It is thought that only program testing was carried out initially and the degradation coincided with the introduction of a new release, which had new required facilities.

New Releases

A second example of the effects of a different new operating system release on system failures is shown in Figure 5.10, on a weekly basis. Quite typically, this user tried out new releases for a short time and initially found them unsatisfactory.

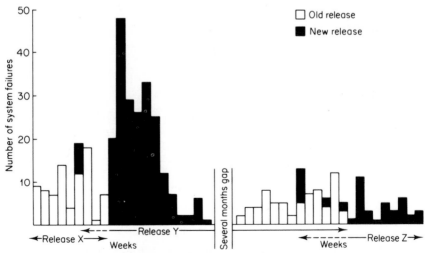

Figure 5.10   Software caused system failures before and after new releases

When release Y was brought into use, there was a significant increase in the number of system failures. Release Z did not make a lot of difference, perhaps because its introduction was delayed more.

RELIABILITY VARIATION COMPARED WITH HARDWARE

The figures given above indicate that the initial software reliability can be expected to be far worse than hardware and the disturbance effects of new releases even more so. However, this is not always the case, and examples can be found, where hardware faults give an equal number or more system failures and, often, more down time. The latter is because hardware faults can incur extended engineering investigation times, whereas most of the software down time is due to recovery time only.

Variations from One Supplier to Another

Table 5.1 shows mean time between system failures, mean down time per system failure and unserviceability for a number of computer systems from various suppliers, separate figures being given for mainframe, other hardware and software. Each of the figures is based on populations of processors: all are fairly large to large, with well established software and are shown in descending order of computer power, the last 4 having competed for certain projects. For 5 out of 6 types of system, the system failure rate is worse on the hardware than the software. In all cases the total down time is higher on the hardware, this being reflected in the unserviceability ratio between hardware and software of 3–18 times. The main point is that, on established systems, at times when new releases are not being introduced, hardware failures and down time are more likely to be predominant but wider extremes, as reflected in Figure 5.9 may still be found on the software.

Long Term Variations

Figure 5.7, besides showing variations in system failures due to software faults, also shows hardware caused system failures. Except for one peak of failures caused by the introduction of a new processor model to the population, it should be noted, that the trend in hardware failures follows that on the software, indicating that some of the failures have probably been attributed to the wrong cause, or new hardware problems have been reproduced by introducing the new software, some possibly due to complementary modifications. It should be noted that, most of the time, system failures due to hardware give more trouble than the software. However, it should again be noted that the graph represents a population average.

Table 5.1 System failures and unserviceability on a number of computers supplied by various manufacturers

	Mainframe			Other hardware			Total hardware			Software			System		
	Mtbsf	Mdtsf	% US	Mtbsf	Mdtsf	% US	Mtbsf	Mdtsf	%US	Mtbsf	Mdtsf	% US	Mtbsf	Mdtsf	%US
1	21.3	0.91	4.1	71.4	0.87	1.2	16.4	0.92	5.3	56.5	0.17	0.3	12.7	0.75	5.6
2	38.5	1.03	2.6	137.0	0.83	0.6	30.0	1.00	3.2	45.5	0.50	1.1	18.1	0.81	4.3
3	37.3	0.80	2.1	89.3	0.63	0.7	26.3	0.76	2.8	28.7	0.12	0.4	13.7	0.46	3.2
4	21.7	0.69	3.1	63.7	0.71	1.1	16.2	0.71	4.2	100.0	0.30	0.3	13.9	0.65	4.5
5	250.0	1.51	0.6	151.5	1.68	1.1	94.3	1.63	1.7	205.0	0.45	0.2	64.5	1.26	1.9
6	119.0	1.93	1.6	178.6	1.44	0.8	71.4	1.75	2.4	65.3	0.33	0.5	34.1	1.02	2.9

Mtbsf = Mean time between system failure in hours
Mdtsf = Mean down time per failure in hours
% US = Percentage unserviceability

Table 5.2   System failures and unserviceability on eight computers of the same type over a 6 month period

	Hardware		Software		System	
	Mtbsf	% US	Mtbsf	% US	Mtbsf	% US
1	15.4	4.6	83.3	0.6	13.0	5.2
2	25.0	3.7	100.0	0.6	20.0	4.3
3	76.9	1.7	202.0	0.2	55.7	1.9
4	22.7	2.1	120.0	0.2	19.1	2.3
5	7.7	6.1	125.0	0.2	7.3	6.3
6	17.9	2.4	115.0	0.3	15.5	2.7
7	12.3	5.8	111.0	0.4	11.1	6.2
8	8.8	4.1	28.6	1.0	6.7	5.1

Variations on Computers of the Same Type

Considering a number of systems of the same type, with established software, the effects of utilisation on reliability can be greater on the hardware. Table 5.2 shows mean time between system failures and unserviceability, for hardware and software on eight systems of the same type. On the hardware there is a 10 to 1 variation in the frequency of system failures and 3.6 to 1 on unserviceability: the difference in variations between failure rates and unserviceability is due to the fact that particular users/engineers have some control on the number of failures. In some cases the engineer investigates every incident, leading to a high mtbsf with long mean down times: in other cases, due to the intermittent nature of most problems, work is continued with frequent short duration stoppages, as the engineer gathers information on the problems, and leads to a lower mtbsf and low mean down times. On the software, there is a 7 to 1 variation in system failure rates and 5 to 1 on unserviceability, again these being less significant than hardware problems.

Short Term Variations

For the system shown in Figure 5.10 the following summary has also been made of hardware and software caused system failures, over the same period.

System failures per week (of 100 hours)

	Hardware		Software	
	Average	Range	Average	Range
Release X	7.3	1–18	8.8	1–18
Release Y (first 6 weeks)	4.2	1–8	30.2	20–48
Release Y (later)	6.4	1–11	4.7	1–12
Release Z	4.3	2–10	4.0	1–11

The above shows similar averages and ranges of variation for both software and hardware, except when release Y was first introduced. An interesting observation is that, when the new software was introduced, the reported hardware failures decreased, again indicating the problems in distinguishing between hardware and software failures. Overall variations on a 4 weekly basis were:

	Mtbsf	Percentage unserviceability
Hardware	8.0–44	1.6– 8.5
Software	2.9–36	0.8– 9.4
System	2.7–19	3.4–11.9

In this case, due to software problems following the new releases, there is a somewhat wider variation in system failure rates due to software; also software failures lead to a considerable short term reduction in serviceability.

SPECIFICATION OF SOFTWARE RELIABILITY

As a summary for when it is necessary to specify software reliability requirements, criteria could be devised for the following:

1. Software correctness—the number of outstanding problems in individual software packages and response times for providing corrections. This may have to be associated with a comprehensive priority scheme which reflects the severity of the symptoms seen by the user and takes into account whether the problems are avoidable.
2. System serviceability—the effects of software errors on system serviceability. As indicated earlier, it is extremely difficult to differentiate between hardware/software system failures and down time for certain types of problem, so it may only be possible to specify overall system serviceability criteria.
3. System reliability—the frequency of system or subsystem failures caused by software errors. Again there is the problem of differentiating between hardware and software faults.

To be realistic, the criteria should also take into account:

1. Brand new software may require less demanding criteria initially and a timescale for improvement;
2. A relaxation in criteria may be required for a short period following the introduction of new releases;
3. Variations caused by different or changes in applications and utilizations;
4. The effectiveness of a manufacturer's support in providing corrections

is dependent on the reproducibility of the problems, which is, in turn, dependent on the information supplied by the user;

5. There may be other requirements to be taken into account, for instance to demonstrate speed/performance: it might be that this can only be achieved at the expense of more outstanding incorrect facilities or poorer system reliability/serviceability.

Chapter 6

Fault Symptoms

CONSEQUENCES OF FAILURES

So far, failures discussed have been in terms of component failures, investigations, incidents, error reports or system failures. System failures represent symptoms or consequences of failures but there are others, where the consequences may be more severe, such as wrong results being produced without any indication, or breaches of security, allowing unauthorized access to data. Other incidents on peripherals can cause the input media to be physically damaged but there are many others whose consequences are not very severe, only causing minor operational disturbances. To determine likely consequences of various incidents, it is useful to consider fault symptoms.

UNDETECTED ERRORS

It is very difficult to obtain information on how often computers make mistakes. The most publicized incidents, such as an excessive electricity bill of thousands of pounds, usually being caused by user program errors. However, during CCA acceptance trials (see Chapter 10), results of all programs are checked and the cause of the problems determined. Analysis of the results of 100 trials, on various types of system, gave the undetected errors shown in Table 6.1.

It should be noted that programs used during the trials were mainly engineering and user type programs which are looking for this sort of fault and do not carry out integrity checks (e.g. sum checks), which may be included in live user programs; hence, in practice, the undetected error rates could be expected to be somewhat lower than indicated.

Processors

Certain of the systems had parity checks throughout the processor, including parity predictions for floating point operations, and error correction on the main storage; on these, no undetected errors were

Table 6.1 Faults giving undetected errors

Device	Undetected error rate
Central processing system	0–30% of faults
Disks and magnetic tape units	10–25% ″ ″
Card punches	30–40% ″ ″
Card/paper tape readers	50–60% ″ ″
Printers	60–70% ″ ″
Paper tape punches	80–90% ″ ″

recorded during the trials but there is still a small probability that they could occur. On large computers, without parity checks in the processor, up to 30% of faults gave wrong results, including most of those in the floating point area. Similarly, on mini computers, without parity checking on the store, the figure was also up to 30%.

Figure 6.1 has been drawn to show the magnitude of the problem and

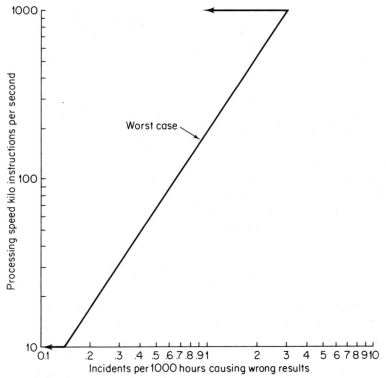

Figure 6.1 Undetected errors on mainframes per 1000 hours

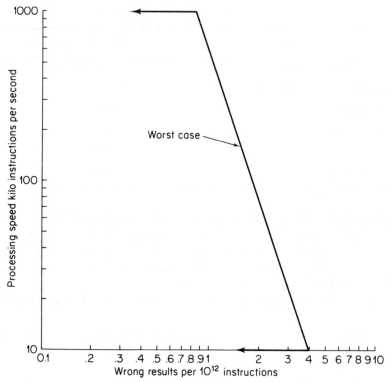

Figure 6.2   Undetected errors on mainframes per 10^{12} instructions

shows worst case undetected errors per 1000 hours versus processor speed, in terms of kilo instructions per second (KIPS), over a range of processors. (The graph is based on worst case data given in Chapter 11 and by assuming that 30% of incidents give undetected errors.) With the trend shown, at 10,000 KIPS, up to 10 wrong results per 1000 hours, possibly one per week, could be expected.

These figures may be considered unacceptable, so it is useful to consider the scale of the problem in different terms. The figures can also be measured in terms of incidents per 10^{12} instructions by the following formula:

$$\frac{1000 \times \text{incidents per thousand hours}}{\text{KIPS} \times 3.6}$$

The above produces the approximate results shown in Figure 6.2. The first observation is that, larger processors with the same sort of checking facilities, are likely to make less mistakes in completing a given amount of work, even though they run it much faster. The next point is that, with 4 or less mistakes per 10^{12} instructions, the computers must surely give far less wrong results than any equivalent manual system.

In general, the effects and consequences of hardware faults depends on whether they are solid, intermittent or of a transient nature. Solid faults can cause numerous programs to produce wrong results (only counted as one incident in Figures 6.1 and 6.2) but they are likely to be soon noticed and suspect jobs can be rerun. Transient faults may produce wrong results but, with a bit of luck, the results will be obviously wrong.

Because most incidents are caused by intermittent faults, wrong results are likely to be generated over a relatively short period, with long periods of correct results in between; so to specify the undetected error rate in terms of one per week (as above) is rather misleading. Other faults, which could lead to wrong results, could either cause a program to be terminated, for example by causing an overflow, or a system to stop.

Peripheral Equipment

Disks

10 to 25% of faults on disks caused errors which would normally be undetected, the lower figures being obtained on units with the most sophisticated checking codes. The faults included reading the wrong record or file, information being written wrongly with correct checking codes and, occasionally, spurious misreads. Some of the faults were due to controllers but others were cured by adjustments to the drive. With the same utilization as trials, and reliability of established exchangeable disks of about 1 incident per 1000 hours per drive (see Chapter 11), 0.1 to 0.25 undetected errors could be expected per thousand hours, that is similar to a small worst case processor; this may indicate that a number of the errors are caused by disk controller faults.

At a typical trials disk transfer utilization of 5%, that is with the disk actually transferring data, and average transfer rate of 300 Kbytes/second, the error rate per drive becomes:

$$1 \text{ undetected error per } 1.7 \times 10^{12} \text{ bits}$$
to
$$1 \text{ undetected error per } 4.3 \times 10^{12} \text{ bits}$$

Note that with 5% transfer utilization and typical transfers taking 3 milliseconds the on-line occupancy of the disk units may be 30%, due to waiting time for access.

Magnetic Tape Units

Again 10–25% of faults caused the wrong information to be obtained on reading. Unlike disks, tape units have automatic read after write but this does not prevent undetected errors from occurring.

With average reliability of, typically, 2 incidents per 1000 hours per drive, 2% transfer utilization and average transfer rate of 80 Kbytes per second, the error rates are:

0.2 to 0.5 undetected errors per 1000 hours
1 undetected error per 0.9×10^{11} bits to 2.3×10^{11} bits

Tape units are normally on-line with a program waiting to be used, and on-line occupancy is likely to be about 20%. As for disk units, with a lower occupancy and utilization the number of undetected errors per 1000 hours would be less.

Card Punches

On these devices 30–40% of faults caused the wrong information to be produced, without being detected by read after punch checks, many of them being by punching the holes outside an acceptable tolerance for the reader.

Card punches generally have a very low occupancy/utilization with typical incidents per 1000 hours of 1.5: undetected error rate 0.45 to 0.60 incidents per 1000 hours. As shown later, undetected error rates are about 1 in 10^6 to 1 in 10^7 cards.

Card Readers

In this case, 50–60% of faults gave undetected misreads due to such problems as double reading of a column, skew, or starting reading in the wrong place. As for other devices, the effects on user work may not be so severe, for instance on reading program source cards, the fault may cause rejection due to a spurious program error.

Card readers, typically, have an incident rate of 2 incidents/1000 hours or undetected error rates of 1 to 1.2 per 1000 hours. With occupancy/utilization of 10% and a 1000 card per minute reader the error rate becomes:

1 undetected error per 5×10^6 to 6×10^6 cards

Paper Tape Readers

50–60% of faults again gave the wrong results, in spite of parity checking on some of the devices.

These readers may have a reliability of about 1 incident per 1000 hours or undetected error rate of 0.5 to 0.6 per 1000 hours at 1% utilization. At 500 characters per second this gives an error rate of:

1 undetected error per 3×10^7 to 3.6×10^7 characters

Printers

Many of the 60–70% of printer faults, which gave wrong results, were due to illegible, half printed characters, which would be questioned by the people reading them; for a number of others, columns of printing were completely missing and, for a few others, one character was found to be missing or wrong in a large printout.

The incident rate of printers is, typically, 5 per 1000 hours at 25% occupancy or undetected error rate of 3 to 3.5 per 1000 hours. At an effective printing rate of 500 lines per minute and 30 characters per line the error rate is:

1 undetected error per 6.4×10^7 to 7.5×10^7 characters

Paper Tape Punches

These have the worst record, with 80–90% of faults causing the wrong characters to be punched or spacing tolerances unacceptable to the readers, causing misreads. In practice, where parity, or sum checks are punched on the tape, many of the problems will be indicated on reading but this does not excuse the information being mispunched.

Tape punches, as card punches, generally have a very low utilization and may have incident rates of about 1.4 per 1000 hours, most of them being undetected errors as indicated above.

Manufacturers' Specifications

Some manufacturers provide expected detected and undetected error rates for certain peripherals, where it is assumed that the tolerances of the devices and media can be at opposite extremes to give rise to random errors, for which no fault can be assumed; an example of these for magnetic tape units, disks, paper tape and card readers and punches is given in Table 6.2. The undetected error rates are variable according to equipment design and type, but paper tape punches come out the worst at 1 in 10^5 to 1 in 10^7 characters for undetected errors. Perhaps many of the incidents quoted earlier are due to these design tolerances being exceeded and cannot be classified as being due to faults.

Overall System

Looking at a typical ADP system, and assuming the same utilization as trials, the range of undetected errors could be as follows, giving 10 to 17

Table 6.2 Recoverable, irrecoverable, detected and undetected error rates, claimed by manufacturers

Device	Recoverable error rate (soft failures)	Irrecoverable error rate	Undetected error rate
Phase encoded magnetic tape units	1 in 10^7 bits in-flight corrected 1 in 2.5×10^8 bits recoverable	1 in 2.5×10^{11} bits	1 in 10^{13} bits
NRZI magnetic tape units	1 in 5×10^7 bits to 1 in 10^8 bits	1 in 10^9 bits to 1 in 10^{11} bits	1 in 10^{13} bits
Disks and drums	1 in 10^9 bits to 1 in 10^{10} bits	1 in 10^{11} bits to 1 in 10^{13} bits	

	Detected error rate	
Card readers	1 in 10^5 cards to 1 in 10^6 cards	1 in 10^6 cards to 1 in 10^7 cards
Card punches	1 in 10^4 cards to 1 in 10^5 cards	1 in 10^6 cards to 1 in 10^7 cards
Paper tape readers (no parity checks)		1 in 10^6 characters to 1 in 10^8 characters
Paper tape punches		1 in 10^5 characters to 1 in 10^7 characters

per 1000 hours, or about one per week:

	Undetected errors/1000 hours
Processor 1000 KIPS	0–3.0
8 magnetic tape units	1.6–4.0
6 exchangeable disk units	0.6–1.5
2 line printers	6.0–7.0
1 card reader	1.0–1.2
1 card punch	0.4–0.6
	9.6–17.3

Again it should be emphasized that, the distribution of these incidents is likely to be such, that many weeks may pass without any problems, then a number of data corruptions may occur within a short period.

USER RECORDED FAULT SYMPTOMS

With day to day fault symptoms recorded by users, there is usually little sign of undetected errors, as most of these affect individual programs which are not checked at the time. The following sections give details of incidents as observed on a number of computer systems and derived from over 2000 user fault reports; each section indicates the percentage of incidents giving particular symptoms.

Processors

Indicated by lights	11%
Indicated by console message	34%
Stopped without indication	28%
Looping or other apparent software fault	25%
Failing to load	1%
Console printing rubbish	1%

These symptoms vary considerably from one computer type to another, according to the design and checking features, but very few give proper indications for more than 50% of processor faults. The main symptoms to note are those which are apparent software faults, where dumps are sent away for analysis, meanwhile the local engineer does nothing.

Peripheral Equipment

Exchangeable Disks

Irrecoverable read errors	38%
Seek errors	6%
Other indicated equipment failure	13%
Dropping off-line	18%
Failing to unload	1%
Failing to load	24%

In the case of the first three categories, the disk pack could be transferred to another unit for reading but, for many, the information would be irrecoverable and necessitate a large amount of spoilt work time in regenerating the information. The faults causing the disks to drop off-line are not necessarily serious, unless the pack holds the software; in this case, the whole system usually grinds to a halt and, once the disk is reconnected, the software has to be reloaded and all jobs restarted. For 4% of the incidents, head damage was recorded. Head crashes are the worst form of disk faults, where a head may crash into the surface, damaging the head and digging up the surface; this does not only destroy the information but may spoil the head flying characteristics, such that any other pack placed on the same drive is damaged, also any damaged pack being located on another drive causes further heads to be ruined. It is not unknown for the latter type of fault to ruin a dozen disk packs and over £2000's worth of heads.

Considering modern disk transports, of 200 Mbyte capacity and transfer rates of 800 Kbytes per second; at one incident per thousand hours, 38% of faults giving irrecoverable errors and average transfer utilization of 2.5 per cent the following irrecoverable rate can be calculated:

$$\text{1 irrecoverable error per } 1.5 \times 10^{12} \text{ bits:}$$

this compares well with typical manufacturers' claims shown in Table 6.2. However, the undetected error rate calculated earlier is not much better. This may be because this type of incident is more predominant in a trials environment or the impact of the disk controller is to produce more undetected errors.

Besides the incidents or hard failures above, which are noted by the operators, recoverable errors or soft failures are likely to occur in larger numbers; these will be recorded in a systems error log, if one is provided, and indicate the number of errors recovered by rereads, repositioning the read/write heads or by the error detection/correction facilities. A measure of the hard and soft failure rate may be in terms of input/output calls; for example, an average figure for 200 Mbyte disks is:

1000s of I/O calls per incident

Hard failures	Soft failures
5000	6

Magnetic Tape Units

Irrecoverable reading/writing errors	22%
Excessive recoverable errors	3%
Other indicated equipment failure	26%
Dropping off-line	8%
Failing to rewind/unload	9%
Failing to load	30%
Operator observed mechanical defects	2%

For most of the categories, the effect of the incidents is to cause the particular program, using the decks, to be terminated and sometimes tapes have to be recreated (45% of irrecoverable errors were on reading). Most of the 30% loading failures should not be serious but, on some systems, the software makes it difficult for alternate units to be assigned. An unknown number of the incidents were probably due to operator errors on loading, or faults on the media, the standard excuse by some engineers for most tape unit problems. For 11% of the incidents a tape wreck was indicated, with most being during loading or rewind/unloading.

For modern tape units, with $\frac{1}{2}$% transfer utilization, in a similar manner to the disks, the irrecoverable error rate can be calculated as:

$$\text{1 irrecoverable error per } 5 \times 10^{10} \text{ bits}$$

This is of the same order as in Table 6.2. However, the undetected error rate quoted earlier is much worse than that in Table 6.2; again, this may be because of the tape controller or the state of the units at the time of acceptance trials.

Other magnetic tape unit statistics collected, for one particular manufacturer's units, indicate the following:

Phase Encoded Units 3-4 irrecoverable errors per million blocks of 4 Kbytes

NRZI Units 10-15 irrecoverable errors per million blocks of 4 Kbytes

The above gives irrecoverable error rates of 1 per 8×10^9 to 1×10^{10} and 1 per 2×10^9 to 3×10^9 respectively, that is somewhat worse than the earlier calculations; also the PE units are much worse than indicated in Table 6.2.

An example of hard and soft failures on modern magnetic tape units is:

1000s of I/O calls per incident
Hard failures	Soft failures
1000	2

Line Printers

Misprinting	28%
Ribbon problems	12%
Paper feed faulty	19%
Other indicated equipment failure	9%
Dropping off-line	5%
Failing to allocate	8%
Paper stacking	10%
Operator adjustment faulty	2%
Printer noisy	6%
Burning smell	1%

The sort of undetected errors observed by the operators are usually when a whole column is dropping, characters permanently misaligned and faint printing due to ribbon faults. The paper stacking problems must have been really bad for operators to report them, as almost no line printers appear to be capable of stacking paper properly.

Card Readers

Indicated misreads	21%
Cards misfeeding	50%
Card wrecks	14%
Failing to allocate	7%
Dropping off-line	8%

Two thirds of the problems on the card readers considered were on card handling, giving misfeeds or wrecks, the wrecks being particularly bad as input data is destroyed. The expected detected error rate given in Table 6.2 is one in 10^5 to one in 10^6 cards read. The table above indicates misfeeding/wrecking occurs at 3 times the rate of misreading.

Console Typewriters

Misprinting	40%
Paper feed	7%
Stopped	33%
Keys faulty	13%
Noisy	7%

Paper Tape Readers

Indicated misreads	17%
Tape feeding problems	33%
Stopped	50%

Card and Paper Tape Punches

As these devices have low utilization, very few fault dockets were available for analysis but incidents were divided approximately equally between mispunching, media handling problems and stopping.

SOFTWARE FAULT SYMPTOMS

To obtain information on software fault symptoms, details from one manufacturer's declared software errors have been analysed; these may bear no resemblance to the relative frequency of occurrence observed by users, for example, one particular fault may give numerous incidents and others very few. However, as software faults are mainly design errors, users do not generally report every incident, especially when the fault is declared in a known error list. One other difference from hardware is that, for certain reported faults, the suppliers change the specification, rather than fix the fault.

Controlling Operating System

The following figures represent the percentage of faults in the various categories:

System crash	26%
Package crash	3%

User program failure	13%
Data corruptions	4%
Security breach	2%
Performance degradation	2%
Facilities	50%

1. System crashes include looping, system stopping without indication, system error print out messages, and faults, where the software has to be reloaded, for example to reconnect a peripheral.
2. Package crashes represent faults which do not stop the whole system but only one of the modules or packages, which has to be reloaded.
3. The user program failures are faults which cause a user program to be terminated, stuck in the system (and lost if the operator does not notice) or unable to use the required resources.
4. Data corruptions represent problems which cause corruptions during data flow and lead to wrong results.
5. Faults in the security breach classification give rise to user access of the wrong file, in certain circumstances, or failure to restrict access.
6. The performance degradation faults include such things as over allocation of resources or the slowing down of input/output.
7. The 50% of faults in facilities are generally avoidable, providing the user is aware of them but some can produce wrong results or program failures, if the user is not aware. They can be further subdivided as follows:

User program procedures and instructions	12%
Job control or operator commands	8%
Input/output formats	7%
Wrong or corrupt messages	15%
Operating procedures	3%
Other	5%

Compilers and Assembler

Most of the faults in these software packages are, again, generally avoidable, providing users are aware but, where the users are unaware, the consequences can be quite severe:

Package crash	8%
Expression not correctly handled	29%
Failure to recognize error	10%
Inaccurate results	5%
Input/output format	16%
Incorrect or false error messages	24%
Other	8%

E

Except for the package crashes, false error reports and a few of the 'other' category, the remainder of problems affect programs at run time and cause false run time errors, wrong results or false program termination. The false errors and messages may not appear to be so severe but one wonders how many hours of programmer time are wasted in looking for false errors in correct programs.

Chapter 7

Down Time and Maintenance Time

DOWN TIME DEFINITIONS

When design reliability figures are available for a computer system, besides the confusion caused over mean time between failures (see Chapter 1) there are equal discrepancies in the other term often quoted, that is mean time to repair or mttr. It is often said that the mttr is of the order of half an hour but, on examination, it is found that this is the average time to diagnose and repair solid faults, with the engineer standing there with spares available. From a users point of view the important consideration is the down time incurred per incident, and this can be broken down to various constituent parts:

1. Machine spoilt work time. When a fault occurs on a computer system it may not be immediately obvious; the systems may be producing wrong results for a period before it is noticed. Alternatively, the fault is likely to occur in the middle of a program, which has to be aborted and thus, productive work lost. It can be difficult to measure machine spoilt work for the former case quoted, so, in assigning down time, the user may prefer to use rerun time, that is the time, after recovery, to successfully reach the same stage of processing as when the fault was observed. The main problem with machine spoilt work is that it is so application dependent and relies on the user employing adequate checkpoint/restart facilities in long running programs: hence, it is usual for a user to limit down time claims for this category to, say, 15 minutes.

   A further category of rerun time is incurred when it is found that previously created files have been lost; this may be caused by the records being unreadable, either due to a fault causing them to be written wrongly in the first place or due to physical damage to the media; alternatively, the directory indicating the location of particular files may be corrupted or lost. The time to restore files is again application dependent and can vary from a few minutes to recreate a magnetic tape to many hours to restore all files on a large disk based system; again, in this area, it is usual to limit down time claims to, say, five hours to restore all files.

2. Operational down time. Whenever a fault occurs which affects operations, there is always a finite time between the operator observing the condition and reporting it to the engineer or starting recovery action; this may include time for fixed close down procedures, automatic recovery attempts, automatic diagnostic procedures or dumps, or the operator analysing console lights, recording the fault and making sure he has not made a mistake.

3. Waiting time. Even if the engineer is on site, he is very rarely standing at the side of the computer waiting for faults to be reported and, if the site is served by an on-call maintenance service, a few hours (or days if reported last thing on Friday) can elapse before he becomes available. Waiting time will be also incurred when the engineer does not have required spare parts on site and when he calls for assistance or advice.

4. Investigation time. This comprises the time to load and run engineering test programs, make repair attempts and rerun the test programs to prove the repair. For solid faults, providing the spares are on hand, the mttr could well be half an hour. For intermittent faults, test programs which actually reproduce the fault may have to be run for an average of 30 minutes and, after a repair attempt, run again for the same period; this may be followed by further repair attempts and test program runs, until the fault goes away or is fixed. Hence, the mean investigation time is quite high and, when subsequent repair attempts are taken into account, the true mttr is even higher.

5. Recovery time. When the engineer hands the system back to the user or it is decided to restart the system without bothering the engineer, recovery time is required for reloading the software and application program, then restarting; this time may vary from a minute or so, to over half an hour, depending on the system.

Down time figures most frequently available from a user represent the time from when the fault is first observed to when a system is restarted or:

Operational down time+Waiting time+Investigation time+Recovery time

that is, excluding machine spoilt work time. Down time figures most frequently available from a manufacturer usually represent investigation time and may exclude some waiting time. When considering reliability and down time figures, it is most important that the figures are correctly matched.

Table 7.1 Down time and failure classifications

Class of failure	Mtbf type	Hours	Down time rate	Hours
Failures seen by the user (350 @ 550 hours)	Mtbsi	28.6	Mean down time per incident (mdti)	1.57
Investigations by the engineer (150 @ 375 hours)	Mean time between investigations	66.7	Mean investigation time	2.5
Actual faults (50 @ 375 hours)	Component mtbf	200	True mttr	7.5
(50 @ 550 hours)			Mean down time per fault	11.0

Matched Down Time and Failure Classifications

Considering the reliability figures given in Table 1.4, typically the total down time could be 550 hours, representing 150 investigations taking 375 hours, and 350 system failures, where an additional 175 hours (including spoilt work) is recorded; these are shown correctly matched in Table 7.1. Usually a manufacturer provides component mtbf figures matched with mean investigation time and very few would admit that the average time lost per fault could be 10 hours or more. Again the effects of intermittent faults should be pointed out, where, if the mean down time for solid faults is as high as 2 hours the 25 solid faults give rise to 50 hours down time and the 25 intermittents give 500 hours; or over 90% of the down time is the result of intermittent faults.

To further emphasize the down time situation and to show the effects of maintainability features, the following sections give actual down time distributions of various systems, supplied by different manufacturers.

INVESTIGATION TIME

Small Computer

Figure 7.1 shows the percentage of investigations between 0 and 1 hours, 1 and 2 hours, etc recorded on a number of small processors of the same type. The systems are covered by on-site engineers and a full set of spares is kept on-site. The equipment is not easily maintainable, a detailed analysis showing an average of about two investigations per fault. The distribution can be considered to comprise a number of normal investigations with a mean investigation time of 2 hours and a few extended investigations, where the on-site spares prove to be faulty and waiting time is incurred, or the local engineer requires assistance for difficult faults, again incurring waiting time; the latter is specially the case, where the user is not prepared to continue working until the fault is

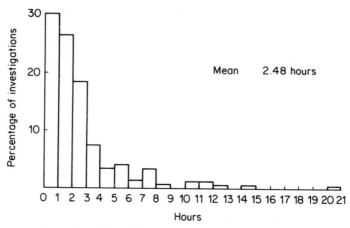

Figure 7.1   Investigation time on small processor A

rectified. To show the differences with other systems, the percentage of investigations are also shown in Table 7.2 in the ranges 0–1, 1–4, 4–8, and 8+ hours; this also indicates the true mttr for this processor is about 5 hours.

Figure 7.2 shows investigations on a different small computer, which appears slightly more maintainable than the former, but is covered by on-call maintenance, with the engineer bringing the appropriate spares with him; the initial waiting time for engineers is not included. This time, the engineers spend a little longer trying to fix faults, in an attempt to avoid being recalled and the normal mean investigation time is 2.43 hours. The number of solid faults and maintainability of this system are reflected by the low number of investigations in the 0–1 hour region—providing the

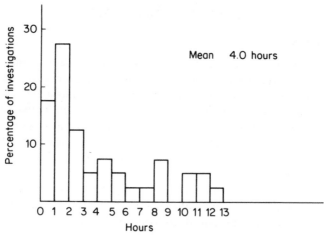

Figure 7.2   Investigation time on small processor B

Table 7.2 Investigation time range of various processors

Type of processor	Investigations per fault	Percentage of investigations in the range of hours				Mean inv. time hours	True mttr hours	Mean inv. time excluding inv. of 8 + hours
		0–1	1–4	4–8	8 +			
A small (Figure 7.1)	2.0	30	52	12	6	2.48	4.96	2.0
B small (Figure 7.2)	1.75	18	45	17	20	4.0	7.0	2.43
C mini (Figure 7.3)	1.5	18	63	13	6	2.75	4.12	2.2
D large (Figure 7.4)	5.0	70	23	5	2	1.21	6.05	1.0
E large (Figure 7.5)	2.0	38	40	13	9	2.85	5.7	1.73

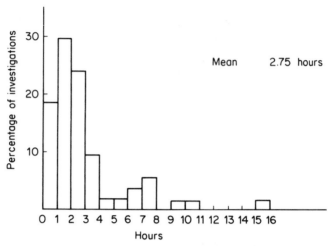

Figure 7.3   Investigation time on mini computer processor C

engineer brings the correct spares, indicated by the symptoms communicated by the operator, solid faults should all be cleared in less than 1 hour, and, if 50% of faults are solid, at 1.75 investigations per fault, at least 28% of investigations should be less than one hour. The problem of bringing the wrong spares is reflected in the 20% of investigation times of greater than 8 hours (see Table 7.2).

Mini Computer

Figure 7.3 gives the distribution of investigation times on a mini computer, again covered by on-call maintenance, but the engineer generally carries a full set of spares, this being possible as there are only a dozen or so in the processor. The systems is slightly more maintainable than the previous one, at 1.5 investigations per fault and normal mean investigation time of 2.2 hours (Table 7.2); however, the lack of solid faults is again reflected by the small proportion of activity in the 0–1 hour region. The benefits of being able to carry the spares is shown by the low value of 6% of investigations greater than 8 hours. Although, as for the other systems being considered, the times given represent the periods spent on site by the engineer, who could go away for a few days, until the spare arrives.

Large Computer

At first sight, the down time on the large processor (Figure 7.4) is ideal, with most investigations being less than one hour, only 2% more than 8 hours and a mean of 1.21 hours; however, this is misleading, as the maintainability of the system is bad, requiring 5 investigations per fault,

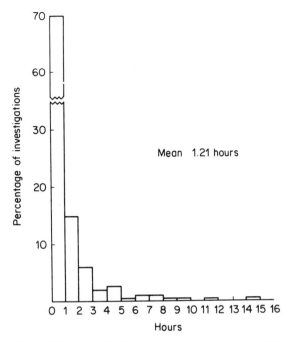

Figure 7.4   Investigation time on large processor D

and many of the short investigations only comprise examination and recording of the lights, which show the state of the machine. The true mttr of this processor is 6.05 hours (Table 7.2) and is only held at this level by the full complement of on-site spares and the higher level of engineering expertise employed. It should be noted that, although the overall investigation time is not excessive, the system suffers from frequent system failures, incurring recovery time not included in Figure 7.4.

Figure 7.5 represents the investigation time on a different large processor with on-site maintenance, this time with an apparent investigation per fault ratio of 2. The normal investigation time is quite low at 1.73 hours, with a high proportion of times below one hour. This performance is marred by the long duration investigations due to difficult faults and spares problems.

The maintainability and fault tolerance of this system is higher than it appears to be, as certain built in features ensure that the system continues working with faults present or automatically recovers from transient fault conditions; for these faults, the evidence is made available to aloow repair during scheduled maintenance periods and this time is not included in Figure 7.5. Considering all faults, the features provided reduce the true investigations per fault, during user operations, to a much lower figure than 2.0 (see Chapter 9).

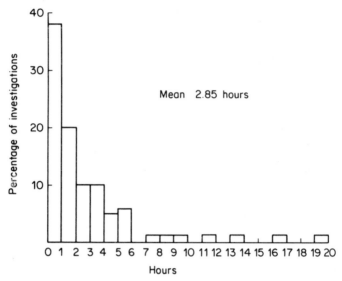

Figure 7.5   Investigation time on large processor E

Peripheral Equipment

The normal investigation time of peripheral equipment is almost always in the 1.5 to 2.5 hour region, that is the same as processors summarized in Table 7.2. Similarly, overall mean investigation time is usually 1.5 to 4.0 hours, but on particular sites has risen to 20 hours or more, over a long period, due to unavailability of spares.

USER OBSERVED DOWN TIME

For each of the investigations, the user observes some additional down time, that is operational down time, waiting time, recovery time and machine spoilt work time. These down times are also observed for incidents, where the engineer is not available or where the user decides to carry on working without engineering intervention.

The sum of operational down time and recovery time usually varies from five minutes to half an hour or more depending on the capabilities of the particular system. The minimum down time in this area is usually in the range from a few seconds to 15 minutes or more, but the average is increased, due to exceptional events, such as the requirement to consult the engineers for certain problems or extended recoveries.

Waiting time not included in investigation time, besides waiting for the engineer in the first place, include delays due to spares not being available or assistance being required, when the engineer has left the site. The waiting time depends very much on the maintenance service being provided; for on-call maintenance, this may provide a guarantee or aim of a response time of anything from 2 to 24 hours.

The actual average waiting time is likely to be somewhat less than guaranteed response time, unless the site is in a difficult location; also, as many of the faults are of an intermittent nature, the users tend to continue attempting to recover, whilst waiting, but this increases the number of incidents recorded.

The waiting time for specialist assistance is reflected in maintenance engineer training policy of one manufacturer, which is:

Normal engineers trained to find –	85% of faults
Installation and support engineers trained to find –	95% of faults
Remainder requiring reference to manufacturing or design authority –	5% of faults

Thus, for 15% of faults some assistance or advice is required and this takes time as the specialists are usually few and far between.

Distribution

Table 7.3 shows down time recorded by users for the five processors shown in Table 7.2.

A On the first system, waiting time is included in investigation time and the engineers investigate every incident, but an extra 5 minutes is recorded for recovery.

B On this processor there is a significant amount of waiting time and the user tolerates 3 incidents per investigation or 5.25 per fault. Overall mean down time becomes almost 10 hours per fault and 1.9 hours per incident.

C On the mini systems, although the mean investigation time per fault is just over 4 hours (Table 7.2), because of the extended waiting time and the average of 4 incidents per investigation, the overall mean down time per fault becomes over 13 hours.

D This large system which proves difficult to maintain has a little additional waiting time, mainly waiting for specialist assistance and an overall incident per fault ratio of 14, leading to an average of 10 hours down time being recorded per fault.

E On system E the waiting time is included in the mean investigation time. An extra 2.5 incidents per investigation are tolerated, but the overall mean down time per fault is only about 6.5 hours. However, because of the other faults cleared during scheduled maintenance periods the true mean down time per fault becomes lower.

Maintainability Effects

When a computer system with good maintainability features is introduced, it is often assumed that the mean investigation time, mean down time per incident and overall down time per fault will be low. The above examples illustrate that this is not necessarily the case. The maintainability features

Table 7.3 Typical down time on various processors

System and mtce. type	Investigations				Operational down time and recovery time			Overall mean down time per	
	Mean invest. time hours	Mean waiting time hours	Investigations per fault	Mean time per fault hours	Mean down time hours	Incidents per fault	Mean time per fault hours	Incident hours	Fault hours
A On site	2.48	0	2.0	4.96	0.08	2.0	0.16	2.56	5.12
B On call	4.0	1.25	1.75	9.19	0.15	5.25	0.79	1.90	9.98
C On call	2.75	5.0	1.5	11.62	0.25	6.0	1.5	2.19	13.12
D On site	1.21	0.10	5.0	6.55	0.25	14.0	3.5	0.72	10.05
E On site	2.85	0	2.0	5.7	0.17	5.0	0.85	1.31	6.55

may ensure that the system continues operation with automatic recoveries for certain types of fault but these tend to be those which would be easily diagnosable anyway: so the more difficult faults may be the only ones which incur down time during user operations and the down time may be further extended due to complications of faults in the additional maintainability circuitry. It appears that the only systems which have low mean down time per incident are those where the users tolerate a large number of incidents without bothering to call the engineers or those with poor maintainability features where 'quick look' investigations are employed only to be recorded as 'no fault found'.

Chapter 9 covers maintainability features in detail and shows that maintainability is not necessarily compatible with the possibilities of economic provision of spares, this being reflected in the extended down times of some of the above apparently highly maintainable systems. Finally, perhaps the most significant down time factor on the systems that are generally reliable and easily maintainable, such as mini computers (see C above), is waiting time for on-call service, which can ensure that these machines incur the longest overall down time per fault.

System Down Time

The down time distributions considered so far are at unit level. When considering down time at system level, the processor figures still apply, but on top of this is other time lost due to peripherals and software. Considering only those faults which cause a system stoppage, on software the mean operational down time plus recovery time is usually about the same as that on the processor, that is between 5 and 30 minutes. The latter also apply for peripheral faults which cause a system crash; although, on a number of systems, there may be an insufficient number of standby peripherals or the on-line test programs may be inadequate, leading to extended investigations, which require dedicated use of the complete processor.

Table 7.4 shows system down time recorded on systems using the five processors considered earlier. The general tendency is for the mean down time per system interruption (mdtsi) to decrease, due to the inclusion of peripherals and software, and the number of incidents giving down time of less than one hour to increase considerably.

A   The first system has no software to speak of and no standby peripherals. The engineer investigates all peripheral incidents as for the processor.

B   This system has some standby peripherals, so the system can sometimes continue operation with faulty peripherals, leading to a lower down time. As for the next system, an insignificant number of software faults, which affect total system operation,

Table 7.4 Typical down time on various systems

| System type | Percentage of incidents, giving down time hours in the range | | | | Mean down time per system interruption hours | | | |
	0–1	1–4	4–8	8+	CPU	Peripherals	Software	Overall
A	36	50	11	3	2.56	1.94	–	2.1
B	80	9	6	5	1.90	1.3	–	1.5
C	75	9	8	8	2.19	1.95	–	2.0
D	90	8.5	1	0.5	0.72	0.35	0.26	0.6
E	83	11	4	2	1.31	0.67	0.17	0.9

were recorded. The largest number of incidents giving less than one hour down time are due to the two incidents per investigation which do not receive engineering attention and the peripheral faults which do not hold up the system operation.

C   Again on the mini systems there are virtually no standby peripherals but the large number of incidents of less than one hour are due to recoveries, whilst waiting for the engineer. This system has the highest proportion of incidents giving more than 8 hours system down time; this is due to the combination of long duration investigations and the extended waiting time on occasions.

D and   For both these systems, the software is fairly well established,
E   but still contributes significantly to the number of short duration incidents. The systems also have an adequate supply of standby peripherals, leading to the lowest average down time due to peripheral incidents.

The figures for systems B to E are the most typical, with the proportion of incidents giving system down time of less than one hour normally being in the range of 75–90%, although this could rise to 95% in the early days, when software problems are predominant. The down time distributions given in this area do not include machine spoilt work, which could add 0.25 hours or more to the mean down time per system interruption.

PERIPHERAL EQUIPMENT DOWN TIME

Table 7.3 indicates mean investigation times in the range 1.2 to 4.0 hours for processing units, or 1.3 to 7.75 hours when waiting time is included. Mean investigation times for peripheral equipment is similar to processors but, when waiting time is added, the mean down time per investigation is usually in the 2.5 to 10.0 hour range and occasionally over 20 hours. The additional time is due to extra time in waiting for spares, where expensive motors and major assemblies are not normally available on site, nor at the local spares depot. The waiting time tends to grow on peripherals, when standby units are available, as there is not so much user pressure to fix the units.

SCHEDULED MAINTENANCE TIME

Scheduled maintenance time is often specified for all electromechanical peripheral equipment for preventive maintenance, that is to change parts and carry out adjustments before operation of the equipment is affected by faults caused by wear or adjustments wandering. Very few processors have maintenance aids which reproduce faults before they affect user operations, so scheduled maintenance time for these is usually used for corrective maintenance, although preventative maintenance may be carried out on such items as fans and filters. This corrective maintenance may be in conjunction with information recorded in the system's error log or the engineers may use the time attempting to reproduce transient or intermittent faults reported by the user.

Manufacturers often require complete dedicated use of the whole system for scheduled maintenance purposes, in order to be able to run any required test programs and, at the same time, to check and adjust peripherals. Typical scheduled maintenance requirements specified by the various manufacturers may bear no resemblance to processor size or configuration, varying from one hour per week to 3 hours per 3 months for mini systems, and 2–4 hours per week to 4 hours per 2 months for systems using small to large processors. Sometimes, on the larger configurations, additional scheduled maintenance is carried out on standby equipment concurrently with user operations. On older systems, daily scheduled maintenance of up to $2\frac{1}{2}$ hours was specified, but this tendency, with certain exceptions, has died away, with users being made responsible for routine cleaning. In some cases, scheduled maintenance is carried out rather on a random basis as dictated by trends of failure patterns indicated in a system's error log. Examples of total scheduled/preventative maintenance times on various peripherals are shown in Table 7.5.

SUPPLEMENTARY MAINTENANCE TIME

Besides scheduled maintenance, supplementary maintenance is required on all systems for the incorporation of modifications and this time cannot be scheduled too far in advance. The mean time to fit modifications is usually between $1\frac{1}{2}$ and 2 hours so, using the figures quoted in Chapter 3, the first large system delivered may require 400 FCOs during the first year, giving up to 800 hours of supplementary maintenance: this could vary from 160 hours during the first month to 30 hours during the twelfth month. Some of the modifications are supplied incorporated on new modules but time is

Table 7.5   Examples of scheduled/preventative maintenance for various mainframe peripherals

	Maintenance time hours					
Device	Per week	Per month	Per 2 months	Per 6 months	Per year	Overall per 1000 hours
Card reader	1.5	5.0				25.0
		3.0	3.0			8.0
Line printer	2.0	4.0	3.0			30.0
	1.3	1.3	2.5			17.3
Exchangeable disk unit	0.8	1.0	1.0			10.7
			0.5	2.5		1.2
Magnetic tape unit	0.5	2.0	3.8	1.2		11.9
		0.8	2.5	2.5		4.1
Typewriter				3.0		1.0
Visual display unit					1.8	0.3

still required to run the processor tests after insertion; others may require numerous wiring changes and take a long time to incorporate, thus giving a similar distribution to investigation times. Modifications are also required on the peripherals but, on large systems, the changes may be incorporated off-line on standby equipment; however, system time may still be required for testing purposes. Even for later systems, where the initial bulk of modifications are carried out during manufacture, supplementary maintenance can still be significant and, along with disturbance faults caused by the changes, can spoil any users plans for running a system on a continuous basis.

Time is required for generating the users operating system for new software releases and for incorporating patches to overcome problems; this time may also be counted as supplementary maintenance.

Chapter 8

Serviceability and Availability Ratios

DEFINITIONS

Serviceability and availability ratios are used to express the overall quality of service over a period. The serviceability ratio (S) is:

$$S = \frac{\text{Up time}}{\text{Up time} + \text{Down time}}$$

where up time (or serviceable time) includes productive time, time used for program development or operator training, and time lost due to operator errors, program errors or problems with media; also time when the machine is switched on and idle.

The availability ratio is sometimes defined in an identical manner to the serviceability ratio but it is preferable to define the availability ratio (A) as:

$$A = \frac{\text{Up time}}{\text{Up time} + \text{Down time} + \text{Extra maintenance time}}$$

where extra maintenance time comprises scheduled and supplementary maintenance time. In the former case, when the term availablity is used, it should be clarified as 'availability during scheduled operational hours'.

On a system obtained for continuous operation, where extra maintenance requiring the whole system is not allowed, the availability and serviceability ratios again equate. In other cases, although supplementary maintenance can prove to be rather an embarrassment, the extra maintenance is carried out at preplanned periods, so for the remainder of this chapter the availability ratio is ignored. However, many of the arguments and statistics given apply equally well to both availability and serviceability ratios.

Serviceability ratios may be available for individual units or systems but, as for failures and down time, different figures may be produced for the same equipment and one has to be careful in carrying out comparisons.

The first ratio to be considered is the engineering serviceability ratio (S_E):

$$S_E = \frac{\text{Serviceable time}}{\text{Serviceable time} + \text{Investigation time}}$$

Dividing the above by the number of investigations during the period under consideration this becomes:

$$S_E = \frac{\text{Mean time between investigations}}{\text{Mean time between investigations} + \text{Mean investigation time}}$$

or dividing by the number of component failures:

$$S_E = \frac{\text{Component mtbf}}{\text{Component mtbf} + \text{True mttr}}$$

Similarly, a user serviceability ratio (S_U) may be calculated, where down time comprises investigation time, plus operational down time, plus waiting time, plus recovery time; machine spoilt work may or may not be included. Dividing by the number of incidents this becomes:

$$S_U = \frac{\text{mtbi}}{\text{mtbi} + \text{mdti}}$$

Table 8.1 shows serviceability ratios for the processor covered by Table 7.1, with an extra entry excluding 15 minutes machine spoilt work for each incident, indicating that, for the same equipment, serviceability ratios varying between 94.8% and 96.4% could be produced.

Table 8.1   Serviceability ratios for a processor

Class of failure X	Mtbx hours	Mdtx hours	Serviceability ratio
Component failures	200	7.5	$S_E = \dfrac{200}{200 + 7.5} = 0.964$
Engineering investigations	66.7	2.5	$S_E = \dfrac{66.7}{66.7 + 2.5} = 0.964$
Incidents seen by the user	28.6	1.42 (excluding spoilt work)	$S_U = \dfrac{28.6}{28.6 + 1.42} = 0.953$
Incidents seen by the user	28.6	1.57 (including spoilt work)	$S_U = \dfrac{28.6}{28.6 + 1.57} = 0.948$

HISTORY

Early Systems

Serviceability ratios have been used on computer systems since the first ones became available. During the 1950s, the first commercially available computers had one input and one output device, and a drum or disk as main storage: they could only do one thing at a time, all programs making use of all equipment, and there was no software. At this time, the serviceability ratio reflected not only the down time due to system failures (all incidents caused a system interruption) but also down time of all equipment and the loss of throughput due to faults.

The next computer systems had magnetic tape units, with some acting as standby in case of failure. They only had the capability to run one program at a time but input/output could be overlapped with processing. To further improve throughput, the slow input/output was often provided by off-line card to tape or tape to printer converters, etc. On the main system, any peripheral incident gave rise to system down time but this was limited when a standby peripheral was available. The calculated serviceability ratio reflected the down time of the minimum configuration required for successful operation and the loss of throughput due to faults; it did not, however, give an indication of down time of all equipment. Separate serviceability ratios were sometimes calculated for the off-line converters.

Multiprogramming

During the 1960s the first computers were produced with basic multiprogramming software, the first ones having the capability of running one main program, one input to tape program and one tape to output program. At this stage, some users continued using a serviceability ratio based on the minimum configuration, which meant that loss of throughput on the input/output streams was not reflected. At this time, to indicate loss of throughput, multiprogramming serviceability schemes were introduced, where the down time was calculated according to the number of programs interrupted. In some cases, standby peripherals were available, so the down time was limited to change over and spoilt work time multiplied by the proportion of programs affected. On later systems, with more varied multiprogramming capabilities, for some schemes, a fixed multi-programming factor was introduced for calculating the down time; this overcame the difficulty of determining what programs were running at times when a peripheral fault affected one out of numerous programs.

Weighting Factors

On systems with the more complex multiprogramming capabilities, where faults carried equal weighting, irrespective of what the particular affected programs were doing, the concept of reflecting the loss of throughput became distorted. A further complication was that facilities became available for enabling systems or individual programs to continue operation in a degraded mode, that is with less than the maximum equipment required for the highest throughput. To overcome these problems weighting factor schemes have been introduced; for these, each item of hardware and controlling software is given a weighting factor, which is determined for a particular application, to reflect the loss of throughput, due to that item failing. Also, a standard recovery time is specified to represent operational down time, plus recovery time, plus machine spoilt work time or, alternatively, a standard spoilt work time factor is used and the actual operational down time and recovery time. An example of weighting factors is shown in Table 8.2: for a processor, software or peripheral incident, where investigation requires dedicated use of the processor, the whole investigation time is counted as down time (weighting factor 1.0): for all system failures a 30 minute standard recovery time applies: the system can continue operation with part of the main storage out of service, but at a lower throughput rate, for example, at 80% throughput with one store module not available, so the down time is multiplied by 0.2: similar weightings are given for peripheral failures, for some, standby devices being available and one can be out, without loss of throughput (weighting factor nil) but the standard recovery time shown is still used for change over to the spare: finally, a fixed five hours is allocated for recovery, in the event of all files being lost. A variation of the weighting factor scheme can be used to represent the minimum configuration approach, that is where the only weighting factors used are 0 and 1, indicating that the system is either considered to be fully working or not working.

The more complex serviceability recording schemes certainly give a more

Table 8.2 Weighting factors and standard recovery times for a simple system

Item	Number of units	Weighting factor for units inoperable					Standard recovery time hours
		1	2	3	4	5	
CPU	1	1.0					0.5
Main store	4	0.2	0.5	1.0	1.0		0.5
Disks	5	0.1	0.2	0.7	1.0	1.0	0.3
Magnetic tape units	5	Nil	0.1	0.3	0.5	1.0	0.2
Line printers	2	0.2	1.0				0.1
Card readers	2	Nil	1.0				0.1
Console	1	1.0					0.2
Operating system	1	1.0					0.5
Filing system	1	1.0					5.0

accurate representation of loss of throughput due to faults but this is associated with the requirement for more detailed recording methods and, for certain complex systems or ones with widely varying work, the ratio is still rather artificial. A further disadvantage of the various recording schemes is that they do not take into account software inefficiencies, due to design faults or hidden overheads.

VARIATION IN RESULTS

Varying Measurement Method

With all the various methods employed for measuring serviceability ratios, even wider variations than those indicated in Table 8.1 can be produced and this can cause wild misinterpretations, when trying to compare different systems. An example of different serviceability ratios obtained by various schemes is shown in Table 8.3: (again for the same system as Table 8.1); this time the serviceability ratio varies between 91.2 and 96.4%. The variations can, of course, be wider than this; for example, with unstable software the ratios could be reduced by much more than 10%. The multiprogramming and weighting factor schemes are each shown to give a typical reduction of about 0.5%, but this is very configuration and time dependent, for example, one store module with a weighting factor of 0.2, out of service for 20 hours in a week of single shift operation could make 10% difference or even higher if the effect on throughput rated a higher weighting factor.

Range of Serviceability Ratios

As indicated earlier the serviceability ratio can be calculated as:

$$\frac{\text{mtbx}}{\text{mtbx} + \text{mdtx}}$$

where x represents incidents, component failures or investigations; so it is clear that the same ratio can be obtained by having frequent failures (low mtbx) plus low mean down time and few failures (high mtbx) and high mean down time. The foregoing is reflected in Figure 8.1 over mdtx from 0.1 to 10 hours and mtbx from 1 to 1000 hours. In a practical situation, the same serviceability ratio can be obtained on a system with different reliability and down times, depending on the attitude of the management, for example on a system with a component mtbf of 200 hours:

1. System A — The user insists that the engineer investigates each incident thoroughly, leading to high investigation times and few incidents per fault, hence high mtbi:

   mtbi = 100 hours, mdti = 2.5 hours, serviceability = 97.6%

Table 8.3 Serviceability ratios for a system (10,000 hours serviceable time)

Down time included	Serviceability ratio definition	Down time hours	Approximate serviceability
Investigation time CPU faults only	CPU engineering serviceability	375	96.4
Hardware (including peripherals) investigation time, whole system down	Minimum configuration hardware engineering serviceability	435	95.8
As above including recovery, spoilt work time, etc	Minimum configuration hardware user serviceability	685	93.6
As above including software	Minimum configuration system user serviceability	860	92.1
	Multiprogramming factor system serviceability	910	91.7
	Weighting factor system serviceability	960	91.2

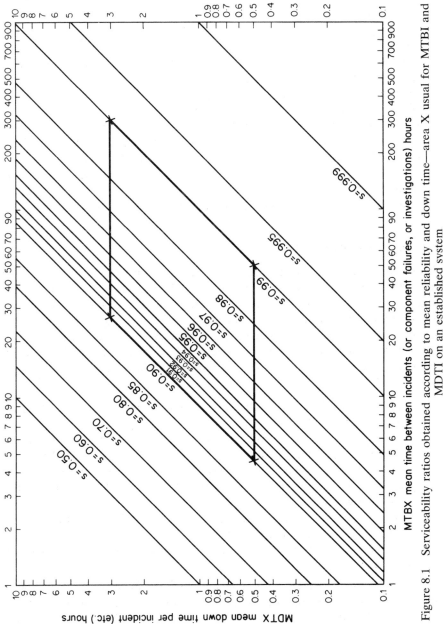

Figure 8.1 Serviceability ratios obtained according to mean reliability and down time—area X usual for MTBI and MDTI on an established system

2. System B—The user refuses to let the engineer on the system to investigate faults during working hours, but continues reloading and restarting the system, leading to numerous incidents per fault but low mean down time:

mtbi = 20 hours, mdti = 0.5 hours, serviceability = 97.6%

Examination of serviceability returns indicates that average serviceability ratios in the range 90% to 99% are obtained for most computer systems.

The mean down time per incident (causing system unserviceability) is usually in the range 0.5 to 3 hours, hence, from Figure 8.1, mean time between system interruptions is in the range 4.5 to 300 hours.

So far, only mean serviceability has been considered but, over short periods, wide variations from the mean occur, depending on the length of the period, also the reliability and down time characteristics and distributions. To cover all events, an infinite variety of serviceability distributions would be required but some generalities can be observed.

Varying Reliability Effects

Figure 8.2 gives a family of curves for serviceability ratios of 90, 93, 96 and 99%, showing, for months of 250 hours serviceable time, the cumulative proportion of months with at least the extrapolated serviceability; for example, at a mean of 90% (see Figure 8.2), 95% of months could be expected to give 81% serviceability or better, or 5 out of 100 months less than 81% serviceability. These curves have been calculated based on the following assumptions (which may or may not be valid):

1. The basic hardware faults are random and follow a Poisson distribution (see Chapter 1);
2. Although faults may have several incidents or investigations, the down time is mainly incurred during one accountable period and the remainder exhibit random occurrences during the other periods;
3. Some standby peripherals are available, thus reducing the overall system down time per fault;
4. Batches of software incidents given a random distribution of occurrences between the periods;
5. The mean down time per random occurrence (mdtx) is 3.5 hours with 8% greater than 8 hours.

The distributions have been checked against measured serviceability figures and have been found to be representative of systems with middle of the road reliability and maintainability, so further analysis can be carried out.

Figure 8.2 represents the effects of varying reliability on serviceability, with a fixed down time distribution. At a mean time between random

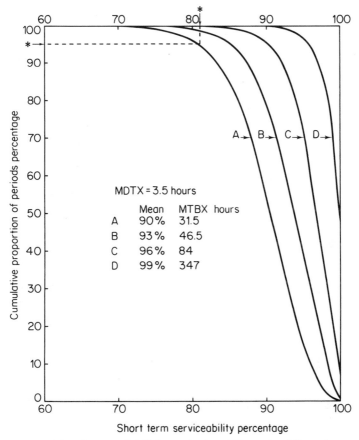

Figure 8.2 Serviceability ratio distributions—fixed down time distribution, fixed hours (250), variable reliability

occurrences (mtbx) of 31.5 hours there is little chance of 100% serviceability being achieved but at mtbx of 347 hours, 48% of months are at 100%. It is interesting to note that at 99% average serviceability, the short term ratio can fall to 90% or, unserviceability ratio to ten times worse than the average.

Varying Period Effects

Figure 8.3 is based on the same assumptions as above, to show the effects of varying the lengths of periods with a fixed average serviceability. The periods considered are weeks of about 60 hours, months of 250 hours and four consecutive months of 1000 hours. The distributions cannot be used to estimate serviceability likely to be obtained by changing a system's

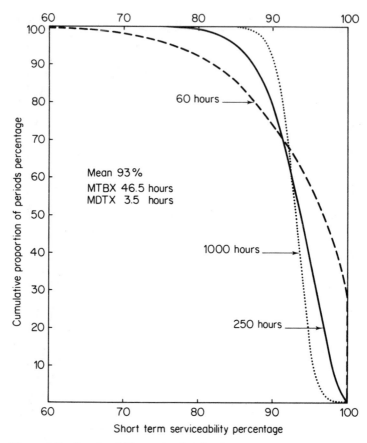

Figure 8.3   Serviceability ratio distribution over different periods
(same down time distribution and reliability)

operational hours (although in some cases they could apply), as different down time and reliability patterns may be introduced by switching on/off at different times or by the different work profile. During the weekly periods, 100% serviceability is obtained sometimes but, to counterbalance this, there are some weeks when very low serviceabilities are obtained; the former is because few faults are expected during 60 hours of operations and the latter due to the effects of long duration faults, where, for example, one 15 hours fault gives 25% unserviceability. At the other extreme, over 1000 hours, the variations from the mean are not very great.

Varying Down Time Distribution Effects

Figure 8.4 shows the effects of fixed reliability, fixed hours and varying down time distributions, where the variations are made up from more and

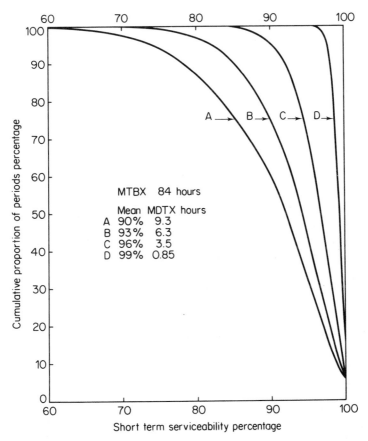

Figure 8.4   Serviceability ratio distribution, fixed reliability, fixed
hours (250), variable down time distributions

more long periods of down time. It can be seen that the effects of a higher
mean down time is to produce a similar distribution to that of a lower
down time and lower reliability over a shorter period—the 93% curve from
Figure 8.4 fits about half way between the 60 and 250 hour curves in
Figure 8.3 or at about 150 hours.

Worst Case Effects

Figures 8.5 and 8.6 have been prepared so that the worst case low
serviceability ratios can be estimated for a range of means and down time
profiles.

90% Confidence Limits

Figure 8.5 gives 90% confidence limits where, for a given mean, the short
term serviceability ratio can be obtained for a cumulative proportion of

90% of the periods under consideration. For example, for a system with a mean serviceability of 96% working 60 hour weeks or 250 hours per month:

1. 90 out of 100 weeks can be expected to achieve 88% serviceability or better (1 in 10 weeks less than 88%).
2. 90 out of 100 months can be expected to achieve 91.8% or better (1 in 10 months less than 91.8%).

Except at 60 hours and 2000 hours, the curves in Figure 8.5 are only drawn up to 99% mean serviceability as they cross over after this point; this is because, over the shorter periods at high serviceabilities, more than 90% of the periods can achieve 100% up time. The example quoted above uses the periods for average down time distributions with a mean of 3.5 hours used earlier. Figure 8.5 can also be used for cases where the down time distribution is really bad over the longer periods shown and, where the down time is exceptionally low, over the short periods shown.

The bad down time distribution can be obtained on a system with no standby peripherals, on-call maintenance with long waiting times, a

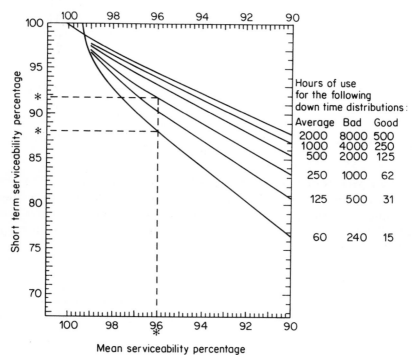

Figure 8.5   90 per cent confidence limits of serviceability

significant number of faults where spares are not available and with maintainability problems, leading to several investigations per fault. In this case the mean down time is 14 hours, representing the mean down time per fault if all faults are cleared during the periods under consideration.

The good down time distribution has a mean down time per random occurrence of under one hour, which can be obtained on a system with duplicate redundant units and few long duration periods of down time, due to lack of spares, service or maintainability problems. The lower levels of mean serviceability may be obtained in the presence of frequent system failures caused by software faults and, providing these exhibit random occurrences, the derived figures still apply. In practice, the confidence limits shown for good down time distributions have also been obtained on systems which have exhibited large numbers of incidents per fault, where these have mainly been of a random transient nature and investigation times have been low, although, in this case the lower apparent reliability has led to a low level of mean system serviceability.

99% Confidence Limits

Figure 8.6 shows 99% confidence limits for the same periods and down time distributions as Figure 8.5. In this case for the system with a mean serviceability of 96% the following apply:

1. For the average down time distribution 1 in 100 weeks can be

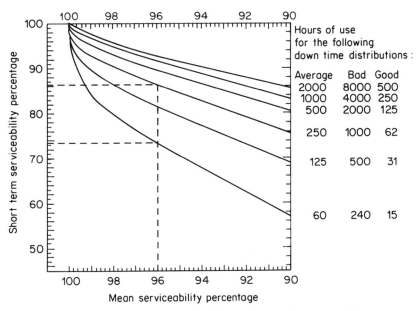

Figure 8.6   99 per cent confidence limits of serviceability

.expected to achieve less than 73.5% serviceability or the same level of 1 in 100 months with a bad down time distribution.

2. For the average case 1 in 100 months can be expected to achieve less than 86.3% serviceability or the same level for 1 in 100 weeks for a good down time distribution.

Although the unserviceability ratio has been mentioned earlier, it should be again stressed that this gives a far better measure of the disturbance caused by faults, rather than serviceability; for example, for 1 above, the unserviceability is 26.5%, or more than six times worse than mean unserviceability.

Chapter 9

Maintainability and Fault Tolerance Features

DEFINITIONS

There is no substitute for high inherent component reliability but various features can be provided or procedures adopted to keep systems going with faults present and to reduce down times; however, reliability and these features tend to go hand in hand. Due to design faults, all systems are initially unreliable and the better the features to identify the faults, the easier it is for the design faults to be found, appropriate modifications to be incorporated and high reliability achieved. Various terms are used to define these features:

1. Maintainability—the ease with which maintenance can be carried out.
2. Fault tolerance—the ability to continue operation successfully even though faults occur.
3. Resilience—the ability to recover and continue to perform successfully following fault incidents.
4. Diagnosability—the ability to diagnose faults.
5. Redundancy—standby units provided to allow reconfiguration or multiplicated units carrying out the same functions concurrently to ensure that a system continues correct operation with faults present on a predetermined number of the units.
6. Reconfiguration—the act of rearranging units.
7. Integrity—the state of being able to continue operation without making undetected mistakes.

There is much confusion on the above terms and many claims made by computer suppliers on facilities provided, so it is necessary to consider the facilities in detail to assess the benefits.

FAULT DIAGNOSIS

The ability to diagnose faults to the faulty component or replaceable module is one of the major claims made by some suppliers and the subject

133

of many technical papers on design of computers and test equipment. The concept of diagnosability of electronics is usually based on the assumption that, under fault conditions, an element will either be permanently 'stuck at 1' or 'stuck at 0', that is faults are solid. Unfortunately, for solid faults on some technologies the elements can be 'stuck between 0 and 1' and drift at will from one state to the other. Also, as indicated in earlier chapters, the majority of incidents that the user sees are the result of intermittent or transient faults, where the fault symptoms are present for a short period of time, so attempts to diagnose a faulty component are of limited use for minimising system down time. Some diagnosability features are limited to identifying a faulty area of the hardware, even for intermittent or transient faults, or identifying whether an incident was caused by hardware or software; these can be beneficial in ensuring that the resources are employed in investigating the right area.

In practice, for solid faults, diagnosis can be carried out by built in self testing facilities, by test programs in conjunction diagnostic hardware which can pin-point the fault or by test program logic in conjunction with functional modularity. As less than 10% of system down time is likely to be due to solid faults, the provision large amounts of extra hardware purely for diagnostic purposes should be questioned, as more time is likely to be lost in sorting out intermittent problems on the extra logic than is saved by its provision.

For intermittent faults, diagnosis is possible by experience in conjunction with failure pattern history recording, sometimes by the experience being built into a history analysis program, or by the ability to reproduce the fault conditions and the replacement of parts by trial and error. The history recording may be by the engineer recording the lights or automatic error logging in conjunction with extra hardware for checking and error indication purposes.

TEST PROGRAMS

Test programs are provided in various forms and there are wide variations in the efforts expended by computer suppliers in the different areas. The test programs can be broadly classified as follows:

1. Diagnostic
2. Functional
3. Exerciser
4. Interaction
5. On-line
6. Timing
7. Compatibility

Diagnostic Test Programs

A number of suppliers, especially those in military and message switching areas, concentrate on providing diagnostic programs, which are at least designed to identify the failing module for 'stuck at' type faults. The diagnosis usually relies on a built-in ability to write directly to certain registers, control the clocking to carry out partial instructions or functions; and read out registers, error triggers and status codes; often this is in conjunction with a separate diagnostic processor or specially designed controlling hardware. A great deal of time and effort has to be expended in developing the diagnostic programs and may involve software simulation on a different processor or physically inserting faults on the hardware being developed. In a simulation, each gate in turn is arranged to be 'stuck at 0' then 'stuck at 1' and a series of tests arranged to identify the failing module (occasionally the failing component), very few being possible as the result of a single test, as various faulty gates give rise to identical failure symptoms. To physically insert faults, inputs to components have to be disconnected or shorted; to facilitate this, special modules may have to be manufactured.

When completed, diagnostic programs are usually aranged to give a print out of the failing module for up to 90% of solid faults and for 2–3 modules for the remainder.

Because of their comprehensiveness, these programs tend to have a very long running time, compared with functional tests, so besides not being much use for intermittent faults, they may be a little slow for carrying out a quick confidence test for ensuring that no solid faults are present.

Functional Test Programs

The most frequently available test program is the functional type, with one being available for each identifiable unit. These programs are initially developed during the equipment design phase to carry out a go/no go test on each function of a unit and, irrespective of the depth of following development, continue to perform a useful purpose in checking our newly built equipment, where multiple solid faults may be present.

The crudest form of functional test programs available follow the following sequence:

PERFORM FUNCTION

IF CORRECT GO TO NEXT FUNCTION

STOP

NEXT FUNCTION

If the function is not performed correctly, the program stops. It is up to the engineer to determine the function being carried out and the results

F

(from program instruction address counter and other registers), and then to determine the faulty area from logic diagrams. Even the crudest programs follow a logical sequence in starting with the simpler functions and not using areas, which have not been checked, for testing other areas. However, the engineer is usually in trouble if the program will not load and start.

These crude test programs are the only ones available on certain mini computers but most systems have the obvious extensions of printing out the function which failed and the result. In either case, the lowest level of test program only carries out one or two simple checks of each function (e.g. all ones and zeros) and is thus only really of use for solid faults, although there are probably means of looping on sections of the program to prove the repair; this in turn may help in reproducing fairly hard intermittents.

These simple programs are recognizable by the small amount of code and short running times (e.g. a few milliseconds for a processor test). However, they have their uses, often neglected on more advanced engineering software, by being able to carry out a rapid test to ensure that no solid faults are present and, in the case of solid faults being indicated on mini computers with very few modules, the fault may be fixed by replacing three or four modules and tests re-run, in the same timescale as running a true diagnostic program.

The more advanced functional test programs have longer running times (e.g. a few seconds for a processor test), carrying out several tests of each function and may attempt to carry out semi-diagnosis to indicate a particular faulty area. These programs can reproduce a higher proportion of intermittent faults, especially when looped to run continuously and can be used for repair of solid faults, in conjunction with module swopping.

Exerciser Test Programs

Many faults which give rise to intermittent incidents are pattern or sequence conscious and the only way of reproducing them is by repeating the particular data patterns or function sequences; some of them may, in fact appear to the user as solid faults in attempting to re-run the same program, but functional test programs do not reproduce the same conditions. Design faults can also be in this category and it is not unknown for some unusual sequence to be encountered years after a system was first introduced. The problem of these sequences can be highlighted by calculating the time taken for all possible combinations of data patterns being manipulated by all possible sequences and combinations of instructions (the time soon becomes infinite) but fortunately certain sequences prove more onerous than others. An example of exerciser test programs, provided by most computer suppliers, is the store test, which may include the following routines (1 and 2 are the functional tests):

1. Addressing test—writing own address in each location then reading and checking.
2. All ones—writing to each location and reading followed by all zeros.
3. Checkerboard pattern (101010 etc. odd rows, 010101 etc. even rows), then inverse.
4. One word ones, remainder zero to every location in turn and complement.
5. Write zero continuously to one location, then write/read one; repeat on other locations.
6. Other worst case patterns (peculiar to particular design/construction) and complement.
7. Random patterns, random addresses.
8. Check of parity or error correction circuits (requires special hardware to force errors).

One pass of a store test can take from less than one minute to more than an hour, depending on routines included and size of store.

For processors, exerciser programs may take the form of pseudo-random instruction sequences and operand patterns; they may last for several hours without repeating the sequences. Others may carry out a variety of functions, summing the results and only checking after several thousand (or million) passes. Further ones may have facilities to incorporate a sequence of events from a user program or software, which is thought to be causing a problem.

Exerciser programs are available for most peripherals. Magnetic tape unit tests include writing/reading a whole tape with fixed or random patterns, writing/backspacing/reading along the tape, and writing/reading variable length blocks.

Disk tests may incorporate routines to write/read the whole surface with various patterns including random ones; then writing and random reads to exercise head switching (and movement for EDS); also variable length writing/reading.

Similar tests are usually available for all the slow peripherals to check all input/output characters in all format positions and to generally stress the mechanism, logic and power supplies.

The exerciser programs, especially those developed over a period to include newly discovered worst case characteristics, can be quite successful in reproducing difficult intermittent faults, but the main snag lies in the time taken; however, this can often be reduced if facilities are available to simultaneously vary equipment characteristics or environment, such as by voltage or timing margins, temperature variations or vibration. On one of the very large complex processors, the combination of exerciser programs, and margins (also constructional and functional modularity and a full set of

Table 9.1   Characteristics of systems with good and bad maintainability

	Good maintainability	Bad maintainability
Number of faults	50	50
Investigations during operational hours and down time	26@2.16 hours = 56.16 hrs	150@2.5 hours = 375 hours
Investigations during scheduled maintenance	40	Small when compared with those during operational time
System failures and recovery time	134@0.16 hours = 21.44	350@0.5 hours = 175 hours
Total down time	77.6 hours	550 hours
Mean down time per incident	0.58 hours	1.57 hours
Incidents per fault	2.68	7
Mean down time per fault	1.55 hours	11.0 hours

spares) has meant that the majority of intermittent faults have been able to be reproduced and fixed within a relatively short period, many within scheduled maintenance periods and a number before the user's work is affected: the extent of this ability is reflected in the fact that 60% of faulty modules are replaced during scheduled maintenance periods, thus increasing the apparent reliability that a user sees and making the system one of the very few where true preventative maintenance of the processor is possible. This is reflected in Table 9.1 compared with the characteristics of a system with poor maintainability (same system as Table 1.4), showing that the overall investigations per fault (during operational hours) is less than 1 at about 0.5 and down time per fault 1.55 hours. One disadvantage is that regular scheduled maintenance is required, thus if the system was required for continuous operation, the down time would be increased by the 40 additional investigations.

Interaction Test Programs

Interaction tests are a different form of exerciser test, designed to reproduce faults caused by changing programs and input/output interaction: they also allow simultaneous testing of peripheral equipment and the processor for scheduled maintenance purposes. The tests require a form of engineering executive program which controls the running of a series of functional or exerciser test programs. The simplest interaction tests may allow only processor, store and channel tests to be multiprogrammed and others may include peripheral tests, but with the program scheduling being rather crude. More advanced test executives will allow multiple copies of one program (e.g. one for each peripheral of the same type) with scheduling, priorities, job control, etc., carried out in a similar fashion to the system's operational software. For reproducing intermittent faults and proving the repair, interaction tests again take rather a long time to run; typically an extra half hour per investigation is incurred by manufacturers who regularly run this type of program. So, unless there is a significant reduction in the number of investigations per fault, more down time may be incurred by running interaction tests for every problem, but on certain mini systems, when waiting time and the reduction in visits by the engineer are taken into account, these tests have lead to a saving in down time.

On-line Test Programs

These are programs which run under the control of the normal system software, concurrently with user operations and can be provided for the following purposes:

1. For testing units without incurring system down time
2. For establishing system integrity
3. As a system interaction test

The most frequently available on-line test programs are for peripheral equipment, and are usually either of the functional or exerciser type. The programs, stored on disk or magnetic tape, are initiated from either the main console or an engineer station (if available) and facilities are normally required to overcome the software scheduling mechanisms to allow specific devices to be selected. These peripheral on-line tests can ensure that engineering investigations can be carried out during prime shift, without incurring system down time and are specially of use on systems requiring high availability. Less common are on-line programs for testing specific areas of main storage, input/output channels and peripherals, such as swopping drums, not normally accessible by user programs, as these require more significant changes to system software. These programs, when run at relatively infrequent intervals, may not have a noticeable effect on the throughput of a large system but, on small systems, the central processor time taken to generate and compare data used in the tests can degrade throughput considerably; for example 10 minutes CP time could be used in generating patterns, writing, reading and checking for a magnetic tape unit exerciser test on a small system.

On certain systems, especially those on military and message switching areas, on-line test programs are provided for ensuring system integrity. In the simplest form, these programs are loaded on the system continuously and automatically scheduled and run whenever the processor would otherwise be idling. The main benefit of this type of on-line test is to ensure that a system does not run for a long period with the presence of solid faults, which can cause corruptions of vast quantities of data. It is not unknown for scientific computers to run for a few days with an unnoticed solid fault present on floating point areas and producing slightly wrong results on most programs. The need for on-line integrity tests disappears when adequate checking hardware is provided on all appropriate areas, but on processors, without built in facilities for ensuring that wrong results are not produced, these tests can save a significant amount of spoilt work time. However, for the latter type of system, intermittent and transient faults can lead to wrong results being produced, as on-line tests running for short periods may not reproduce and indicate the faults. The simplest form of this type of test can lead to a significant degradation in throughput of users work (e.g. 10%), due to the time required to swop the program out, whenever a higher priority user's job requires attention from the processor. More advanced tests have built in scheduling which arrange for the programs to be run at specific intervals (e.g. once every 10 minutes) for a specific period (e.g. 2 seconds) or number of passes, with the interval and period being variable to suit the needs of a particular project or to enable the programs to be run more frequently when a hardware fault is suspected.

A combination of processor and peripheral on-line tests can provide a good system interaction test, especially for faults caused by interaction of the hardware and controlling software; they are also useful for commissioning and acceptance tests for establishing the viability of a new system. However, it is not recommended that this form of interaction test is run on a regular basis, concurrently with user operations, as more down time is likely to be incurred, due to recovery from system crashes caused by the interaction, than is saved by reproducing and repairing intermittent faults within a shorter timescale.

Timing Test Programs

Special test programs or routines in general purpose engineering programs are sometimes available for measuring timing of computer hardware in the following areas:

1. CPU times for individual or sequences of instructions
2. Input/output transfer rates via channels
3. Disk rotation, head movement/switching times and transfer rates
4. Magnetic tape unit transfer rates, stop/start time, length of interblock gaps, rewind time, etc
5. Slow peripheral transfer rates, etc

These programs are useful for initial checking of equipment specifications on new equipment, revealing faults caused by timing changes, checking that adjustments have been carried out correctly and for ensuring that the specification is still met, following design changes.

Compatibility Test Programs

Card reader and paper tape reader tests are always produced to read the output produced by card and paper tape punch test programs respectively; this not only provides the required functional tests but also ensures compatibility, in ensuring that the punching tolerances produced by the punches are acceptable for the readers.

On magnetic tape units and disks, the devices are usually set up using a special calibration tape or disk, but sometimes special test programs are provided as an additional check that information written on any device can be read on any other of the same type. To check full compatibility with one specific series of data patterns can take a long time on a large configuration: for example, with 20 exchangeable disks, assuming the first read pass is on the drive which wrote the information, 20 write passes, 20^2 or 400 read passes and 380 pack changes are required; this can take several hours. Other compatibility tests write part of the disk or tape on one device, which is read on the next device and more written, with the process continuing until the media is again transferred to the initial device for reading data produced by all others; this provides a quicker check of compatibility. In either case, there are limitations in having the ability of reproducing the obscure pattern conscious compatibility faults, which can severely disrupt user operations.

HARDWARE TESTERS

Hardware testers are available in various forms, varying from simple self testers, through exercisers to diagnostic and test processors. The simpler self testers carry out a quick check that a particular area of a computer is free from solid faults and are initiated at periods, varying from once each time the system is started to every time a particular function is used. They are, of course, not much use for reproducing and indicating intermittent faults but can save significant amounts of spoilt work time by establishing integrity, in the event of solid faults being present. In the more advanced form, the testers may be in the form of a microprocessor on each replaceable module or unit, having the capability to be enhanced into exercisers and diagnostic processors.

Exercisers

Exercisers are sometimes provided for peripherals, storage units, channels and control units, and may be either built-in or portable, with one provided for each type of device. The simpler forms generate fixed patterns or function sequences, without checking facilities and are provided to enable equipment to be set up correctly in the first place, or in conjunction with scheduled maintenance.

The most sophisticated exerciser testers can be arranged to generate and check various function sequences and test patterns, and may provide diagnosis for solid faults. When used in an off-line mode, they can enable certain intermittent faults to be reproduced, reducing engineer's time and minimising unit down time, without any reduction of the user's throughput (as incurred by on-line test programs).

Maintenance Processors

Engineering test processors are the natural extension of self testers and exercisers, with the additional flexibility and intelligence, which can be harnessed for the following purposes.

1. To carry out a quick check of the system before software is loaded, then to load the system,
2. For monitoring equipment status and environment, and recording/indicating error conditions,
3. Following a system crash or unit failure, to interpret the state of the system, determine recovery procedures and assist in recovery,
4. To act as a diagnostic processor, especially useful when test programs cannot be loaded on the main system; they can also be used for on-line debugging of software faults,
5. To control on-line or pseudo off-line exercising and test program running,
6. For analysing recorded error conditions to determine scheduled maintenance requirements and likely locations of faults,
7. Processing engineers commands, monitoring/displaying operations, providing facilities for altering information stored on the system etc.

A properly organized maintenance processor can reduce investigation time and recovery time, especially when it has its dedicated input/output equipment and storage facilities but, usually, it can only be economically justified on the larger systems.

MODULE TESTERS

Module testers, for testing circuit board modules, are occasionally provided as on-site maintenance aids and, almost always, at module repair depots and manufacturing plants. The testers are generally designed to find the 'stuck at' type solid faults and can vary in complexity from a simple functional tester, where the fault has to be located by an engineer, to a fully programmed diagnoser, capable of diagnosing 80 to 100% of faulty components, depending on module complexity and the effort put into the design of the tester.

As the testers are only designed to identify solid faults, the overall usefulness at fault finding is dependent on the maintainability features on the system, which can lead to from 1.25 to 5 modules being replaced per fault; assuming that 50% of faults are solid and the tester is 100% efficient, the following applies for 100 faults:

	A	B
Modules replaced	125	500
Solid faults identified	50	50
Intermittent faults not identified	50	50
Nothing wrong	25	400

In the case of A, on 60% of modules no fault is found; in the case of B, 90%, with 67% and 11% of these, respectively, being still faulty. The options, adopted by various manufacturers at this stage, include:

1. Return the modules to the field and hope for the best,
2. Return to the field but indicate details of reported fault conditions in records for particular module (only possible where modules have serial numbers); more detailed investigations carried out if the module is returned for repair a second time,
3. Return to the field with label attached, indicating fault conditions. This practice has been used by some manufacturers but stopped, as the local site engineers tended to send the modules back for detailed investigations,
4. Return to the field with a secret mark; this prevents the problem given by 3 but previous reported fault symptoms are lost,
5. Carry out more thorough testing by exercising and applying vibration and margins, either on the module tester or in a working processor; this technique, in conjunction with oscilloscope measurements, is being adopted as the standard test method on many modern systems, with tests/measurements taking a number of hours and operation in a processor a number of days,
6. Scrap the modules. One manufacturer, with module replacements as category B above (90% no fault found), adopted a policy of scrapping all modules replaced, but these were very small and inexpensive to manufacture. For larger modules, it has been observed that local site engineers have physically destroyed modules, with production costs of over £100, to avoid them being returned to the field again, with intermittent faults present. On larger systems, with even more expensive modules, (e.g. £1000) manufacturers tend to take them out of circulation, in the hope that, some day, a means may be found of reproducing the faults.

As indicated above, module testers do have their limitations, but it should be emphasized that solid faults on a complex module can be identified to component level in a matter of minutes, compared with more than an hour using manual methods, hence saving considerable resources at a module repair depot or manufacturing plant.

CONSTRUCTIONAL AND FUNCTIONAL MODULARITY

Constructional Modularity

To be maintainable, equipment should be constructionally modular, so that parts can be replaced easily. Most of the electronics on computers is constructionally modular, with the components being mounted on replaceable modules. Often core storage sections have had, driver, sense and addressing areas as easily replaceable units, but the core stack, including numerous controlling diodes, have tended to be in large units: in one case, where the core stack comprised half a computer bay, an engineer was observed to take 8 hours to repair a solid fault, even though a spare was on-site; because of the cost of the unit and the problems in transporting it to the repair depot, the engineer was reluctant to replace the unit, until he was absolutely sure that the fault was in the core stack. Almost all mini computers, and a number of larger systems, have core stores mounted on the same type of replaceable module as the processor.

The more modern semiconductor memories are inevitably mounted on replaceable boards, generally making them more easily maintainable than large system core stores, providing, of course, working spares are available.

Power supplies are sometimes wired in as components on the computer frame; in other cases, the power unit can be easily detached. On many systems, the main wiring is on a large wire wrapped backplane, which, although extremely reliable, cannot be replaced if, say, corrosion is found. Other systems have a multi-layer printed circuit board backplane, which can be unplugged and replaced.

Functional Modularity

Although much of the computer system electronics is constructionally modular, it is not always functionally modular. The first computers had valves as the replaceable items, which could be replaced very quickly but, because of the small circuit content of the valve, more than one replacement was often necessary before a fault was repaired. The early transistor systems tended to have standard modules containing a number of standard gates, with the functions being determined by the backplane wiring: this meant that few different spare modules were required, but there was a fairly low probability, that the module replaced, was the faulty one. On systems constructed from integrated circuits, the same problems have been encountered by having a small number of standard modules or where the integrated circuits, themselves, have been the replaceable elements.

With the move towards faster computers, with integrated circuits using medium scale integration, the tendency has been to produce larger modules with a high degree of functional modularity. Mini computer processors, including store and I/O channels, are likely to be constructed from 3–10 different types of module: in this case, an engineer can often carry all types of module with him, ensuring a low mean investigation time and a typical investigation per fault ratio of 1.5. On the larger systems, there may be 100 or more different types of module, each with 100 or more integrated circuits: these present a fair degree of functional modularity, but full spares provisioning at each site, of say £50,000 or more, may not be economically possible, leading to excessive waiting time for spares. On the larger modules, although the system down time can be minimized, there is still the problem of reproducing and diagnosing the fault off-line or at the spares depot; when this is not organised properly, many of the spares can have uncured intermittent faults present.

Even when a system is constructed from large constructionally and functionally modular units, and repair procedures are adequate, maintainability problems may arise through the architecture, say by having common timing and separate common control (and inevitably separate common power supplies), where almost any fault could be on a particular functional area board, or the timing board, or the control board. The best way to explain optimum modularity is in terms of the following simple example (see Figure 9.1):

Assuming functions A, B, C, D, control and timing are required.

METHOD 1—The unit could be constructed using small standard modules, giving lots of interconnections, poor maintainability but low spares costs and low waiting time for spares.

METHOD 2—using functionally modular boards, giving fairly good maintainability, but problems due to common control or timing, high spares costs and, possibly, high waiting time for spares.

METHOD 3—using identical modules on a bit slice principle for function, control and timing (a basic simple clock may be required to synchronize the functions), giving good maintainability, reduced spares costs and, perhaps, low waiting time for spares.

Method 3 may not be possible, in many cases, but has been achieved to some extent: for example, certain mini computers are available as 8, 16, 24, 32 etc, bit systems, using identical modules. At least one of the larger system suppliers has adopted this optimized functional modularity approach to a reasonable extent and, although this leads to a larger number of components, maintainability is as good as mini computers (better than 1.5 investigations per fault, 2.5 incidents per fault and total down time per fault of under 4.5 hours). Also, partly because of the improved maintainability, design problems were sorted out more easily and optimum reliability achieved; Chapter 3 indicated

146

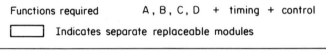

Functions required   A , B , C , D   +   timing   +   control

☐ Indicates separate replaceable modules

Method 1   Large number of standard modules connected via backplane

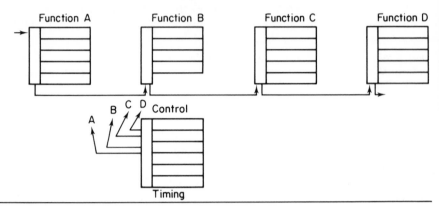

Method 2   Standard functional modularity

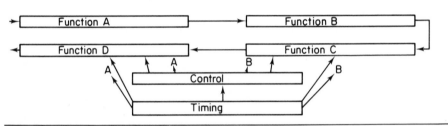

Method 3   Optimized functional modularity   CO = Control   T = Timing

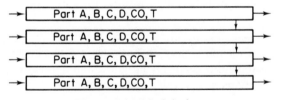

Figure 9.1   Modularity

that processors with the largest number of components could produce the best reliability.

Functional modularity has also been employed at system level, by having a processor which is slowed down, to produce the lower powered processor in the range, or by having a single peripheral controller, which has a microprogram loaded, such that it acts either as a disk controller, or a magnetic tape controller, or a slow peripheral controller. The end effect is again an overprovision of components with low utilization, good reliability, low spares costs, less maintenance training but a rather high production costs for the slower processors or controllers with the lower utilizations. Similarly, on the peripheral equipment, the same devices are sometimes used at varying transfer rates and capacities.

Large Scale Integration

With the move towards LSI, each integrated circuit may represent the equivalent of one or more circuit modules on previous computers with potentially a higher level of reliability, providing the quality is good and the design logically and electrically correct under all circumstances.

In many cases, the LSI integrated circuits are highly functionally modular, providing very good maintainability, with the ultimate concept being a complete microprocessor on a single chip. For larger systems, the chips may be mounted on replaceable modules providing an even higher degree of functional modularity, such that, in the event of a fault, the investigation per fault ratio should be very low. However, almost every module in the processor is likely to be different and there may also be a large number of different LSI circuits. In this case, it is unlikely that spares will be kept on site so, again, the most maintainable systems are likely to have the longest down times, due to waiting time for spares. To minimize the down time over a period, the reliability goals must be achieved by ensuring that the chip design is as near perfect as possible, implying very high development costs with more emphasis on design automation and simulation; also when the systems are constructed, the quality control procedures should be even more perfected to avoid extended burn-in times.

Whatever techniques are used in the design process, it is unlikely that *all* LSI chips will be completely logically correct. Such an assumption is almost synonymous with expectations of initially writing completely error free software. However, a much higher success rate can be expected where the design is based on known architecture or circuit logical sequences. When logical errors are found, it is not just a matter of a few wire changes on a module but a design change in the basic artwork used in the integrated circuit manufacturing process and an associated delay of perhaps several months. The delay can be minimized by employing uncommitted arrays in the chips such that, in most cases, only the top layer of the circuits will need to be changed. Because of the difficulties, there may be a trend not to include retrospective modifications on all systems excepting those which appear to be encountering the particular problem.

Problems may also be encountered due to the circuits being electrically incorrect, leading to more design changes. Although the design simulation should minimise this type of change, as the quality control tests cannot normally measure individual gate propogation delays, etc. in the middle of an LSI chip, the combination of extremes of design tolerances and marginal gates are likely to lead to intermittent type incidents. If these exhibit random transient failures, the user may suffer from frequent system stoppages but may continue operation until the engineer arrives with the correct spare module.

To help to overcome problems caused by logical errors, a manufacturer may opt for producing a relatively small number of standard LSI chips which are connected together to produce the required functions, such that most logical changes can be made outside the integrated circuits. In this case, the basic replaceable unit can still be a circuit board, representing a high level of functional modularity, providing good maintainability at system level but associated spares provisioning problems. Also with the small number of standard integrated circuits, the manufacturing process and quality control tests should become more easily perfected but the behaviour of individual gates could present difficulties, especially in attempting to find faults at the spares repair depot where, in this case, the chips themselves do not represent a high degree of functional modularity. This can lead to even higher spares turnover costs or the tendency to keep modules in circulation with transient faults present and not to replace them unless a user particularly complains.

In order to minimize spares costs, the basic replaceable units can be plug-in integrated circuits but, if the functions are spread over a number of chips, maintainability in terms of investigations per fault may be quite poor and, because of the need to make frequent chip changes, there is a potential reliability hazard on the micro-contacts required for this sort of application.

Whatever method of construction is adopted for large scale integration computers, there are potential maintainability problems and the real successes are likely to be more dependent on the quality of the initial design, manufacturing and testing processes. Also, as these devices usually have quite a high heat dissipation, if they follow the same trends as earlier technology, where the incident per fault ratio increases with heat (see Chapter 4), the cooling method becomes one of the most critical factors.

Certain large processors are now available where the potential high reliability of LSI is demonstrable: examination of these indicates far superior engineering than earlier systems and much more extensive quality control. However, they do suffer from the maintainability hazards mentioned above.

MARGINS

On earlier computers, facilities were generally available to vary the voltage supplies to the electronics, with a view towards varying the equipment characteristics, in order to help in reproducing intermittent faults. The variations were generally controlled by a switch, which simultaneously varied the supply to the whole machine. Similar margins have been available for core stores on relatively modern systems and are quite effective in reproducing certain kinds of faults.

Voltage Margins

Voltage margins are not provided for the general logic on many modern computers, as it is said that varying the complete supply simultaneously, provides self compensation from one circuit to the next so, unless the effects of varying the margins is to alter the thermal or timing characteristics, they may not help in reproducing faults, until the design limits are reached. There are exceptions, however, where voltage margins are very successful: in this case, the supplies are independently variable to individual replaceable modules, where under test program control, the margins can be varied dynamically, up or down on one or more modules, as required. The latter type of margins is one main reason why the better system, reflected in Table 9.1, achieved an investigation per fault ratio of less than 1, with 60% of faulty modules being replaced during scheduled maintenance periods.

Timing Margins

On other types of computer, many faults give rise to transient/intermittent timing problems, so timing margins are often provided on modern systems. The simplest timing margins are in the form of facilities to vary the clocks up or down by switch or potentiometer control: these are quite useful but the more maintainable systems allow the margins to be again varied dynamically under test program control. On one processor, with the latter type of facilities, it has been observed that they can actually enable diagnostic tests to diagnose certain intermittent faults. Other timing margins have been in the form of small capacitors, which can be plugged into test points on suspect modules.

Temperature Margins

Because of the possible effects of varying temperatures (see Chapter 4) it is felt that localised temperature margins could be one of the most useful maintainability aids. The only area where temperature margins appear to have been provided is for certain military type computers.

Other Forms of Margins

Other forms of voltage or timing margins can be implemented by the provisions of special test boxes or circuit boards, which can be plugged into the equipment, when a fault is suspected. These are sometimes provided for testing input/output buses. They are especially useful for introducing timing skews and reduced signal levels on common bus systems, where an extremely large number and variety of equipment can be connected, which could give rise to transient data pattern problems.

ERROR DETECTION AND CORRECTION

Parity Checking

A limited number of modern processors, channels and peripheral controllers have parity checking along all data highways and arithmetic pipeline units, even to the extent of predicting parity for floating point operations. The major benefit of the parity checking is to provide data integrity and, as indicated in Chapter 6, this is extremely successful.

Instruction and Unit Retry

On maintainability and diagnostic grounds, the parity checking is extremely successful in pin-pointing solid faults and for providing a failure pattern for certain intermittent faults. Along with parity and validity checking on microprogram or instruction decoding operations, the data path parity checking can allow instruction or unit (e.g. channel) retry for transient faults, thus providing a fault tolerance feature, which allows operations to continue until a preventative maintenance period. In certain cases, the retry can lead to considerable savings in operational down time but, if the fault is solid or of a pattern conscious intermittent nature, the retry is of little use.

An indication of the effectiveness of instruction retry could be presented from details given in a systems error log, where the ratio of detected hard failures to retried soft failures is typically 1 to 10: however, solid faults and fairly hard intermittents can clock up hundreds of retries, to distort the picture, before the system stops. The limitations and disadvantages of instruction retry are:

1. The data highways may only represent 10% of the processor logic and all instruction failures are not retriable.
2. In order to facilitate the parity checking and retry, numerous additional registers are required at strategic points, and extra logic is required for the checking and retry arrangements. The additional logic gives a reliability hazard, as more components are provided than are required to carry out the required functions. The normally easily diagnosable faults are made easier by the checking facilities, but difficult faults can be made more difficult, by the complications of false indications and intermittent faults in the checking circuits.

The checking facilities provide more enhanced diagnosability features when used in conjunction with correct functional modularity. However, because of the series maintainability logic reliability hazard, it is better if some form of checking can be applied as parallel maintainability logic, around a functional area, such that a fault in the extra logic does not normally cause a system failure.

Main Storage

Core storage units on the larger systems have generally had parity checking provided to identify single bit failures, assuring data integrity and, because stores represent a large array of symetrical logic, the pattern of parity failures is most useful for identifying faulty driver circuits, sense amplifiers, faulty locations etc. Parity checking on mini computer core stores is of less use, as both X and Y drivers tend to be common through all storage planes, and the probability of multibit errors approaches that of single bit errors.

Error Correction

Error correction on main storage was first provided on core stores, giving an extremely useful fault tolerance feature, as shown by the following example, for 1 megabits (128 Kbytes) of store:

Faults/1000 hours	0.3
Percentage of correctable faults	87%
Percentage of non-correctable faults	13%
Non-correctable faults/1000 hours	0.04
Incidents per fault (non-correctable)	5
Incidents per 1000 hours	0.2 (1.5 no error correction)
Incidents per fault (all faults)	0.67

Error correction is being provided on semi conductor stores for most of the medium/large systems currently being sold. These stores are generally of high functional modularity and, because most of the faults are in the active storage elements, where faults can be easily identified, maintainability is very good and a low incident per fault ratio is achieved. The early MOS stores had a worse inherent reliability than core stores, but this has now improved considerably. An example of the effects of error correction on an early MOS store is as follows, for 1 megabits:

Faults/1000 hours	0.71
Percentage of correctable faults	93.4%
Percentage of non-correctable faults	6.6%
Non-correctable faults/1000 hours	0.047
Incidents per fault (non-correctable)	1.7
Incidents per 1000 hours	0.08
Incidents per fault (all faults)	0.11

The above indicates that, the effectiveness of error correction is much better than core stores, but this is nowhere near the 99%+ figure often shown in theoretical papers. The latter tend to ignore power unit and common logic faults.

Semiconductor stores are more volatile than core stores and can be subject to more transient type incidents. Where only parity checking is provided, the majority of these are detected, but certain failure modes can cause multiple errors, which may or may not be detected. Where error correction is not provided, the transient faults give rise to a higher incident per fault ratio than above, and the incident rate, seen by the user, can be worse than core stores. On most types of small capacity semiconductor stores, the incident rate may still be tolerable but, for stores of greater capacity than, say 1 megabits, error correction is highly desirable. The foregoing applies also to mini computer stores, where error correction is not always available.

Error detection/correction is often provided on disk units and in-flight correction for single track failures on phase encoded magnetic tape units. These ensure a better fault tolerance or, at least, an improved fault incident rate when compared with earlier devices of lower capacity or slower transfer rate.

FAULT RECORDING

History Recording

Parity checking on the electronics can help in pin-pointing faults, as indicated above, but in providing a means of reproducing intermittent/transient faults, their use is restricted by the amount of complex analysis required—in certain cases this may be carried out by an analysis program.

History recording, available on one of the more easily maintainable systems for a number of years, and now being introduced on others, provides a record of the last 30 or so operations, including functions and data. In the event of a fault incident being detected, the history recording can be entered in the system's error log. Later, the sequence can be incorporated in a test program to assist in reproducing function sequence or data pattern dependent faults. The history recording, being recorded in parallel with normal operations, does not necessarily reduce operational reliability and can also be used for more effective retry facilities, or in identifying system failures caused by software faults.

Error logs

Almost all modern systems, including minis, have an error log facility, where, in the event of an equipment failure being detected, location, status information, content of registers and failure modes can be dumped to a disk for later analysis.

Information on peripheral equipment incidents normally represents the largest amount of recorded data. Besides assisting in fault diagnosis, the trend in detected and corrected errors can be used to determine preventative maintenance requirements: this enables the preventative maintenance to be carried out when required, rather than at predetermined intervals, thus reducing disturbance failures as described in Chapter 2.

The benefits in assisting in the diagnosis of processor, channel or peripheral controller faults depends, to a great extent, on the information recorded which, in turn, depends on the error and status checking circuitry in the units. In certain cases, the recorded information is of minimal use but, in others, 5000 error triggers, history recordings, complete register contents and parity status may be recorded, providing enhanced maintainability.

The information recorded for storage failures, gives the location of the failure and, where error detection/correction is provided, often enable the appropriate failing modules to be replaced during preventative maintenance periods.

Error log analysis programs are becoming more popular, where the program attempts to diagnose faults to module level, from information given in the error log: this can be quite successful for certain types of faults, but these are the ones which are easily diagnosable, anyway.

Console and Display Facilities

Most systems have consoles with facilities for displaying data, instructions, status, memory addresses, condition codes etc, with associated switches for selection purposes, also facilities for stepping through a program at a variable rate. The more maintainable ones have facilities for displaying more information and several items simultaneously or dynamic displays, giving a continuous display of all relevant information, rather than a snapshot at one point in time. It is also likely that any displayed information can be dumped in the error log.

REDUNDANCY AND RECONFIGURATION

Redundancy in the form of replicated circuits is not often met on commercial computer systems. Sometimes a number of power supply units are connected in parallel, the current rating being such, that one or more can fail and the remainder can carry the load. A limited number have important data paths duplicated, mainly for data integrity purposes and, in the event of a miscomparison, a retry can take place to overcome transient failures: alternatively a quick diagnostic test can be carried out to determine if a solid fault is present, and one path busied out if necessary.

Problems in incorporating a large amount of replicated circuits include cost, the requirement for splitting the circuits for testing purposes and the likelihood of all circuits failing when a design deficiency is met.

Quite often, standby equipment is purchased or a system is designed, so that it can work on less than a full complement of resources. The system can then be reconfigured to overcome certain intermittent faults, which cannot be found, or solid faults for which no spares are available; also to allow system operation to continue until a convenient preventative maintenance period. The main reconfiguration possibilities are:

1. Main stores or buffer stores—by re-arranging absolute addressing, busying out sections, avoiding or modifying interleaving. In one case, in the event of a store parity failure, before arranging reconfiguration, which carries a performance overhead, the location is tested to determine if the fault is solid or transient; for a transient fault, the information is dumped in the error log and the failing program or software module reloaded, without reconfiguration taking place. Often, when part of the store is busied out, the operating system has to be reloaded.
2. Processor functional units, such as high speed multiply units, storage access translation mechanisms for virtual storage—generally a software simulator is used employing alternative hardware.
3. Alternate paths to input/output channels, controllers or main storage. With appropriate error detection, these can often be brought into use without abandoning programs or without requiring the operating system to be reloaded.
4. Standby peripheral equipment, controllers or channels. Normally, when standby peripheral equipment is brought into use, the particular user programs have to be re-run, at least from the point of failure.
5. Multiprocessors—the effectiveness of multiprocessors depends very much on the application. In message switching systems a 'hot' standby is usually available, which accepts the data input, processes it, updates files but does not output the information, unless the active master computer fails: these systems are susceptible to hardware or software design problems which are likely to bring both systems down.

   General purpose multiprocessor systems cannot normally justify this 'hot' standby concept and either the tasks are dynamically allocated to available processors, or particular processors are dedicated to specific application areas. In these cases, often a failure of the controlling processor or the operating system leads to a complete system stoppage.

Reconfiguration of the various hardware units is best organized via a specially designed reconfiguration panel or console, which can provide a flexible, visually controllable means of minimizing operational errors, when alternate equipment is connected.

RECOVERABILITY

Modern large scale computers have many facilities to aid recovery, following a failure, for example:

1. Fast reloading of the operating system—following a hardware or software caused system failure, on reloading the operating software it is necessary to check the integrity of the system and, with large data bases, this can take a relatively long time: to reduce this time, the integrity checks are carried out concurrently with restarted user programs. Certain systems, with the faster recoveries, ignore the integrity checks, in the hope that corruptions can be detected by the appropriate application programs and recovery organized then.

2. Conservation of queues, so that failing tasks can be automatically restarted from the appropriate queue. User programs in the execution phase can be re-entered in the input queue after a system crash or a failure affecting a single program, thus avoiding the problem of sorting out the output documentation to determine which jobs have been completed successfully.

3. Duplicate directories of files—a major problem is the integrity of the file directory, as this is often being swopped in and out of the processor continuously, and can easily have omissions. If the directory is lost, many hours may be required to reconstitute files.

4. Modular system construction, where hardware or software elements are self checking and maintain a record of data until the next modular element has passed it on.

   The best example of this is a front-end or network processor, which can continue communicating with remote terminals, after the main or next in-line processor system has gone down and to, at least, permit graceful degradation or, even better, to allow incoming communications to continue by the provision of bulk storage.

5. System design—by appropriate design methods, a system can be organized such that failures of only critical software modules or hardware units necessitate reloading of the operating system. There is nothing more annoying than a requirement to reload the operating system to reconnect peripheral equipment or terminals.

MAINTENANCE ORGANIZATION

Maintenance Charges

Basic prime shift maintenance charges for computer systems generally vary from about 4% of the capital cost pa for the larger systems to 8%–10% pa for mini computers. These charges are fairly consistent on systems of the same capabilities but with wildly varying reliability characteristics.

However, it could be said that training and other overheads provide a constant factor. Out of these charges, the maintenance organizations are normally expected to be self sufficient and maintenance arrangements can be based on a compromise between spares costs, manpower costs and user observed reliability/serviceability. At any point in time, the capital cost of spares, for a system with a large base, is likely to vary from 3% to 10% of the initial equipment capital costs. Initial stocks and replacements are generally covered by the field service budget.

Resources Required

On certain of the functionally modular large systems, on-site spares equivalent to 30% of the processor modules may be required to assure serviceability levels. These larger systems still tend to have on-site maintenance engineers, which are sometimes difficult to justify on economic grounds. For example, a not too reliable system with 20 peripherals may have 40 engineering investigations per 1000 hours at an average time of $1\frac{1}{2}$ hours each: this is equivalent to about 2 investigations or 3 hours per shift week.

Preventative maintenance requirements are on top of this and can increase total maintenance time requirements by 3 to 6 times so full time attendance still may not be justified. However, on-call maintenance with, perhaps 2 hours waiting time, is not generally tolerable to large system users. On systems with poorer maintainability features, the more difficult faults are generally repaired by back-up specialists and the best maintenance arrangement could be on-call by specialists, providing these could be located on a fairly local basis.

At the other extreme, mini computers, with a large base, may have a machine/man ratio of up to 10 and on-call maintenance. In this case, the average mini may have 2.5 investigations per 1000 hours or 1 per 10 weeks. Hence, an engineer may deal with about one corrective maintenance call per week. However, besides preventative maintenance and travelling time, these engineers are normally responsible for installing new systems.

There is a current trend on medium/small systems to provide facilities for remote diagnosis, where the system can be accessed by a remote terminal at the field service centre. The aim of the remote diagnosis is to enable an engineer to be able to go along to the site with just the right spares. These systems suffer from the same diagnosability problems mentioned at the beginning of this chapter, that is possibly not much use for the majority of problems but suitable for solid faults when, after all, a spare part is almost certainly required. The remote maintenance feature could be especially useful for examining error logs, to determine preventative maintenance, and for the interrogation by experienced support staff, for diagnosis of difficult hardware or software faults.

The corrective maintenance manpower requirements, given earlier in this section, are based on averages and, as indicated below, much more effort can be required in the short term.

EFFECTS OF MAINTAINABILITY AND FAULT TOLERANCE FEATURES

Measurement

As indicated on a number of occasions, measures of maintainability and fault tolerance can be the following:

$$\frac{\text{Engineering investigations}}{\text{Number of genuine faults}} \text{ or Investigations per fault}$$

and

$$\frac{\text{Incidents affecting user operations}}{\text{Number of genuine faults}} \text{ or Incidents per fault}$$

plus, of course, the associated down time which, as indicated in Chapter 7, is better measured as the overall down time per fault. Table 9.2 provides a summary of what could be regarded as good and bad maintainability, with the down time excluding waiting time for on-call service. The effects of fault tolerance features are to reduce the figures by ensuring that the investigations or incidents do not impact upon user operations.

Short Term Effects

The figures quoted in the investigation or incident per fault ratios are average values: it is also useful to consider short term effects.

Figures 9.2 and 9.3 represent 90% and 99% confidence limits of the number of incidents or investigations in a period, related to mean faults, and incidents or investigations per fault. (The graphs are derived from a formula given in 'Analysis of computer system reliability and maintainability', R Longbottom, *The Radio and Electronic Engineer*, **42**,

Table 9.2   Measurement of maintainability

Maintainability classification	During scheduled operational hours		
	Investigations per fault	Incidents per fault	Overall mean down time per fault hours
Outstandingly good	<1	<2	2.0
Good	1.5	3.0	4.0
Fairly bad	3.0	6.0	7.0
Bad	6.0	12.0	10.0

IPF = Incidents or investigations per fault

E.g. 20 faults expected in a period at 1.5 investigations/fault so 30 investigations expected. The actual number of investigations in equal periods should be 39.5 or less for 90 percent of periods, or more than 39.5 for 10 percent of periods.

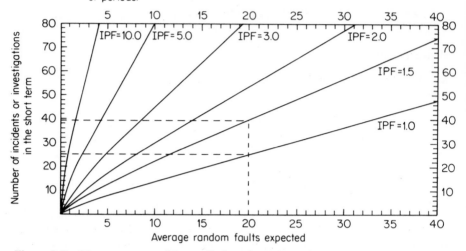

Figure 9.2   90 per cent confidence limits of number of incidents or investigations in a period related to average faults expected

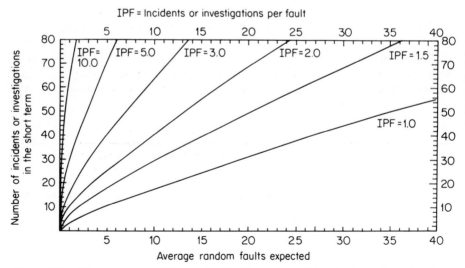

Figure 9.3   99 per cent confidence limits of number of incidents or investigations in a period related to average faults expected

No. 12, December 1972). The graph for IPF=1 is derived from Poisson distributions. Examples of the use of the curves are:

Case 1—A maintenance organization being planned, using reliability predictions derived from component counts and component failure rates. If, say, 20 faults per month are expected and it is desired to provide sufficient resources to provide total coverage on 90% of occasions, the resource requirements may be planned on the basis of 25 faults per month, representing 90% confidence limits of a Poisson distribution (Figure 9.2, IPF=1). If the system has good maintainability, requiring an average of 1.5 investigations per fault, actual investigation visits should be planned on about 40 vists per month or, with fairly bad maintainability and an IPF of 3, on the basis of over 80 visits per month.

Case 2—A user expects an average of 10 incidents a month on a system which gives 5 incidents per fault, 2 faults are expected per month; extrapolating from 2 faults and IPF of 5 indicates that, on 10% of months, more than 22 incidents can be expected, rather than about 14 had all incidents been of a random nature. Figure 9.3 indicates that, on 1% of months, more than 40 incidents could be expected.

The above show that, the effects of intermittent faults is not only to produce more incidents, but also to make short term effects more severe due to the bunching effect of incidents around a prime fault. The results derived from Figures 9.2 and 9.3 apply to fairly long periods of time (e.g. at least a week); in the shorter timescales more incidents are likely to be carried over from one period to the next, reducing the diversity of the distribution. In a similar fashion, when incidents are caused by use dependent design faults, as long as the particular method of utilization continues, the incident rate can be fairly consistent. On the other hand, when considering site to site variations in the presence of software or hardware design faults the overall effect is similar to Figures 9.2 and 9.3 when it is assumed that the incident per fault ratio is very high, say 10 or more. For example:

A system failure rate of 15 incidents per month is expected, which at IPF=10 is equivalent to 1.5 faults per month. 10% of systems can expect 36 incidents and 1% can expect 73 incidents.

Anyway, computers which are designed for high maintainability and fault tolerance, generally achieve the best reliability from all points of view and less diversity of problems.

Chapter 10

Acceptance Trials

THE NEED FOR TRIALS

When a computer system is delivered, it will have undergone some form of pre-delivery factory testing but, in certain cases, this is very limited, not necessarily geared up to the requirements of the design and, with drop-shipped peripherals or new software, the ordered configuration may not have been tested as a system (see Chapter 3).

On delivery, installation and commissioning is likely to take anything from a day, for a mini computer system to, typically, four weeks for a large mainframe system. During this time, as the various items are being assembled, others are tested. At the end, there is likely to be some acceptance procedure, which may be a limited subset of pre-delivery tests but, quite often, the only requirement is for all the engineering tests to run, without any other specific criteria. During the whole period, records will be kept of all engineering activity and spares used, but it is unlikely that a detailed log will be kept of all incidents, nor assessments made of the impact of any deficiency upon the user's work.

After the above, the user is normally expected to sign an acceptance certificate. In many cases, the next stage is for the user to attempt to generate and load the operating software; even if software has been run during the commissioning period, it is unlikely that it is the same version or the same format required by the user.

With these standard procedures, it is likely that a certain number of manufacturing and assembly defects, and significant design deficiencies, will be present on hand-over; also odd options missing or of the wrong type, equipment damaged and documentation wrong. From the contractor's point of view, the system is covered by a warranty but, after official acceptance and payment, there is not the same urgency to overcome user difficulties. So, from the user's point of view, it is useful to have a formal acceptance procedure, designed to meet his particular requirements, before payment is made.

An ideal form of acceptance trial would be one in which it could be established, for both hardware and software, that all facilities are provided and that the claimed reliability and performance specifications are being met; also, that support services are adequate.

Reliability Trials

Considering random failures, a reliability trial can be devised with durations being determined by the Exponential or Poisson Distrubutions (see Chapter 1).

For example, a reliability trial of 500 hours failure free running is required on a computer, where the claimed mean time between random failures is 1000 hours. Using the Exponential Distribution, the probability of failure free running, or probability of success $P_s(e^{-a})$ is:

$$\text{where } a = \frac{500}{1000}, P_s = 0.607$$

or there is approximately a 40% chance that one or more faults will occur and cause the trial to fail, i.e. a risk that the contractor is unlikely to want to take. (The 'risk' concept in acceptance trials is derived from 'Statistical properties of computer acceptance tests', Barnett, V. D. and Ross, H. F. (1965), *Ir Statist Soc A,* **128,** 361–394)

Similarly, if the true random mtbf is 250 hours, the probability of success is:

$$\text{where } a = \frac{500}{250}, P_s = 0.135$$

or there is a 13.5% chance that a system 4 times less reliable than expected will pass the trial, a risk that the customer is unlikely to want to take.

The only way to reduce the risks taken by both contractors and customers is to have a trial of duration such that more than one fault is likely. This time the Poisson Distribution can be used to determine durations and risks involved.

For example, again assuming random failures with mtbf of 1000 hours and a trial of 5000 hours, with criteria accept if 0–5 faults, reject if greater than 5. Considering the following Poisson Distributions:

Number of faults X	Mean 10.5 Probability of up to X faults P (0–X)	Mean 2.62 Probability of up to X faults P (0–X)
0	.000	.073
1	.000	.264
2	.002	.513
3	.007	.732
4	.021	.875
5	.050	.950

If five faults are observed the trial passes. As indicated above there is a probability of .05 of 0–5 faults occurring where the mean is 10.5 or, to put it another way, the user has a 5% risk of accepting a system with a true mtbf of:

$$5\% \text{ user risk} = \frac{5000}{10.5} = 476 \text{ hours true mtbf}$$

If more than five faults are observed the trial fails. In the second case above, there is a 95% probability of 0–5 faults occurring, where the mean is 2.62 or, the contractor has a 5% risk that the system will be rejected with a true mtbf of:

$$5\% \text{ contractor risk} = \frac{5000}{2.62} = 1908 \text{ hours true mtbf}$$

Table 10.1 shows the approximate 5% and 95% confidence limits of Poisson Distributions for various numbers of faults; also trial durations and mtbfs for 5% risk, where the expected mtbf is 1000 hours. It can be seen that, the longer the trial, the less the risk to both parties, and a trial of 25 times the mean time between random faults is considered to be a suitable test. However, in the case shown, this means a trial of 25,000 hours or about three years of continuous operation. For a mini processor, with a claimed mean time between random faults of 10,000 hours, about 30 years would be required, or 30 processors for a year.

Besides the time required, the other snags in conducting reliability trials are:

1. A new system is subject to early failures (see Chapter 2) and this may require up to 12000 hours for the reliability to stabilize.

Table 10.1 Duration of a reliability trial based on confidence limits of the Poisson distribution, with user's and contractor's risks

Number of faults observed	True mean where probability of 0–X faults is		1000 hours expected mtbf 0–X faults allowed		
			Trial duration	Customer's 5% risk of accepting	Contractor's 5% risk of rejection
X	0.05	0.95	hours	Mtbf hours	Mtbf hours
0	2.94	0.05	500	170	10000
1	4.76	0.36	1000	210	2810
5	10.5	2.62	5000	480	1910
10	16.9	6.17	10000	590	1620
25	34.7	18.2	25000	720	1370
50	63.3	40.0	50000	790	1250
100	117.6	84.7	100000	850	1180

2. Reliability is utilization dependent. In certain cases it may be possible to utilize equipment at a higher level than expected and reduce the length of testing. Other forms of accelerated testing may be possible, by varying margins and the environment, but it is doubtful if sufficient information could be obtained to validate this procedure.

3. New hardware and software are subject to design failures (see Chapter 2, 3 and 5), so a reliability trial may not be valid unless the actual user's production work is run on the system, with all expected variables, such as data or operational sequences. On systems with fully developed and dedicated single applications, such as message switching or payroll, it may be possible to carry out reliability trials at system level, occasionally reducing the trial to manageable proportions. On systems with a variable number of tasks, it may only be valid to measure reliability on individual units.

4. Because of intermittent faults, it is likely that the fault rate may appear to be higher than it actually is and detailed analysis of every incident would be required to ensure that only prime faults are counted (see Figure 1.2). If one could be certain of the utilization, a trial based on incident rates may be possible: this could be based on the random fault rate and incident per fault ratio (see Chapter 9 and Figures 9.2 and 9.3). Table 10.2 shows approximate 5% and 95% confidence limits of this incident distribution, for various numbers of incidents based on five incidents per fault, also trail durations and mtbi's for 5% risk, where the expected mtbf is 1000 hours and mtbi 200 hours.

Compared with Table 10.1, Table 10.2 indicates a higher divergence. For example, at a trial of 25 times the mtbi (5000 hours) the two 5% risk points are 0.42 and 3.1 times the mean, respectively, against 0.72

Table 10.2 Duration of a reliability trial based on confidence limits of incident distribution with user's and contractor's risks

Number of incidents observed	True mean where probability of 0–Y incidents is approximately		200 hours mtbi 5 incidents per fault 0–Y incidents allowed		
			Trial duration	Customer's 5% risk of accepting	Contractor's 5% risk of rejection
Y	0.05	0.95	hours	Mtbi hours	Mtbi hours
5	25	0.75	1000	40	1330
10	36	1.85	2000	56	1080
25	60	8.2	5000	83	610
50	95	23	10000	105	430
100	153	59	20000	130	340
125	173	85	25000	140	290

and 1.37 times the mean, for a trial of 25 times the mtbf. Even at a trial duration of 25,000 hours, the points are 0.70 and 1.45 times the mtbi. The figures indicate that, by basing the trial on incidents, the contractor's risks become greater than the customer's and the minimum length reliability trial is only achievable by resolving incidents, to determine real random faults.

5. Because engineering actions can affect the number of faults or incidents observed, it may be necessary to take down time into account; the usual way of achieving this is by measuring serviceability. Barnett and Ross (see reference earlier in this chapter) show that a trial of 25–50 times the mtbf is required for a reliability trial, where serviceability is used as the criteria: in this case, failures were assumed to be random and down time to follow Exponential or Gamma Distributions. The results are reasonably valid if incidents are again resolved to determine real random faults.

Facilities Testing and Performance Measurement

As far as the hardware is concerned, Chapter 3 indicated that many machine hours of operation are necessary to stabilize the design and remove the majority of logical errors: these errors mainly lead to an apparent lower reliability, rather than making it appear that facilities do not work properly. Some of the engineering test programs are specifically designed to check that facilities work properly and others to measure speeds of equipment but they do not necessarily check all combinations or sequences of facilities which may be met under specific applications. To achieve the latter, ideally, the application programs should be run under the computer's operating system control.

As indicated in Chapter 5, it is virtually impossible to check out all software facilities in a finite time and readily avilable means are not normally available for measuring software performance. Also, with the software continuously being changed, a set of tests designed for one release of software may not be valid for the next release. The only way of determining the acceptability of software is to run it for extended periods, with the real live application programs but, on most new systems, these have not been fully developed when the new computer system is delivered.

Support Services

To determine the effectivenesss of support services also requires an extended period of time. As the hardware and software support services generally have separate maintenance and services contracts, this can be covered by having suitable criteria in these contracts, such as serviceability levels, response times and levels of outstanding problems allowed (see Chapters 5 and 8). Long term hardware and software reliability levels may also be able to be specified in the maintenance and services contracts.

PRACTICAL ACCEPTANCE TRIALS

It should be fairly clear now, that the ideal form of trial cannot be achieved in practice, for establishing that reliability, facilities and performance meet predetermined specifications. A further obstacle arises through economical considerations and, if the acceptance trials impose significant financial overheads on the computer supplier, the user can be expected to pay.

Acceptance trials are highly desirable on many new computer systems and should take into account the following practical considerations:

1. The trial should be specified in the contract and should have a mechanism for rejection of the system if the specified criteria are not met.
2. The trial should not impose too much of a financial burden on the user, so time and effort in preparation and implementation may have to be limited.
3. The user should be responsible for determining the content of the trial, which should include user work or other programs providing similar or more exhaustive utilization. The user should be responsible for observing the trial, checking the output and determining whether the tests are successful.
4. Adequate records should be kept of the progress of the trial and of all unexpected incidents.
5. The contractor should be responsible for investigating unexpected incidents and for repairing or correcting faults, or for providing acceptable explanations.
6. The hardware/software configuration used during the trial should normally be that which will be used afterwards. The trial should show that all identifiable items are provided.
7. The trial should attempt to show that the broad hardware and software facilities are provided and, with limited testing, that not too many detailed facilities do not work as expected.
8. It is unlikely that the trial can establish that predetermined long term reliability criteria can be met but, because of the extremely high failure rate, which can be encountered when equipment is not assembled or commissioned correctly, (see Chapter 2), attempts should be made to ensure that the equipment is fairly free from these early failures, especially the intermittent variety.

   Reliability hazards caused by incorrect hardware or software design should receive particular attention under 3 to 7 above and, if these cannot be overcome within the duration of the trial, it should be possible to reject the system or to apply some conditional acceptance.

   Particular attention should also be given to faults which cause loss of integrity, breaches of security or physical damage to user provided media. (See Chapter 6.)

9. Any required compatibility with other systems, or within the new configuration, should be established, including exchangeable magnetic media.

10. Hardware performance (speed) specifications should be measured and attempts made to establish software/system performance. Where benchmarks are used for choosing or sizing a system, these should be included in the trial, with a contractual requirement to achieve the same or projected performance.

CCA'S STANDARD PROCEDURES

The Technical Services Division (TSD) of the Central Computer Agency was formed in 1958 (at the time known as the Technical Support Unit or TSU) to provide a professional engineering consultative service on computer systems obtained for Government Departments. Later, with developing new techniques, software specialists and communications experts were recruited to provide the necessary consultations in these areas and direct assistance where required.

TSD has various different branches which are responsible for carrying out detailed appraisal of software, equipment and systems from most manufacturers: different branches cover the various software areas and packages, others cover peripherals, technology, communications, large systems, mini systems, data preparation systems, microprocessors, accommodation planning and post installation work. A Technical Support Officer, generally with a software/system or hardware/system background, is nominated for each project, to provide advice at all stages of procurement from feasibility study, through operational requirement specification, to choice and sizing of the system. The same officer is responsible for specifying and supervising the acceptance trials and, in many cases, he may also be the appraisal officer for the particular system or, at least, some major part of it.

The computer systems are procured using a standard contract, controlled by the CCA Contracts Division. The Contracts Division also acts on an agency basis for Research Councils, Universities and NHS Hospitals: in conjunction with the contract, these bodies also receive TSD consultative and acceptance trials' services.

Hence, it is with this very broad background that trials are carried out. In fact, between 1958 and 1979, TSD have been responsible for specifying and supervising trials on over 1600 systems and enhancements, including most types supplied by the major mainframe and mini computer suppliers. The trials' procedures have evolved over the years, with the current procedures described below. The procedures are also under constant review and, currently, providing TSD appraisal activities do not reveal major problems, trials on the smaller systems are only carried out on the first one or two systems of a type, then devolved through other standard procedures to the user/supplier.

The method, procedures, conditions and broad criteria of success are specified as part of the standard contract. Detailed tests with specific criteria are included in a schedule, prepared by TSD for each system. The standard procedures allow for factory and site trials, each of up to 100 hours nominal duration. Factory trials are generally only held on early production models, to ensure that the system is not shipped to site with major design problems present. If the system does not pass a trial by the third attempt the contract is terminated.

The trials consist of two parts known as Demonstrations and Cyclic Testing.

Demonstrations

The demonstrations follow a logical sequence, making no assumptions as to whether particular facilities operate correctly: this eases the identification of any incidents which occur as the testing becomes more complex. The phases of the demonstrations are:

D1 Microprogram Load/System Start Up

This phase is generally very short, with the microprogram being loaded from floppy disk or cassette tape, if appropriate, followed by the the loading of any software required for the next tests.

D2 Processor/Store/Input—Output Tests

This phase comprises running the appropriate engineering functional test programs on the processor, store and input/output channels. Various timing measurements are made, using oscilloscopes and engineering timing programs. Standard benchmarks are also run as part of this phase but, at a later stage, when the operating software is loaded. A check is also made of switches and lights to ensure that all work correctly.

D3 Peripheral Equipment Tests

Functional engineering test programs are run on each peripheral sub-system in turn. Transfer rate and other speed/capacity measurements are made; operational modes and formats, also error detection and correction are tested; lamps and switches are also checked on each unit; a test is also run attempting simultaneous operation of all peripherals.

A compatibility test is run on magnetic tape units and exchangeable disks, to ensure that information written on one device of a type can be read on all others. An ideal compatibility test, for example on magnetic tape units, would be to write a whole tape on each unit and read it on all others. This is not always practicable, for instance for 10 units, 100 passes are required, which could amount to several hours work. So it is usual to write part of a file on each unit but, firstly, reading data written by the other units. Where a large number of devices are provided, a random selection of them is made, at the time of the trial, for the compatibility runs.

D4 Job Mix

Usually, this demonstration comprises of a standard set of programs biased towards the particular application area, e.g. scientific (mainly FORTRAN), ADP (mainly COBOL). User benchmarks may be also run as part of this phase.

D5 Fault Tolerance, Resilience and Reconfiguration Tests

These tests are generally carried out under operating system control to ensure that the various units can be switched out without interference, that the system can be reconfigured and that a minimum system is capable of supporting operational work. The system may also be switched off/on for various periods and combinations of any motor alternator sets tried.

D6 Special Testing

Special hardware, or more normally, software testing is included in this phase. The aim in this area is to provide subsets of tests for the operating system, languages, conversion products, communications, data management, editing and testing aids, user diagnostics and emulation.

Duration

The nominal duration of demonstrations is normally in the range 4 to 40 hours, according to system size and complexity.

Criteria of Success

The criteria of success, for demonstrations, is that all should be completed successfully in the nominal duration + 100% allowance (e.g. total time 8 to 80 hours) also that any timing is within 95% of specification. The extension is given so that any faults can be corrected and further attempts made, even for the longer demonstrations.

For early production systems, additional D6 and benchmarking phases may be carried out after the formal initial trial, with appropriate stage payments made as the required facilities are provided, or performance goals achieved: the dates for these are, of course, specified in the initial contract and title is not taken for the system until these are complete.

To assist in this phase of testing, CCA are developing as synthetic benchmark generator to ensure that the work profile can be accurately simulated for cases where the application programs are not fully developed.

Cyclic Testing

Programs Used

The cyclic testing part of the trial is mainly geared towards exercising the complete configuration, with optimum interaction and utilization. A test cycle is made up of the following types of tests, each of approximately 15 minutes duration, when timed in a stand alone mode, where short programs can be combined to make up one test or longer ones sub-divided. The 15 minutes was chosen to ensure that a reasonable amount of program re-run time is carried out following an incident.

1. Stand alone engineering tests. These are included in the cycle as they are often the only programs available which test all hardware functions, data paths and storage locations. Where possible, the remainder of the tests are run in a multiprogramming mode, under the operating system, configured according to the user's post trial requirements. By intervening these engineering tests, it can be ensured that the operating system is reloaded at regular intervals.
2. Peripheral and system exerciser tests, normally engineering tests with high worst case utilization. Sometimes manufacturers' software/system exerciser tests can be made available.
3. User programs. It is not very often that the user has developed his application programs for the new system or the work is of a continuously varying nature, but programs from earlier systems and suitably amended benchmarks are often included. In collecting user programs, one has to be careful that they fulfil some useful function, as the tendency of users is to provide short programs, with outer loops to extend running time, little variety of data patterns, no checks of consistency and vast quantities of uncheckable printed output. The best forms of user programs for ADP applications is a suite of tests say data vet, sort, calculate, output, each stage including a comparison with a master output contained on a disk or tape file and program interdependencies controlled by the job control card system. On certain of the large scientific systems, similar suites of live production programs are sometimes available.
4. System utilities. Copy utilities are very useful for providing high utilization of peripherals, controllers and channels, with low CPU utilization (engineering peripheral tests and other user type peripheral tests often use excessive amounts of CPU time for data generation and checking). After several copy phases, the output can be checked with

a compare utility and, in the event of failure, the appropriate failing tape or disk file can be located.

5. Standard test programs written in high level languages. TSD has designed and written sets of test programs, mainly in FORTRAN, COBOL, ALGOL and BASIC, to overcome the deficiencies in user provided programs and to provide transportable, engineering exerciser like programs which can run under operating system control, maximizing utilization.

Processor tests have little input and output and use as many functions as possible. Floating point programs use a wide range of different numbers, without underflow or overflow, and attempt to carry forward any normally undetected errors to the final answer, which is designed to be easily checkable. Fixed point programs occupy all bits in a word with various patterns and are adjustable to suit different word lengths.

Store tests occupy as much store as required (if there is a program maximum, two or more programs can be run concurrently) and use the whole word length with different bit patterns. They can also be used for exercising paging systems by ensuring that the required page is not in the main store.

Magnetic tape unit tests are organized to heavily utilize the driving mechanisms by continuous writing, back spacing and reading. Other disk and tape tests again use various data patterns and can be arranged to write and read long files, or to utilize a number of files and randomly switch between them. Further disk tests use random access methods to ensure adequate head movement or track switching.

Slow peripheral tests (for card readers and punches, paper tape readers and punches, VDUs, typewriters and line printers) emulate engineering tests with appropriate patterns and can employ the full character set. Besides central site equipment, these are useful for testing remote communications equipment.

To emphasize the range of these, a set of programs written in FORTRAN are reproduced in Appendix 1. These were written in 1970 and have gradually been brought into use on all mainframe and mini systems along with programs written in other languages. They have been adopted as standard tests by many computer system suppliers.

Duration

The different tests are normally arranged to make up a cycle of 2 to 10 hours, according to size of system and, at least as far as processors are concerned, there is no problem in ensuring full and varied utilization of even the largest processor. Some doubt is often raised on the ability to schedule specific peripherals or storage areas, but the system scheduler can usually be defeated by de-allocating units or by careful arrangement of program loading sequences.

Criteria of Success

The test cycle is run on a repetitive basis such that, if no faults occur, six complete cycles are run. One criterion of success is that each test has to be completed successfully 6 times in succession: this means that if one test is interrupted because of a fault, after possible engineering intervention, it has to be run for a further 6 times: if a hardware or software fault causes a complete system stoppage, all programs in the execution phase have to be re-run a further 6 times. Thus the penalty for failures becomes greater as the trial progresses and any previously unnoticed early failures can often be repaired without penalty. The six re-runs are also useful for reproducing intermittent faults.

The second criterion is that the cyclic testing should be completed in the nominal duration + 50% (e.g. 6 × 10 hour cycles + 50% = 90 hours). This extension is allowed as part of the objective of ending the trial with a good working system, and also ensures that a limited number of purely random faults, occurring in the latter part of the trial, are not solely responsible for failure.

Supervisor's Role

On the smaller systems the TSD Supervisor normally has a general hardware/software system background and may have some user assistance. On the larger systems two or more TSD officers are present with the supervisor having either software/system or hardware/system expertise and his assistants complementary experiences. The other TSD specialists are on-hand or on-call as appropriate. The Supervisor's role is to ensure that adequate records are kept, to see that the output is accurately checked, to observe system operations and contractor's representative's maintenance actions, to provide rulings on individual test failures, along with determining any revised program running sequences. It may be considered that ruling on all occurrences could be agreed prior to the trial but, unfortunately, computer systems are far too complex for all eventualities to be forecast. Also, any one apparently unsuccessful test or demonstration could be caused by factors outside the contractor's control, for which no penalty is given, so the Supervisor's role is characterized by persistent discussions or arguments on all possible causes of (or excuses for) occurrences, be it, operator or program errors, stationery faults, dust, variations in environmental conditions or mains surges—or even the fly which someone claimed to have seen fly between the lamp and the photocell on a paper tape reader!

The Supervisor is also responsible, in conjunction with the user, for making acceptance recommendations to the Contracts Division. This includes assessing the impact on any unexplained incidents or uncleared faults on the user's application and deciding upon any conditional acceptance conditions.

Records

The main records kept include a log for recording significant occurrences, demonstration timing measurements, starting and stopping times. An incident docket is issued by the Supervisor for every unexpected occurrence and the contractor's representative is required to provide a written answer. A tick sheet is kept of the progression of cyclic testing, to determine which tests are completed successfully and which have to be rerun. Where a large number of programs are run, output checking tick sheets may be provided. On complex systems, a record of peripheral utilization may be kept but this is often pre-specified in the test schedules.

Test Schedules

The test schedules are prepared by TSD, in conjunction with the user, in advance of the trial and include:

1. Schedule 1. Nominal and extended running times, contractural trial's date; list of hardware and modification state; list of software and release level; list of documentation relevant to particular tests; list of maintenance and modification records, software notices etc., to be provided before the trial starts; configuration diagrams.
2. Schedule 2. Demonstration test summary; separate sheets (standard where possible) for each demonstration phase and each type of unit or software package, indicating purpose, criteria of success, method and estimated duration.
3. Schedule 3. Cyclic testing, giving test name, programs used, purpose or description, stand alone elapsed time, CPU time and peripheral utilization, devices used, store occupancy and criteria of success (including any timing measured for consistency, allowable corrected errors etc).
4. Schedule 4. Cyclic testing running order (e.g. which batches of tests have to be loaded together), permitted rearrangements and, where appropriate, reconfiguration and peripheral changes required for each cycle.
5. General notes, giving specific requirements and interpretations of testing rules for the particular system.

Trials' Results

Pass/Fail Ratio

One way of judging the effectiveness of a trial is to determine the pass/fail ratio. On CCA's most recent 400 trials the results were:

Pass	62%
Conditional pass	24%
Fail	14%

So, a significant number fail or receive a conditional pass, when part of the purchase price may be held back until the conditions are met. Just under half of the trials were on mini computer systems and, remarkably, the percentage failures and conditional passes were similar to above. With the minis having much shorter trials and smaller configurations, this is probably another indication of their poor quality. Analysis of reasons for failure and conditional passes on the most recent scientific mainframes and minis gives the following:

CAUSE OF TRIAL FAILURE	NO.
Software would not support system	4
Performance requirements not met	2
Incorrect program results	1
Excessive software deficiencies	2
Excessive incidents (miscellaneous hardware and software)	13
Excessive incidents CPU	7
Excessive incidents peripherals	4
Lack of support	1
Hardware configuration inadequate	1
	35

Seven of the above had major system deficiencies and should not have been offered for trial and the remainder were caused by excessive incidents, indicating inadequate commissioning and trials' preparation.

REASON FOR CONDITIONAL PASS	NO.
Software missing	3
Equipment not delivered	5
Wrong equipment delivered	1
One or two peripherals faulty (generally not accepted)	15
Software deficiencies	7
Unexplained incidents	11
Documentation	3
Damage/cosmetics	4
Safety	3
Test program deficient	1
Specified demonstration not carried out	1
	54

The missing items above were generally declared before the trials started, as were some of the software deficiencies. The remainder were mainly observed as the trial progressed and acceptance made subject to the deficiencies being corrected. Of particular note are safety problems, these mainly being equipment covers which could be easily opened to expose dangerous voltages or moving parts, and acceptance only given when assurances had been made that the problems would be overcome. In many other cases the safety modifications were already in hand.

Ten years earlier, 25% of trials failed, the improvement being due to more reliable modern equipment, manufacturers carrying out better preparations and the current tendency to give conditional acceptance, to enable the user to make use of part of the configuration.

Pre-Trial Activities

As the manufacturers know, in advance, the content of the trial, and are encouraged to carry out proper preparation and rehearsal, most of the trials should not fail. So, even for the trials which have passed, one should look further to see what additional effort was put in and what faults were cleared during the trials.

Manufacturers are required to provide a master output for the trial and, therefore, are required to run all demonstrations and at least one complete cycle before the trial starts. This normally ensures that, with investigation and fault clearance times, a minimum period at least equal to the trial duration is run before the formal trial. Because of the required preparations, very few trials are held on the due date, and slippages on the larger systems are often several weeks: this ensures that equipment has a far longer burn-in time than the nominal trial duration. Furthermore, when the contractually binding trials are specified, the manufacturers normally ensure that higher level support specialists are on hand to sort out problems, against the normal field service personnel, who are usually responsible for standard commercial system installation or cases where CCA trials are devolved to the user or manufacturer. In spite of this higher level of support and extended running times, the systems also benefit from the more intense output checking, record keeping and questioning approach of the official Supervisor.

Faults Rectified During Trials

During the trials, a large number of faults are identified and rectified, this being reflected in a detailed analysis carried out on the results of 100 acceptance trials ('Acceptance trials of digitial computer systems', R. Longbottom and K. W. Stoate, *The Post Office Electrical Journal* **65**, 2, July 1972). These trials comprised some 2300 hours of running on 88 different systems, with over 800 peripherals, and 23 out of the 100 trials failed.

Figure 10.1 shows reliability, as recorded during demonstrations and cyclic testing on all units collectively. The fault rate during the

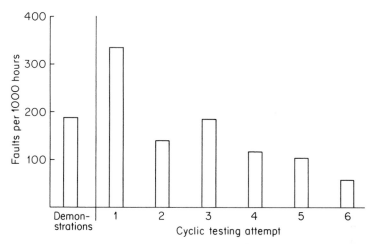

Figure 10.1   Reliability as recorded during acceptance trials for 399 faults on various units (from *The Post Office Electrical Engineers' Journal*)

demonstration period is less than at the beginning of cycles, as the utilization is lower. There is a build up of faults in the third cycle, these being due to the electromagnetic peripherals wandering out of tolerance due to the high activity. It should be remembered that, when a fault is observed, a test is restarted at attempt 1, helping to trap any further faults which develop after the device is re-adjusted.

Of particular significance during demonstrations, 4% of disk and tape systems were found to be incompatible and 1.5% of units were found to be running at the wrong speed. Also of importance are the faults which caused normally undetected errors, details of these being given in Chapter 6.

Figure 10.2 shows details of intermittent faults recorded during the trials, where 95 faults gave rise to 278 incidents. The figure shows, quite clearly, that six cycles appears to be reasonable for reproducing intermittent faults. For the trials' programs it was calculated that, the mean time between repeat incidents is 20–30 minutes of running the failing program. About half of the intermittent faults occurred whilst running user programs and only 20% of these were indicated in engineering tests run as part of the trial, although, in most cases, these engineering tests were run alternately with the failing programs.

When a trial fails, there is often a considerable delay before the second trial, as the contractor ensures that the faults are rectified and tries to determine that no other significant problems are present. About 10% of systems which fail the first trial also fail a second time and even more testing and rehearsal takes place to avoid the contract being terminated. Since 1958, on two occasions, third trials have failed and equipment has been completely rejected and alternative equipment chosen. In numerous

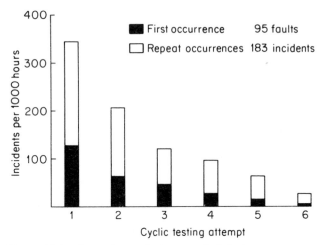

Figure 10.2   Intermittent faults recorded during acceptance
trials (from *The Post Office Electrical Engineers' Journal*)

other cases (some not meeting the conditional acceptance requirements),
processors have been upgraded to the next model, additional or different
store, peripherals or communications processors provided or the price
reduced.

Advantages and Disadvantages of CCA's Type of Trials

The main advantages of CCA's standard trial's procedures are:

1. The trial's content is specified and trial supervised by computer system
   professionals. Besides the obvious advantage of the tests being
   organized by someone with experience of the system, as most
   arguments take place between the Supervisor and the contractor,
   when the system is eventually accepted, the user and the contractor
   can start off on a reasonably friendly footing.
2. The test schedules identify clearly, what is to be tested and the
   criteria of success.
3. The trial is not a reliability trial but the objective is to end up with a
   good working system: in practice this objective is generally met.
4. The equipment utilization during the trial is normally higher than the
   user could achieve at early stages of a project.

The main disadvantages of the trial's procedures are:

1. The manufacturers know in advance what programs are to be run and
   this may not have the same content and variety as user work. This is
   overcome, to some extent, by the high utilization and variety of jobs,
   where up to 400 different programs have been included in a trial.

2. The trials may be of a relatively short duration. As indicated earlier, the extra preparations and rehearsals by the manufacturer compensate for this. Also, on early production models it is CCA policy to carry out more extensive software and benchmark testing after the formal trial.
3. Extra effort is required by all concerned in the preparation and running of the trial; this may incur higher costs.

In order to compare the above advantages and disadvantages, it is useful to examine other forms of practical acceptance trials.

Previous Standard CCA Trials

Prior to 1968 CCA carried out similar types of trials, over similar durations, with demonstrations and cyclic testing, but one of the main criteria was that the serviceability ratio measured (see Chapter 8) should be not less than 93%. A second performance ratio was measured as:

$$\text{Performance ratio} = \frac{\text{Number of failure free tests}}{\text{Total tests}}$$

where a test was deemed a failure for serious incidents or for a succession of minor problems. The ciriterion for this ratio was not less than 96%.

The new trial's procedure was devised to go away from the reliability measurement concept, to make the trials easier to record, to make them more flexible (e.g. in allowing partial acceptance), and to make the test less dependent on the efficiency of the maintenance engineers (the best test for these being regarded as comparisons with specific serviceability criteria given in the maintenance contract).

GSA PROCEDURES

A further trial's procedure is to let the contractor install a system to his satisfaction, then hand it over to the user for a trial comprising normal live operational work. Such a procedure is specified in the standard General Services Administration (GSA) contracts used by American Government Departments. The standard criteria are that the system should achieve 90% serviceability over a 30 day period and the trial has to be completed within 90 days. The same procedure is also adapted as standard by many European Governments. The advantages of this procedure are:

1. The trial can comprise up to 720 hours of running.
2. The programs run comprise real live operational work and the contractor does not know the content in advance so he is not in a position to tune the system to avoid pitfalls.

The disadvantages are:

1. The users may not have sufficient new operational work to fully

utilize the system. (Programs such as those given in Appendix 1 can be included to ensure a higher utilization.)

2. The user may not have previous knowledge of the system, so he can be easily mislead; or he may take a particularly hard line and make unreasonable allocations of time.

3. The concept is essentially a reliability trial. With the average system having a potential serviceability of at least 96%, the 90% criterion is not very good, from a user's point of view: also, over 720 hours, there is, typically, a 5% chance that a system giving 85% will be accepted or one giving 94% will be rejected.

To overcome the last deficiency, in special cases, trials have been negotiated requiring 95% or more over 90 days and other criteria included to cover the frequency of system crashes; also requirements have been specified to run benchmarks, to meet predetermined criteria and to include software facilities testing.

The best form of trial is probably a CCA like trial followed by the GSA type with tighter criteria. In certain cases, this procedure has been adopted by CCA.

Chapter 11

Practical Reliability Calculations

ELECTRONICS

General

Chapter 1 showed the basic concepts of the standard method of calculating reliability of electronic equipment, based on component counts. The problems of defining failures were also explained and amplified in other chapters, highlighting maintainability considerations. Chapter 3 showed that reliability differences of mainframe and mini processors using integrated circuits was up to 142 : 1, based on a per IC basis, with variations being caused by IC complexity, speed of operation, environment and design quality. It was also shown that processors of equivalent speeds could be more reliable when constructed using a greater number of ICs; also, the effect of higher utilization was to decrease reliability even of the electronics.

With these variations, it is difficult to see how meaningful predictions can be made, unless they are based on previous experience of using the same components and established design and quality control procedures. The difficulties are amplified by examining the prediction method for integrated circuits, given in the MIL Handbook 217B: this can show the following variations of reliability derating factors:

Multiplication
Factor

1 to 2.5   *Complexity factor*, this being based on an average complexity difference of 4 to 1 in the number of gates per IC.

1 to 4.0   *Environmental factor*, being the difference in calculations for ground benign and ground fixed applications, where benign, amongst other things, implies full air conditioning: this factor also takes into account the reliability variations due to different internal IC temperatures.

1 to 150   Quality factor, depending on the design, manufacturing and

quality assurance. This range covers all components from standard commercial, to the best military ones; so, the range on computer systems could be expected to be somewhat less.

Central Processing Units

Figure 11.1 has been drawn to reflect the practical situation of central processing units (less store) and shows engineering investigations per 1000 hours versus processor speed in kilo instructions per second (KIPS—see

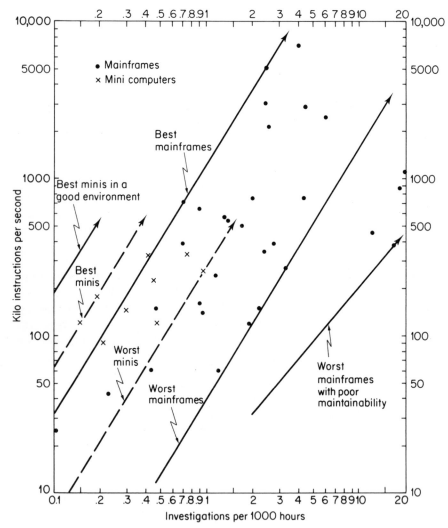

Figure 11.1   Central processing unit (less store) investigation rates vs. processor speed for established populations

Appendix 3 for definition). Each of the points shown represents one type of mini or mainframe processor, all of which are still in service. Many of the figures are derived from large populations of machines but a few are based on a small number of installations.

Current information on microprocessors indicates that they follow the same trend as the slower mini computers.

The mainframes are generally all in good environments so, the differences at a specific speed can be considered to be due to design/quality and maintainability. The difference between the best and the worst mainframes shown is about 8 to 1 and between the best and least maintainable of about 34 to 1. As the reliability of the population of the worst systems does not accurately reflect the position of a single established system (see Chapter 2), the various factors affecting the investigation rates are considered to be in the following range:

Quality Factor (average)	Multiplication Factor
Good	1
Medium	2
Poor	5

This represents average reliability differences of single machines over the first 10 to 12 thousand hours of service and assumes that the processors are not first production models. Likely average reliability differences on a shorter term basis are given later.

Maintainability Factor	Multiplication Factor
Good	1
Fairly bad	2
Bad	4

Figure 11.1 represents investigation rates and the above equivalent investigation per fault ratios of 1.5, 3 and 6 respectively. These factors may not be proportional to processor speed, having far less effect on the smaller systems, which only have a relatively small number of replaceable modules, against hundreds on the large systems.

The mini processors can be considered to be in an average of good and bad environments so, the best minis in a good environment can be assumed to be as shown in Figure 11.1 and the environmental factor as derived from MIL Handbook 217B as follows. On microprocessors with very low heat dissipation, many environments can be considered to be good, as the heat output from a system is one of the major factors which determine the environment.

Environmental Factor	Multiplication Factor
Good	1
Medium	2
Poor	4

This factor includes all the variations indicated in Chapter 4 and, with real worst case environments, the factor could be expected to be much higher.

As indicated in Chapter 3, utilization can affect reliability of processors but this may be mainly where the quality is poor. However, the following factors are considered suitable for including the effects of utilization, especially in the early life of a product:

Utilization Factor	Multiplication Factor
Very low	0.25
Low	0.5
Medium	1.0
High	2.0

Considering only early failures, which can be expected on any new machine, irrespective of whether it is a new type of model or not, the following factors have been derived for processors of varying quality. The multiplication factors each represent averages for single machines on a shift year (2000 hours) basis.

Quality Factor on a Shift Year Basis (burn-in failures only)	Multiplication factor for each 2000 hours of service						
	1	2	3	4	5	6	7
Good	1.5	1	1	1	1	1	1
Medium	4.5	2.5	1.5	1	1	1	1
Poor	10	7	5	4	3	2	2

Also, as shown in Chapter 2, design failures on the early production models further degrade the reliability and the following worst case factors could apply to the first of the new models delivered.

Quality Factor for the first Shift Year (design failures only)	Multiplication Factor
Good	2
Medium	2.5
Poor	3

These design stabilization quality factors generally only apply to the first production models delivered, over the first 6 months or so. In other cases, further factors may apply to subsequent years, depending on particular manufacturer's procedures and these sometimes alter the early failure characteristics. Overall, the combination on the various quality and utilization factors should cover most variations met in practice.

Example

Considering two processors, both medium utilization, working in a good environment but one with good and one with bad maintainability, the following range of investigation rates could be obtained from delivery of the first system. It is assumed that both processors have a speed of 1200 KIPS, giving the best investigation rate from Figure 11.1 of 1 per 1000 hours.

Investigations per 1000 hours for new type of processors

Shift Year

	1	2	3	4	5	6	Av.
Good quality Good maintainability	3	1	1	1	1	1	1.3
Poor quality Poor maintainability	120	28	20	16	12	8	34

Main Stores

Figure 11.2 shows the range of investigations per 1000 hours for core stores of varying speeds. This time, the difference between the best and the worst of a particular speed is about 10 to 1. Because of the symmetrical and fairly modular construction of core stores, the maintainability, as far as investigation rates are concerned, is somewhat better than processors. Overall maintainability factors of 1 to 2 could generally be assumed and quality factors as for processors, but more being of medium quality.

Core stores on mini computers tend to be at about the medium point, or slightly worse but it should be pointed out that the investigation rates relate to 1 megabits (128K bytes) or store, and mini computers normally

184

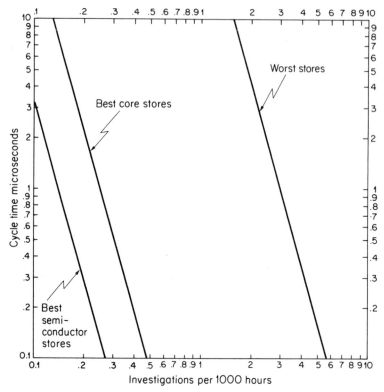

Figure 11.2 Main store (including basic control and power supplies) investigation rates vs. store cycle time per megabit or 128 K bytes. Note the effect of error correction is that many of the investigations will be carried out during preventative maintenance periods

require less store than their mainframe counterparts. However, mini computer stores are generally on easily replaceable modules, with good maintainability, indicating relatively poor quality, even allowing for the figures being for systems in medium environments.

Figure 11.2 also reflects investigation rates of semiconductor memories, where some of the poorer implementations have been as bad as the worst core stores. On the other hand, the better ones show some improvement over the best core stores. With the rapidly developing technology, in this area, further improvements are likely.

The reliability figures given are for stores without error correction, and, when provided, the error correction gives a considerable reduction in investigations during operational hours (see Chapter 9). Incident rates for stores with error correction are given further consideration later in this chapter.

Architectural Considerations

The reliability figures given in Figure 11.1 for central processing units, in fact, include failures outside the real central processor area, for some of the input/output functions. On certain processors, these functions are an integral part so, where they are carried out in identifiably separate units, the reliability figures have been included in the total, to ensure that like with like is being compared. In certain cases, some of these units can be duplicated for resilience purposes, so it is necessary to separately identify their reliability. The stores, whose range of reliability is shown in Figure 11.2, include the basic control and addressing circuitry, but sometimes part of the control is also integral with the processor.

Figure 11.3 has been drawn to identify the range of processor structures and potential reliability of the various units. The dotted lines show the main areas covered in the processor figures given earlier. Figure 11.3a represents the simplest structure, where all the input and output is via the CPU. In this case, the given reliability figures for the CPU and store apply. Figure 11.3 also gives details of approximate integrated circuit populations, to give an indication of potential reliability of the various areas. For all structures, the relative component content of the fast peripheral controllers is quite high and cannot be ignored in reliability calculations.

The second structure employs direct memory access for certain of the input/output functions with other I/O being connected via the CPU. In this case, extra logic is required for the DMA and store interface unit, the latter being responsible for arbitration between store access requests. For this structure, the CPU represents 0.6 to 0.8 of the whole processor logic.

Figure 11.3c shows the third, currently most popular structure, which, besides the store interface, has more complex input/output control, to carry all data directly to store. This control may comprise separate complex fast channels and slower multiplexing channels, or a large I/O processor. In this case, the CPU comprises 0.3 to 0.75 of the main logic.

Overall, as a general case, based on the IC counts given in Figure 11.3, when separate store interface or main peripheral multiplexors can be identified as part of the main processing facility, they can each be considered to be at the following ratios, relative to and included in the reliability figures given in Figure 11.1:

Basic	0.1
Fairly complex	0.2
Complex	0.3

Where the peripheral multiplexing is divided into fast and slow channels, they can be considered to be in the range 0.1 + 0.1 to 0.1 + 0.3, two channels being the maximum included for the Figure 11.1 reliability calculations.

The current position on microprocessor systems is that the largest

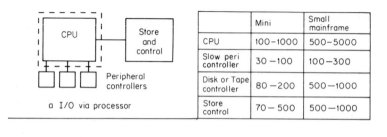

	Mini	Small mainframe
CPU	100–1000	500–5000
Slow peri controller	30–100	100–300
Disk or Tape controller	80–200	500–1000
Store control	70–500	500–1000

a I/O via processor

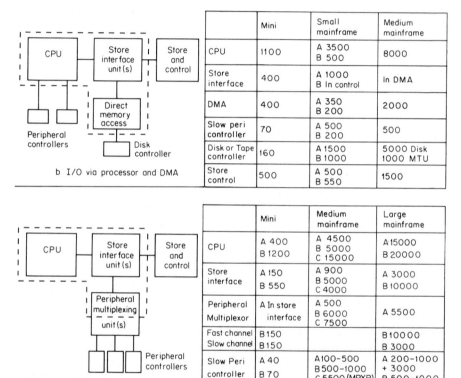

	Mini	Small mainframe	Medium mainframe
CPU	1100	A 3500 B 500	8000
Store interface	400	A 1000 B In control	In DMA
DMA	400	A 350 B 200	2000
Slow peri controller	70	A 500 B 200	500
Disk or Tape controller	160	A 1500 B 1000	5000 Disk 1000 MTU
Store control	500	A 500 B 550	1500

b I/O via processor and DMA

	Mini	Medium mainframe	Large mainframe
CPU	A 400 B 1200	A 4500 B 5000 C 15000	A 15000 B 20000
Store interface	A 150 B 550	A 900 B 5000 C 4000	A 3000 B 10000
Peripheral Multiplexor	A In store interface	A 500 B 6000 C 7500	A 5500
Fast channel Slow channel	B 150 B 150		B 10000 B 3000
Slow Peri controller	A 40 B 70	A 100-500 B 500-1000 C 5500 (MPXR)	A 200-1000 + 3000 B 500-1000
Disk or Tape controller	A 150 B 150	A 500-1000 B 1000-5000 C 5500	A 6500 Disk 1000 Tape B 2000-5000
Store control	A 180 B 300	A 2000 B 2500 C 1500	A 1500 B 3000

c I/O via peripheral multiplexing unit(s)

Figure 11.3   Architectural considerations

component count for one of the 16 bit word varieties represents about 50% of the smallest mini computer shown in Figure 11.3a, in each area, but the architecture may follow one of the other forms. Others, of course, have far fewer integrated circuits with the trend, rapidly approaching, one integrated circuit for the total system electronics.

Peripheral Controllers

On the medium/large mainframes, from Figure 11.3, the proportion of integrated circuits, relative to the main processor, is mainly between 0.2 and 0.3 for disk controllers and around 0.1 for magnetic tape unit controllers. Reliability figures for the more complex controllers mainly indicate the following:

Disk controllers	0.15 to 1.4 investigations/1000 hours
Magnetic tape controllers	0.1 to 1.0 investigations/1000 hours
Communications multiplexors and front end processors	0.08 to 1.0 investigations/1000 hours

The controllers are of varying complexity, according to facilities provided and peripheral speeds, so the range of reliability figures does not appear to be as great as on processors: one reason for this may be that the controllers are provided on a range of medium to large processors, so larger quantities are provided relative to any one processor model, providing more information to sort out design deficiencies. Alternatively, as the controllers are likely to be less reliable on the faster systems (see Chapter 3), the effort in attempting to improve the designs on these may produce a better average, with the bulk of controllers being provided on the slower systems.

Bearing in mind that the average medium/large processor may have a speed of about 400 KIPS, with best case reliability of 0.5 investigations per 1000 hours, the relative reliability of controllers can again be assumed to be:

Basic	0.1	
Fairly complex	0.2	times the main processor reliability
Complex	0.3	

The smaller mainframes have component counts, for disk and tape controllers, from 0.2 to 1.4 times the processor. The larger ratios are where the controller is for devices normally provided on the more powerful systems. Similarly, on mini computers, the range is 0.1 to 0.8, indicating that the controllers are sometimes nearly as complex as the processor. In these cases, further relative reliability complexity ratios can be found.

In many cases, a slow peripheral controller is provided for each device, so the reliability is very high, when compared with the peripheral, and can be ignored. In a few cases, a slow peripheral multiplexor is provided in addition to the main system peripheral multiplexing unit, typically, this having a similar reliability to the other fairly complex controllers.

Examples of Relative Reliability

The following examples of reliability show how the above relationships work in practice.

1. Medium System 400 KIPS

	Investigations/ 1000 hours		
	No.	Ratio of total	Ratio of IC count
CPU	0.25 ⎤	0.36 ⎤	0.57 ⎤
Store interface	0.08 ⎬ 0.7	0.11 ⎬ 1.0	0.14 ⎬ 1.0
Peripheral multiplexor	0.37 ⎦	0.53 ⎦	0.29 ⎦
Peripheral controller (average disk, tape and slow multiplexor)	0.31	0.44	0.22

At 400 KIPS, the overall processor reliability is quite good at 0.7 investigations per 1000 hours but is degraded somewhat by the relatively poor quality peripheral multiplexor which, based on the IC count, ought to give about 0.13 investigations per 1000 hours, if of equivalent quality to the CPU. Similarly, the peripheral controllers could be better.

2. Medium System 270 KIPS

	Investigations/ 1000 hours		
	No.	Ratio to CPU	Ratio of IC count to CPU
CPU (including store interface and peripheral multiplexor)	3.34	1.0	1.0
Exchangeable disk controller	1.15	0.34	0.5
Magnetic tape unit controller	0.24	0.07	0.1
Communications processor	0.69	0.21	0.6

This time, the processor is of poor quality (Figure 11.1 indicating a best case of 0.4 investigations/1000 hours at this speed). The peripheral controllers also appear not to be as reliable as they could be—based on the relative IC counts they could achieve 0.2, 0.04 and 0.24 investigations per 1000 hours respectively.

The above examples serve to show that each manufacturer can have his troubles and it is unlikely that all equipment from one supplier will be of the same quality and maintainability.

Investigation Times

Mean investigation times for the central processors given in Figure 11.1 are in the following ranges:

Medium/large mainframes	0.5 to 5.3 hours
Small mainframes	1.9 to 5.2 hours
Mini processors	2.1 to 4.4 hours

These times do not include waiting time for engineers for on-call maintenance. Chapter 7 showed that the normal mean investigation time for processors is about 2 hours. When the average investigation time is less than 2 hours, it is because of maintainability problems, where many of the investigations are of very short duration to gather evidence. The only recorded mean investigation times of under 1.5 hours, for the populations of processors shown in Figure 11.1, are near the worst mainframe line and, those with bad maintainability are mainly about 1 hour. In these cases, the bad maintainability is greatly influenced by functional modularity (see Chapter 9) and little time is lost waiting for spares.

The investigation times which are significantly higher than 2 hours have a large proportion of extended down times of 8 hours or more, influenced by waiting time for spares, maintenance procedures and quality of engineers. The quality of engineers is relative to the requirements of the particular system: on the most reliable processors the engineers have little opportunity to practice their skills, so the down time is likely to be high.

Overall mean investigation times can be assumed to be dependent on the down time distribution, affected by the factors as described above:

Down time distribution	Mean investigation time hours	
Good	1.0	
Medium	2.5	+ waiting time for engineer
Bad	5.0	

Where on-site service is available for microprocessors, the mean investigations times are also in the above range. In certain cases the system has to be returned to a repair depot, leading to an out of service time of a day or more.

Peripheral controllers also have investigation times over the same range as processors. Mean investigation times on stores are generally in the 1 to 3 hour range, as spares for the least reliable parts are usually available. However, when the stores can be reconfigured, so that the system can continue operation with part of the store busied out, the spares may not always be readily available, so the bad down time distributions can still be encountered.

Incidents and Down Time as seen by the User

The number of incidents per investigation is highly dependent on what the user is prepared to tolerate and, as indicated in Chapter 7, the typical range is from 1 to 4. As a practical figure on modern systems, it can be assumed that there are 2 incidents per investigation. Hence, the mean

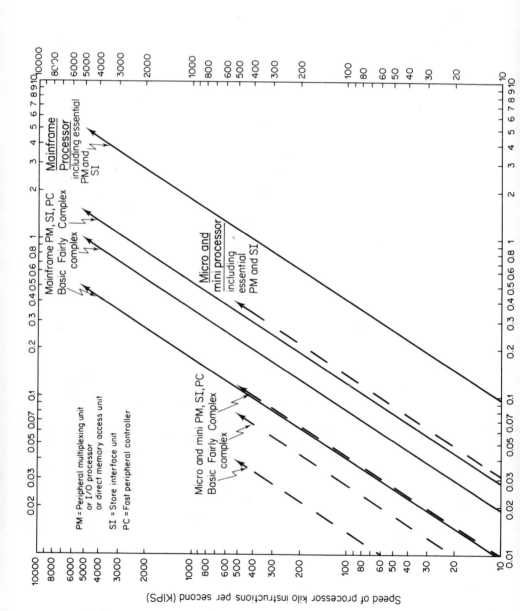

Derating factors multiply by:

Environmental factor		Maintainability factor		Utilization factor	
Good	1	Good	1	Very low	0.25
Medium	2	Fairly bad	2	Low	0.5
Poor	4	Bad	4	Medium	1.0
				High	2.0

Quality factors

Early failures

Shift year (2000 hrs.)

Quality	1	2	3	4	5	6	Av.
Good	1.5	1	1	1	1	1	1
Medium	4.5	2.5	1.5	1	1	1	2
Poor	10	7	5	4	3	2	5

Design failures (new products only)

Shift year

1	2	3
2	Depends on
2.5	suppliers'
3	procedures
	see text

Down time and waiting time

Down time distribution	Mean down time per incident (mdti) Hours	+ Recovery & spoilt work time etc.
Good	0.5	
Medium	1.25	
Bad	2.5	

On call maintenance & waiting time for engineer

Add $\dfrac{\text{response time}}{2}$ to mdti

Possibly add additional incidents but with recovery & spoilt work time etc. only

Figure 11.4 Reliability predictor for processors (less store) and peripheral controllers showing best case incidents per 1000 hours vs. processor speed also derating factors

investigation time per incident can be assumed to be:

	Mean investigation time per incident	
Down time distribution	hours	
Good	0.5	
Medium	1.25	$+ \dfrac{\text{waiting time}}{2}$
Bad	2.5	

On top of the down time shown, it is also necessary to add recovery time and spoilt work time etc. (see Chapter 7). Where extended waiting time for engineering services is incurred, a further two incidents per investigation may have to be allowed but, for these, only recovery time etc. applies.

Figure 11.4 has been drawn to summarize a practical prediction method for the main electronics. This shows the best case incidents per 1000 hours

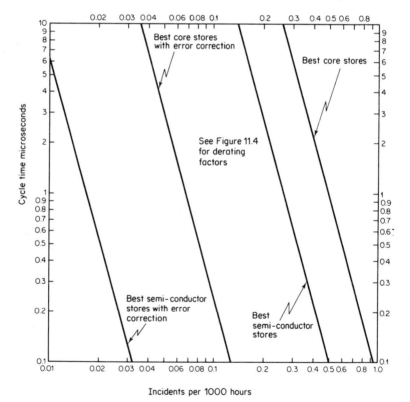

Incidents per 1000 hours

Figure 11.5   Reliability predictor for main stores including basic control and power supplies, per megabit (128 K bytes), showing incidents per 1000 hours vs. store cycle time. Derating factors in Figure 11.4 apply

versus kilo instructions per second for the processor, also peripheral multiplexing units, store interface units and fast peripheral controllers, again assuming two incidents per investigation. For ease of reference, Figure 11.4 also summarizes the derating multiplication factors and mean down time expectations.

Similarly, Figure 11.5 provides a summary of likely best case incidents per 1000 hours versus cycle time for main stores, with the derating factors shown in Figure 11.4 applying. However, as indicated earlier, the maintainability factors are more likely to be between 1 and 2. Figure 11.5 also shows likely best case reliability, where error correction facilities are provided.

PERIPHERALS

The analysis of peripheral failures is generally more difficult than processors, as the recording tends not to be at the same standards. With most of the peripheral failures being recorded in the error logs, on the larger systems, the users need not report every incident. The engineers generally complete a fault docket when any engineering attention is given, but do not necessarily report the time that a device is waiting for attention or spares.

Exchangeable Disks

Table 11.1 provides a summary of various reliability statistics on disk units of different capacities and on different manufacturers' systems. The first two columns are for engineering activity, where the mean investigation time is in the same sort of range as processors. The third column, in conjunction with the first, represents user recorded authorization for engineering activity, where the waiting time included increases the mean down time to between 7 and 8 hours. The last two columns represent the case where users are supposed to record every incident, except the one denoted E, which is derived from error log analysis. It is clear that all incidents are not recorded, many of those missing likely to be failing to load or dropping off-line (see Chapter 6), for which a recording may be made after several incidents. Each of the three sections shown represents an advance in technology where, in spite of greater capacity and increased transfer rate, the reliability remains surprisingly consistent. The disks with the best reliability figures are derived from systems which have large quantities of disks, so the average utilization is less than normal. Overall, the best case reliability with medium utilization can be considered to be:

0.4   investigations per 1000 hours
1.2   incidents per 1000 hours (all incidents)

Table 11.1 Reliability of exchangeable disk units

Device		Investigations per 1000 hours	Mean inv. time hours	Mean inv. time including waiting time hours	Incidents per 1000 hours	Mean down time per incident hours
8 Mbytes	1	0.4	1.6			
150 KB/sec	2				1.12	3.6
	3				0.53	8.4
30–60 Mbytes	1	0.4	3.9		0.23	10.0
300 KB/sec	2	0.55	3.1		0.48	8.9
	3	0.41		7.9		
	4	0.7	2.0			
	5	0.62		7.8		
	6	0.45	3.8			
100–200 Mbytes	1				0.86	8.3
800 KB/sec	2	0.46		7.5		
	3	0.53				
	4	0.33		8.0	0.77E	

E—As indicated in error log.

Table 11.2 Reliability of magnetic tape units

Device		Investigations per 1000 hours	Mean inv. time hours	Mean inv. time including waiting time hours	Incidents per 1000 hours	Mean down time per incident hours
30–60 KB/sec	1	0.49			1.37	3.5
Up to 800 bpi	2		2.1		0.71	7.6
NRZI	3	0.8			1.7	5.6
recording	4				8.0	0.8
	5				3.8	2.5
	6	0.75				
80–160 KB/sec	1	0.7	2.8		0.93	3.1
1600 bpi	2	1.5	1.9		2.8	5.8
PE recording	3	1.2		6.6	34.0	
	4					1.1
	5	0.83	1.5			
	6	1.2		8.8		
80–320 KB/sec	1				2.1	5.2
1600 bpi	2				3.0	6.9
PE recording	3	0.6		7.4	$\begin{cases} 0.96 \\ 5.7E \end{cases}$	2.3

E—As indicated in error log.

Factors Affecting Reliability

The quality, maintainability, and environmental factors given earlier can also be assumed to apply, but maintainability and quality are generally good to medium. Site to site reliability variations, typically of 8 to 1 are found, due to variations in utilization, and the utilization factors given earlier were mainly based on peripherals.

In many cases, the same disk drives are supplied at different capacities and different track packing densities, with the higher density ones giving somewhat worse reliability, mainly in the area of detected transfer errors (see Chapter 6) so the following capacity/speed factors can also be assumed to apply:

Capacity/Speed Factor	Multiplication Factor
Low	0.7
Medium	1.0
High	1.5

Mean investigation times (excluding waiting time) appear to be:

	Mean investigation time	
	per investigation	per incident
Down time distribution	hours	hours
Good	1.5	0.5
Medium	3.0	1.0

The disk units shown in Table 11.1 have a high proportion covered by at least prime shift on-site maintenance, and for a number of them, the down time only represents the period within this maintenance cover. For the disks, the down time distribution including waiting time is similar to the worst figures shown in Table 7.2, except those over 8 hours sometimes include a few in the 50–100 hour range and perhaps one at 250 hours. Overall, the following mean waiting times will often apply, and, of course, the combination of investigation and waiting times give a bad down time distribution by anyone's standards.

	Mean waiting time	
	per investigation hours	per incident hours
Waiting for spares	4.0	1.33
Waiting for engineer	mean response time	$\dfrac{\text{mean response time}}{3}$

Disks on mini computers sometimes give the same sort of reliability as those in Table 11.1, although most are of a lower capacity, slower transfer rate and lower utilization. In certain cases, disks identical to those on the mainframes are provided giving a similar reliability but, in other cases, equivalent devices are of poor quality and worse reliability.

Magnetic Tape Units

Table 11.2 provides a similar summary to that on disks for magnetic tape units of varying technology vintages. Although there is a greater variation in investigation rates, the newer forms of unit gave similar best case figures Overall, the best case reliability for medium utilization can be considered to be as follows. As for all other peripherals, it is assumed that there are 3 incidents per investigation.

0.7   investigations per 1000 hours
2.1   incidents per 1000 hours

The incident rate for magnetic tape units ignores misloading incidents on the new self loading units. These problems can generally be easily overcome but can make the incident rate double the above figure or more. Mean investigation times can be similar to disks so the figures given earlier apply, except the tape units tend to be biased towards the 1.5 hours mean. Similarly, the waiting time can be considered to be as for disks. The tape units are also highly utilization dependent and, it is clear from Table 11.2, that certain ones have severe maintainability and quality problems, this being further emphasized by the variations in environmental specifications given in Chapter 4.

Mini computer magnetic tape unit reliabilities generally appear to be somewhat better than the mainframe units, but the utilization and speed of operation is generally very low.

Peripheral Summary

Other peripherals have similar characteristics to the disks and tapes but, in certain cases, the utilization is very low, so their reliability appears to be much better. In other cases, the investigation times can be slightly lower. Table 11.3 summarizes the best case reliability characteristics of the most popular peripherals, adjusted for medium utilization and speed. Also, for convenience, the reliability derating multiplication factors are repeated with the table. The range of down times are shown for investigation time only and also including waiting time for spares. This waiting time is more likely when standby peripherals are available. In order to determine the real mean down time per incident, it may also be necessary to add spoilt work and recovery times plus a proportion of the response time in waiting for engineering attention.

Table 11.3 Reliability predictor for peripheral equipment showing best case investigations and incidents per 1000 hours and associated investigation times and waiting times—medium utilization, medium speed
*Normally better as utilization is usually low to very low

Device and speed/capacity for current production units	Investigations per 1000 hours	Mean investigation time hours	Mean inv. + waiting (for spares) time hours	Incidents per 1000 hours	Mean inv. time per incident hours	Mean inv. time + spares waiting time per incident (see also below) hours	
						Range	Average
Exchangeable disks 100 MB, 800 KB/sec	0.4	1.5–3.0	5.5–7.0	1.2	0.5 –1.0	1.83–2.33	2.08
Magnetic tape units 160 KB/sec PE	0.7	1.5–3.0	5.5–7.0	2.1	0.5 –1.0	1.83–2.33	2.08
Fixed disks or drums <10MB. >1MB/sec	0.47	2.0–4.0	6.0–8.0	1.4	0.67–1.33	2.0–2.67	2.33
Card readers 1000 CPM	1.7*	1.5–3.0	5.5–7.0	5.1*	0.5 –1.0	1.83–2.33	2.08
Card punches 100 CPM	2.0*	2.0–4.0	6.0–8.0	6.0*	0.67–1.33	2.0–2.67	2.33
Line printers 1000 LPM	1.8	1.3–3.0	5.3–7.0	5.4	0.43–1.0	1.77–2.33	2.05
Paper tape readers 1000 CHPS	1.2*	1.3–2.0	5.3–6.0	3.6*	0.43–0.67	1.77–2.0	1.89
Paper tape punches 100 CHPS	1.9*	1.3–2.0	5.3–6.0	5.7*	0.43–0.67	1.77–2.0	1.89
Typewriters	1.3*	1.0–2.0	5.0–6.0	3.9*	0.33–0.67	1.67–2.0	1.84
VDUs–character	0.2	1.0–2.0	5.0–6.0	0.6	0.33–0.67	1.67–2.0	1.84

Derating factors multiply by the following

Environmental factor	
Good	1
Medium	2
Poor	4

Maintainability factor	
Good	1
Fairly bad	2
Bad	4

Utilization factor	
Very low	0.25
Low	0.5
Medium	1.0
High	2.0

Speed/capacity factor	
Low	0.7
Medium	1.0
High	1.5

Quality factors

Quality	Early failures shift year (2000 hours)						
	1	2	3	4	5	6	AV
Good	1.5	1	1	1	1	1	1
Medium	4.5	2.5	1.5	1	1	1	2
Bad	10	7	5	4	3	2	5

Design failures (new products only) shift year		
1	2	3
2	Depends on	
2.5	particular supplier's	
3	procedures. See	
	text	

Mean down time per incident—add recovery and spoilt work time.

For on-call maintenance add $\dfrac{\text{Response time}}{3}$. Possibly add additional incidents but with recovery and spoilt work time etc. only.

H

EXAMPLES OF PREDICTIONS

Example 1   Determining Air Conditioning Requirements for a Mini Computer System

Considering a basic mini computer system with 32K bytes of core store, a typewriter and a paper tape reader (from Figures 11.4 and 11.5, and Table 11.3) the reliability prediction is given in Table 11.4. It is assumed that the system is covered by on-call maintenance and, as standby units are not provided, the total mean waiting time for service amounts to a further 4 hours per investigation or 1.33 to 2 hours per incident depending on the type of unit.

Considering the environment with the following factors:

Good × 1   Full air conditioning
Medium × 2   No air conditioning but switch off when too hot
                 for people or when environmental design specification
                 limits approached (see Chapter 4)
Poor × 4   No air conditioning, dirty environment, run
                 in excessive temperatures and humidities

The resultant reliability and serviceability becomes:

Environment	Incidents/1000 hours	Serviceability
Good	3.43	0.989
Medium	6.86	0.978
Bad	13.72	0.956

In this case, it is likely that the 6.86 incidents per 1000 hours and 2.2% unserviceability could be tolerated, so air conditioning would not be necessary. However, the amount of time lost due to switching off, when too hot, should be checked (see Chapter 4), as this could override the other considerations.

Example 2   Mini versus Small Mainframe Comparison

Table 11.5 shows a comparison between a mini system and a small mainframe, with a larger configuration than considered above. The quality and maintainability differences are as may be found in practice but it is assumed that both systems have the same down time distributions and response times. The example shows that the small mainframe can have a better reliability than the mini system, with the unserviceability ratios being:

Mini   3.1%
Small mainframe   2.1%

Either of the above average unserviceability figures would probably be adequate but, in a more adverse environment, neither may be acceptable.

Table 11.4 Reliability prediction for a basic mini computer system environment to be determined

Unit	Basic incidents per 1000 hours	Derating factors				Resulting incidents/ 1000 hours	Mean down time/ incident hours	Down time per 1000 hours
		Qual	Maint	Util	Speed			
CPU 300 KIPS	0.28	2	1	1	–	0.56	1.25 + 2.0	1.82
32KB store 1 μs	0.12	2	1	1	–	0.24	1.25 + 2.0	0.78
Typewriter	3.9	2	1	0.25	0.7	1.37	1.84 + 1.33	4.34
Paper tape reader 300 CHPS	3.6	2	1	0.25	0.7	1.26	1.89 + 1.33	4.06
Total						3.43	3.21	11.0

Table 11.5 Mini vs. small mainframe comparison—good environment

Unit	Basic incidents per 1000 hours	Derating factors				Resulting incidents/ 1000 hours	Mean down time/incident hours	Down time per 1000 hours
		Qual	Maint	Util	Speed			
Mini CPU 300 KIPS	0.28	2	1	1	–	0.56	3.25	1.82
64KB store 1 μs	0.24	2	1	1	–	0.48	3.25	1.56
Typewriter	3.9	2	1	0.25	0.7	1.37	3.17	4.34
Disk low speed	1.2	2	1	0.5	0.7	0.84	2.08 + 1.33	2.86
Mag tape low speed	2.1	2	1	0.25	0.7	0.74	2.08 + 1.33	2.52
Card reader low speed	5.1	2	1	0.25	0.7	1.78	2.08 + 1.33	6.07
Line printer low speed	5.4	2	1	0.5	0.7	3.78	2.05 + 1.33	12.78
Total mini						9.55	3.35	31.95

Small CPU 100 KIPS	0.42	1	2	1	–	0.84	3.25	2.73
96KB store 2 μs	0.30	1	1	1	–	0.30	3.25	0.97
Typewriter	3.9	2	1	0.25	0.7	1.37	3.17	4.34
Disk med speed	1.2	1	1	0.5	1	0.6	3.41	2.05
Mag tape med speed	2.1	1	1	0.25	1	0.53	3.41	1.81
Card reader low speed	5.1	1	1	0.25	0.7	0.89	3.41	3.03
Line printer low speed	5.4	1	1	0.5	0.7	1.89	3.38	6.39
Total small mainframe						6.42	3.32	21.32

With the unreliability mainly being dependent on the peripherals, with 3 incidents per investigation and about 1.5 investigations per fault, the example shown indicates 1.4 to 2.1 faults per 1000 hours or about 3 to 4 faults per shift year.

Example 3   Microprocessor Reliability

A microprocessor of equivalent speed 100 KIPS (see Appendix 3), with 8K bytes 1 μsec store, of medium quality, good maintainability, low utilization, working in a good environment (that is good for a low heat system—see Environmental Factor earlier) the reliability could be:

$$(CPU\ 0.14 + Store\ 0.49 \times \tfrac{8}{128}) \times 2 \times 1 \times 0.5 \times 1 =$$

0.171 incidents per 1000 hours

At 2 incidents per investigation or 3 incidents per fault this gives 0.057 faults per 1000 hours. With the processor switched on 40 hours per week or 2000 per year, this gives 0.114 faults per year or 1 fault per 9 years. These calculations do not include the peripheral equipment which could be expected to lead to far more frequent faults, depending on quality, utilization etc.

The above examples indicate how reliability can be estimated for simple systems but, on larger configurations with standby units, more detailed calculations are required: Chapter 12 gives a method for estimating reliability and serviceability of complex systems.

SOFTWARE RELIABILITY PREDICTIONS

Computer suppliers normally refuse to give any predictions for software reliability, neither for the number of errors that a user is likely to encounter nor for the likely effects on total system operations. This attitude is perfectly understandable, as it is impossible to foresee and cater for all user requirements or to ensure that errors are not present which cause total system failures. On the other hand, the same manufacturers are often prepared to give hardware reliability predictions, normally ignoring many of the complications explained in this book and, in the event of design failures being encountered, see that the appropriate modifications are worked out and incorporated, thus tending to ensure that the predicted reliability is obtained in practice. In the case of software, where most of the errors are classified as design failures, users who are encountering a particularly high level of problems are generally given favourable treatment and those who shout the loudest even more so: the point is that, eventually, an acceptable level of reliability is made to happen.

The main reason why manufacturers refuse to give predictions is, as explained in Chapter 5, because it may be so bad initially, so susceptible to variations with utilization, and subject to frequent redesign, ensuring that the reliability takes a long time to reach a reasonably acceptable level. With the current trend for manufacturers to claim that their new software is of superior design, some mutual understanding should be made with the users on the likely levels and trends in reliability so, at least, the users can make adequate plans or, at most, the manufacturers cannot be accused of misrepresentation. It is with this view in mind that the following predictions are given, not for the full variety of errors, which are dependent on the way that a user expects the software to behave, but for the relatively simple prediction of total system reliability.

When the software is first written, the initial reliability will vary according to the quality of the design, quality assurance procedures, size and complexity of the software, also quality of the people employed and whether the particular hardware to be used is established or of a new type.

The rate of improvement is dependent on the built in maintainability, quality of support, number of installations, frequency of new releases and amount of software rewritten.

As far as individual sites are concerned, there will be wide variations due to utilization, including according to the speed of processor and configuration complexity. The rate of improvement is likely to depend on the frequency and variety of changes in user workloads and configurations. Also each user can expect more problems on first delivery, due to early failures.

Table 116 shows the range of controlling software currently available on mini, micro computers and mainframe systems, in terms of the number of instructions used against the particular system type. Each class of software is shown over a range of instruction counts, representing competing systems giving similar facilities. The table also shows the likely average system failure rate, over the first year of delivery to the first users. A similar failure rate could apply to software of different sizes as, just like processors, the larger systems can be more reliable than smaller ones, offering the same facilities and performance. The table also indicates relative sizes and reliabilities of control programs used in software driven peripheral controllers and communications processors.

Also shown in Table 11.6 are the likely derating factors, which, along with the average failure rates, have been derived from the figures given in Chapter 5. The first factor covers variations with time over the lifetime of the product and indicates a 100 to 1 improvement in the average yearly reliability. Very few systems are likely to encounter the worst failure rates shown, as the majority, of course, are normally delivered after the first year of the new software product, but each new hardware configuration can expect to reveal new problems during its first year, so the early failure factor of 2 is shown for the later deliveries: for example, the following

Table 11.6 Reliability predictor for controlling software
(Based on information given in Chapter 5)

Initial reliability of new software

Type of controlling software	Size of processor	Thousand instructions	System failures per 1000 hours	
MINI & MICRO SYSTEMS				
Elementary Executive	Medium	0.25–1	0.4	
Basic Executive	Medium	1–4	1.5	Control programs for software driven peripheral controllers and communications processors are also normally within this range
Extended Executive	Medium	4–16	6	
Basic Operating System	Medium	16–64	25	
Extended Operating System	Medium	64–256	100	
TYPICAL MAINFRAME SYSTEMS				
Executive	Small	4–16	6	
Small Scale Operating System	Small/ Medium	16–64	25	
Medium Scale Operating System	Medium	64–256	100	
Full Scale Operating System	Medium/ Large	256–1000+	400	

Derating Factors

	Variations with time							Early failures
	Year (from delivery to first user)							First year of any hardware configuration delivered after year 1 of software product multiply by 2
	1	2	3	4	5	6	6+	
Multiplication factor	1	0.2	0.1	0.05	0.03	0.02	0.01	

Multiply each of the yearly figures by the following factors

Initial quality		Maintainability and frequency of change		Utilization and user changes	
Bad	2	Bad	2	Very high	4
Average	1	Average	1	High	2
Fairly good	0.5	Fairly good	0.5	Medium	1
Good	0.25	Good	0.25	Low	0.5
				Very low	0.25

Note that the maintainability and utilization factors can change on a year by year basis.

could apply for a large operating system on the very first system delivered, and for one delivered at the beginning of year 2:

	Average System failures per 1000 hours in year						
	1	2	3	4	5	6	6+
First system	400	80	40	20	12	8	4
System delivered year 2		160	40	20	12	8	4

The next factor is for the initial quality, where most of the larger operating systems delivered over the last few years have been in one of the first three categories. The final factors cover variations, given earlier, which are within the control of the supplier and the user respectively. For each of these areas, the factors could be expected to vary on a year by year basis, according to changes made in the particular year: for example, an operating system or major applications package, produced for one particular user, may have a factor of 1 for the first year and 0.25 for the second and subsequent years, providing the initial design is not changed by the issue of new releases, with varying facilities. Each of the figures calculated represents a yearly average and, in the case of general purpose software, short term variations, due to new releases or changes in workload, can be expected, an indication of the likely level of variation being shown in Chapter 5.

Example of Software and Hardware Predictions

Considering two first production mainframes of 1200 KIPS with 512K bytes, 500 ns core stores, without error correction, both systems being of medium utilization and working in a good environment, the following could apply (derived from Figures 11.4 and 11.5, and Table 11.6) on a yearly basis where, for the hardware, this is assumed to be 4000 hours of operation.

Best system, good quality and maintainability	System failures per 1000 hours for years					
	1	2	3	4	5	6
CPU	4	2	2	2	2	2
Store	4.8	2.4	2.4	2.4	2.4	2.4
Total mainframe	8.8	4.4	4.4	4.4	4.4	4.4
Software fairly good initial quality, otherwise average	200	40	20	10	6	4

Worst system	System failures per 1000 hours for years					
	1	2	3	4	5	6
CPU poor quality and maintainability	148	36	20	16	16	16
Store poor quality, fairly bad maintainability	89	22	12	9.6	9.6	9.6
Total mainframe	237	58	32	25.6	25.6	25.6
Software average	400	80	40	20	12	8

In the first case, the software reliability obviously gives the greatest difficulties over the first five years, the hardware then starts to become the least reliable. In the second case, the hardware and software reliabilities are somewhat closer over the first four years, the hardware then becomes predominant. Note that the latter results are similar to those in Figure 2.6 for the processor and Figure 5.6 for the software.

QUALITY OF SERVICE FROM A USER'S POINT OF VIEW

When a new computer system is being obtained, although the manufacturer may not be prepared to contractually commit to specific figures, reliability and serviceability should be discussed so that, at least, the user can set his own standards to decide when he should start complaining about quality of service. The main areas where these standards can be set are:

1. System level—system serviceability ratio and frequency of system failures. Chapter 12 provides a method of estimating these figures for most types of system.
2. Software package level—the number of outstanding problems and response times for providing corrections (see Chapter 5).
3. Hardware unit level—unit availability, embracing the frequency of engineering intervention, corrective maintenance time, preventative maintenance during scheduled hours and response time for engineering services.

Table 11.7 gives an example of how unit availability standards can be estimated. The basic investigation rates and times are derived from Table 11.3, assuming medium quality, good environment, medium speed, medium to low utilization and good maintainability. The down times shown are average investigation times, including waiting time for spares and, for the on-call maintenance, it is assumed that the mean response time is 3

Table 11.7   Unit availability including preventative maintenance

Unit	Mtce type	Per 1000 hours	Mean down time	Down time/ 1000 hours	PM time/ 1000 hours	Mean	500 hr. month	3000 hr. 6 month
			Investigations				**% Availability**	
							Worst case	
Exchangeable	On-site	0.8	6.25	5.0	1.2	99.4	92	97
disk unit	On-call	0.8	9.25	7.4	1.2	99.1	90	96
Magnetic tape	On-site	1.4	6.25	8.8	4.1	98.7	88	95
unit	On-call	1.4	9.25	13.0	4.1	98.3	87	95
Card reader	On-site	1.7	6.25	10.6	8.0	98.1	87	94
(low utilization)	On-call	1.7	9.25	15.7	8.0	97.6	86	93
Line printer	On-site	3.6	6.15	22.1	17.3	96.1	82	91
	On-call	3.6	9.15	32.9	17.3	95.0	79	89
Typewriter	On-site	1.3	5.5	7.2	1.0	99.2	91	97
(low utilization)	On-call	1.3	8.5	11.1	1.0	98.8	89	96
Visual display	On-site	0.4	5.5	2.2	0.3	99.7	94	98
unit	On-call	0.4	8.5	3.4	0.3	99.6	93	98

hours. The preventative maintenance (PM) times are derived from Table 7.5: these cannot be taken as typical as there is so much variation between different makes of unit but, in this area, the manufacturer should provide the information. The mean availability is derived from the total investigation, waiting and PM times per 1000 hours. Finally, the worst case availability figures are derived from the 99% confidence limits for bad down time distributions given in Figure 8.6, over periods of 500 and 3000 hours. The worst case figures could, of course, be even worse over shorter periods or with poorer quality equipment but, on the other hand, with high quality equipment and better than average service, they could be much better.

Chapter 12

Practical Reliability and Serviceability Calculations for Complex Systems

UNITS IN PARALLEL AND IN SERIES

Units in Parallel

When considering reliability and serviceability of systems with standby units, the following formulae are often quoted:

m = mean time between incidents of a single unit

d = mean down time per incident

s = serviceability of a single unit = $\dfrac{m}{m+d}$

u = unserviceability of a single unit = $\dfrac{d}{m+d}$

M = mtbi dual system = $\dfrac{m^2 + 2md}{2d} \simeq \dfrac{m^2}{2d}$

D = mdti dual system = $\dfrac{d}{2}$

$$S = \text{serviceability of dual system} = \frac{(m^2 + 2md)/2d}{(m^2 + 2md)/2d + d/2}$$

$$= \frac{m^2 + 2md}{(m+d)^2}$$

$$= \frac{(m+d)^2 - d^2}{(m+d)^2}$$

$$= 1 - u^2$$

Similarly, U = unserviceability of dual system = u^2.

Also for a triplicated system:

M = mtbi triple system $\simeq \dfrac{m^3}{3d^2}$

D = mdti triple system = $\dfrac{d}{3}$

$$S = \text{serviceability of triple system} = 1 - u^3$$
$$U = \text{unserviceability of triple system} = u^3$$

The basic problem with these sort of calculations is that they do not cover the case where, say, 2 out of 3 units are required. To cover these calculations, the binomial distribution is more appropriate:

$$(s + u)^n$$

where n is the number of units,

s considered as the probability of a unit working, and

u considered as the probability of a unit not working.

For the binomial distribution, the probability of exactly y units working out of a total of n is:

$$\frac{n!}{y!(n-y)!} s^y u^{n-y}$$

For example, three magnetic tape units are provided, each giving an expected serviceability ratio of 0.9876 and 2 are required for a working system. The probabilities of 3, 2, 1, 0 working are:

y	Probability
3	0.96326
2	0.03628
1	0.00046
0	0.00000

Or the probability of at least two units working is 0.99954.

Appendix 2 gives details of a program for calculating serviceability of units in parallel, for use on a programmable calculator.

Units in Series

If a number of devices are all required for correct operation, the items can be considered to be in series and the overall probability of working considered to be the product of individual unit serviceability ratios. For example, a central processing system could be assumed to have the characteristics as shown in Figure 12.1.

In order to estimate overall failure rates, the incident per 1000 hour figures can be added so it is useful to use a formula for calculating serviceability based on the same figures, rather than mean time between incidents:

$$\text{Serviceability} = \left(\frac{d.ik}{1000} + 1\right)^{-1} \qquad \text{Unserviceability} = \left(\frac{1000}{d.ik} + 1\right)^{-1}$$

where ik represents incidents per 1000 hours and d represents mean down time per incident

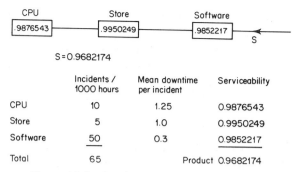

Figure 12.1 Serviceability of units in series

An alternative method for estimating system serviceability is to calculate the overall incidents per 1000 hours and mean down times to determine the result. For the example in Figure 12.1 this gives a ratio of 0.9685230 against 0.9682174. Over the range of calculations normally carried out, the difference is well within the error in unit reliability estimates but the series chain method is considered to give the most accurate result.

Recovery Factor

The most important factors to be considered in configuring a system are the consequences of a failure; although the configuration appears likely to give a high serviceability, some recovery action may be required after a failure, during which time none of the devices may be available for normal work. This recovery factor is often more important than the time lost due to all units being unserviceable.

The recovery procedures depend on the type of failure and tasks being undertaken by the different devices in a specific application. For example, the parallel chain of magnetic tape units, considered earlier, could be used alternately for reading and writing and the following types of failure and recovery times could apply for 10 incidents:

Type of failure	Operator action mins	Unit recovery action mins	Total action mins	No of incidents	Total recovery time mins
Unit off line	2	1	3	4	12
Writing failure	2	4	6	3	18
Reading failure	2	8	10	3	30
				10	60

Mean recovery time = 6 mins.

For use in serviceability chains, a recovery factor, representing the probability of recovery action not taking place, can be calculated from the mtbi, or incidents/1000 hours and mean recovery time. For the equipment above, given a mtbi of 100 hours, the recovery factor of each unit is:

$$\text{recovery factor} = \frac{100}{100 + 0.1} \quad \text{or} \quad \left(\frac{10 \times 0.1}{1000} + 1\right)^{-1}$$
$$= 0.999$$

The recovery factors of all units in use can be assumed to form a series chain, e.g. for the two tape units, the overall recovery factor is $0.999 \times 0.999 = 0.998$. This overall recovery factor can then be multiplied by the system serviceability ratio to provide an overall system serviceability ratio, representing the probability of a system working and not carrying out recovery action. So, the real representation of the parallel chain of the three magnetic tape units is as indicated in Figure 12.2. Hence, the overall serviceability is $0.99954 \times 0.998 = 0.99754$, a significant reduction, especially when the unserviceability ratios are examined, which give a 5 to 1 variation:

Unserviceability parallel chain only   0.00046
Unserviceability with recovery factor 0.00246

Note that in calculating parallel chains, the unit serviceability should normally be derived from incident down time, excluding recovery time (as given in Figure 11.4 for the electronics and Table 11.3 for the peripherals). In series chains, the unit serviceabilities can include recovery times but it is often wise to consider them separately, as a major benefit from carrying out this type of prediction is to help in designing the optimum recovery techniques.

Complex Areas

Many systems can be expressed directly as series and parallel chains. However, there are some complications when items are cross connected in some way. For example, Figure 12.3a shows one difficult configuration;

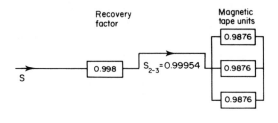

S = 0.99754

Figure 12.2   Serviceability of units in parallel

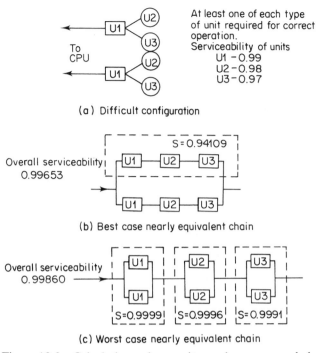

(a) Difficult configuration

(b) Best case nearly equivalent chain

(c) Worst case nearly equivalent chain

Figure 12.3   Calculations where units can be cross coupled

Figure 12.3b is one near equivalent but does not include the working configuration of both U1s with U2 from one half and U3 from the other; Figure 12.3c assumes full cross connection. The true figure for overall serviceability should be 0.99771, or about half way between the two serviceabilities produced. Parts of a total system, which cannot be expressed as series or parallel chains may be able to be shown as worst case equivalents, and if the parts prove not to be a critical area, an estimate of true serviceability can be made. If the area does prove to be critical, more detailed calculations can be made, to cover all possible working states.

TOTAL SYSTEM CALCULATIONS

When carrying out total system calculations, it is very easy to be too optimistic about the reliability and recovery features of the system, so it is useful to be able to see if the result is typical. Figure 12.4 shows the percentage unserviceability of a number of established mainframe and mini computer systems (showing minimum configuration system serviceability, excluding spoilt work time). Some are large populations but others are averages of one or two systems over a long period. The serviceability of smaller systems, which could be much better, is reduced by lack of standby

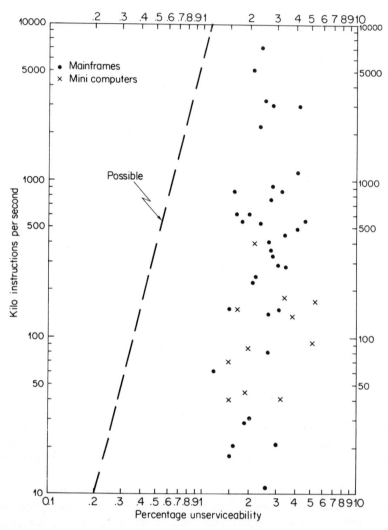

Figure 12.4   Unserviceability of general purpose computer systems
(single processor, minimum configuration, excluding spoilt work time)

peripheral equipment and, sometimes, by poor response times for on-call maintenance.

Medium Sized System

Considering the fairly simple medium sized configuration shown in Figure 12.5, the procedure for carrying out the calculations are as follows. All the figures used are derived from those given in Chapter 11 and are averages for the hardware and over years 4 and 5 after first release of the software. The environment is assumed to be good and the system covered by on-site

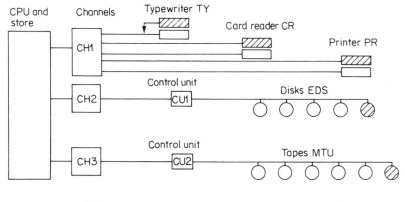

Figure 12.5   Fairly simple medium sized configuration

engineers. On this occasion, the serviceability ratios calculated exclude spoilt work time on individual programs, only system recovery time being considered.

Processor, Store, Channels and Peripheral Controllers

Characteristics—400 KIPS, core store 4 megabits 1 μsecond cycle time, good maintainability, medium utilization, medium quality, medium down time distribution. From Figure 11.4 this gives the following for the processor:

incidents/1000 hours $1 \times 2 = 2$
mean down time/incident   1.25 hours

The processor figure includes two channels and, assuming that the disk channel is complex and the tape channel simple, the CPU and channels give 1.2, 0.6 and 0.2 incidents per 1000 hours respectively. The extra channel and tape controller are also assumed to be simple and the disk controller fairly complex. From Figure 11.5 the store reliability is 0.49 × 4 × 2 = 3.92. The serviceability of each unit is:

	Incidents/ 1000 hours	mdti	Serviceability ratio
CPU	1.2	1.25	0.99850
Channel 1	0.2	1.25	0.99975
Channel 2	0.6	1.25	0.99925
Channel 3	0.2	1.25	0.99975
Disk controller	0.4	1.25	0.99950
Tape controller	0.2	1.25	0.99975
Store	3.92	1.25	0.99512

218

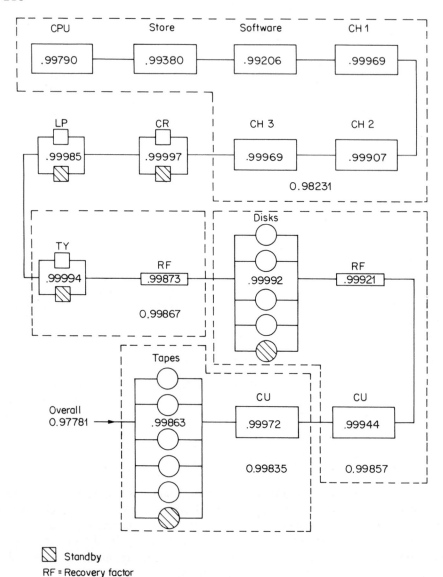

Standby

RF = Recovery factor

Figure 12.6   Equivalent chains for configuration in Figure 12.5

Software

Characteristics—full scale operating system, average quality and maintainability, and medium utilization. For the average of years 4 and 5 of the product, the reliability estimate from Table 11.6 is:

400 × 0.04 = 16 incidents per 1000 hours

Following these failures, the system will have to be reloaded, but sometimes the directory of files or queues may be lost, resulting in more down time. For example, for 100 incidents:

	No of incidents	Recovery time	Total recovery time
Normal stoppages	90	0.3 hrs	27 hrs
Directory of files etc lost	10	2.3 hrs	23 hrs
	100		50 hrs

Mean recovery time = 0.5 hours

Software reliability and serviceability:

16 inc/k hrs, 0.5 hrs mdti, serviceability = 0.99206

Recovery Factors for Processor and Store

Assuming that processor failures also result in the same proportion of loss of directories, the mean recovery time is also 0.5 hours. For all store failures, it is assumed that the processor stops, resulting in the normal recovery time of 0.3 hours but loss of files only occurs for 2% of the incidents, giving an overall mean recovery time of 0.34 hours. The recovery factors and overall unit serviceabilities then become:

	Incidents/ 1000 hrs	Mean recovery time	Recovery factor	Unit serviceability		Overall serviceability
CPU	1.2	0.5	0.99940	× 0.99850	=	0.99790
Store	3.92	0.34	0.99867	× 0.99512	=	0.99380
	5.12		0.99807	0.99363		0.99171

Recovery Factors for Channels

The channel failures are also assumed to give rise to a system stoppage with recovery time of 0.3 hours. Disk channel failures could give rise to corruptions of the directories, when they are being transferred backwards and forwards to disks, but this is ignored.

	Incidents/ 1000 hrs	Mean recovery time	Recovery factor	Unit serviceability		Overall serviceability
Channel 1	0.2	0.3	0.99994	× 0.99975	=	0.99969
Channel 2	0.6	0.3	0.99982	× 0.99925	=	0.99907
Channel 3	0.2	0.3	0.99994	× 0.99975	=	0.99969
	1.0		0.99970	0.99875		0.99845

Recovery Factors for Peripheral Controllers

For these, it is assumed that the software is sufficiently resilient to allow reconnection of the controllers after an incident but, as half of the incidents are subject to engineering investigations, which require dedicated use of the system and software reloading afterwards, the mean recovery time is 0.15 hours.

	Incidents/ 1000 hrs	Mean recovery time	Recovery factor	Unit serviceability		Overall serviceability
Disk controller	0.4	0.15	0.99994	× 0.99950	=	0.99944
Tape controller	0.2	0.15	0.99997	× 0.99975	=	0.99972
Total	0.6		0.99991			0.99916
System failures	0.3					

Overall Mainframe and Software

The overall incident rates, recovery factors and serviceabilities are:

	Incidents/ 1000 hrs	System failures/ 1000 hrs	Recovery factors	Overall serviceability
Software	16	16	0.99206	0.99206
CPU and store	5.12	5.12	0.99807	0.99171
Channels	1.0	1.0	0.99970	0.99845
Total	22.12	22.12	0.98985	0.98231

Peripheral Equipment

Characteristics—all medium speed, good maintainability; disks, tape units and printers medium utilization; card readers and typewriters low utilization; magnetic tape units and typewriters medium quality, others good quality. The reliability and down times from Table 11.3 (assuming worst case down time shown) and serviceabilities are:

Unit type	Incidents/ 1000 hours	Mean down time/ incident	Unit serviceability
Disks	1.2 × 1 × 1 = 1.2	2.33	0.99721
Tapes	2.1 × 1 × 2 = 4.2	2.33	0.99031
Printers	5.4 × 1 × 1 = 5.4	2.33	0.98757
Card readers	5.1 × 0.5 × 1 = 2.55	2.33	0.99409
Typewriters	3.9 × 0.5 × 2 = 3.9	2.0	0.99226

Considering the overall reliability and serviceability:

Unit type	Number provided	Number required	Overall incidents/ 1000 hours	Overall serviceability
Disks	5	4	4.8	0.99992
Tapes	6	5	21.0	0.99863
Printers	2	1	5.4	0.99985
Card readers	2	1	2.55	0.99997
Typewriters	2	1	3.9	0.99994
Total			37.65	0.99831

Recovery Factors for Peripherals

For this system, it is assumed that on-line test programs are available to test peripherals concurrently with user operations, otherwise for up to 1 in 3 incidents, between 1.0 and 3.0 hours investigation time (see Table 11.3) could be expected as a series factor, assuming the maintenance contract only covers operational hours. However, a number of these investigations could be deferred until the preventative maintenance period but because units would be out of service for a longer period, the mean down time per incident would increase. Also, with the on-line test programs, it is not necessary to overwrite the operating system for testing purposes, which would give the equivalent of a system failure.

1. Disks—in this case, as spoilt work is not being counted, the recovery factor depends very much on the application and on the way that the system software, queues and directories are split up between the disks. Assuming that the application uses many different independent files, which can be recovered individually without causing much delay in total system operation, then the recovery factor can be ignored. On system disks some spare capacity is usually available for other user files, so sometimes no effective recovery time will be incurred; but whenever errors occur on reading the software, the unit drops off-line or the pack has to be transferred to a different unit, system failure is likely to occur and, besides software reloading time, there will be other delays. If two system disks are assumed, with 60% of incidents giving rise to system failures, the recovery factor could be:

system failures/1000 hours	$2 \times 1.2 \times 0.6 = 1.44$
mean down time per incident	$0.3 + 0.25 = 0.55$
recovery factor	$= 0.99921$
overall serviceability	$0.99921 \times 0.99992 = 0.99913$

2. Typewriters—as this is the system controlling device, sometimes faults may cause a system failure and, on other occasions, the complete

system may have to be taken over for testing purposes. On other occasions, it should be possible to unplug the typewriters and connect the standby. Assuming system failures are incurred for 25% of the incidents and each time 1 hour investigation time applies, the total system failures and recovery factor is:

system failures/1000 hours	$0.25 \times 3.9 = 0.975$
mean down time per incident	$0.3 + 1.0 = 1.3$
recovery factor	$= 0.99873$
overall serviceability	$0.99873 \times 0.99994 = 0.99867$

3. Other peripherals—for this particular system and configuration, it is assumed that incidents on the printers, card readers and magnetic tape units do not lead to system failure, real delays in overall system operation or occasions when the software has to be overwritten for testing purposes, so no recovery factor has been calculated.

Overall Peripheral Subsystems and Complete System

The complete system series and parallel chains are represented in Figure 12.6 and the total system calculations in Table 12.1. Compared with Figure

Table 12.1 Calculations for a complete medium-sized computer system

Unit	Incidents/ 1000 hours	System failures/ 1000 hours	Recovery factor	Overall serviceability
Disk controller	0.4	0.2	0.99994	0.99944
Disks	4.8	1.44	0.99921	0.99913
Disk subsystem	5.2	1.64	0.99915	0.99857
Typewriter	3.9	0.975	0.99873	0.99867
Tape controller	0.2	0.1	0.99997	0.99972
Tapes	21.0	–	–	0.99863
Tape subsystem	21.2	0.1	0.99997	0.99835
Printers	5.4	–	–	0.99985
Card readers	2.55	–	–	0.99997
Total peripherals	38.25	2.715	0.99785	0.99542
Mainframe (including channels)	6.12	6.12	0.99777	0.99017
Software	16.0	16.0	0.99206	0.99206
Overall system	60.37	24.835	0.98772	0.97781

12.4, the overall unserviceability ratio of 2.2% is reasonable for a system of this size but could be somewhat worse by having on-call maintenance, not having a full set of standby peripherals or less effective on-line test programs. On the other hand improvement may be possible by providing main store with error correction to give 0.5% higher serviceability.

Serviceability and Reliability over Short Periods

Although the figures are calculated over two years, with improving reliability, an idea of the short term serviceability can be derived from Figures 8.5 and 8.6. Assuming that the system is used for 250 hours per month, the short time serviceability could be:

10% if months less than 94.5%
1% if months less than 90.1%

Similarly, an idea of the short term system failure rate can be obtained as indicated in Chapter 9.

	Incidents/ 1000 hours	Incidents per fault	Faults/ 1000 hours
Hardware	8.835	3	2.945
Software	16.0	10	1.6
	24.835		4.545

This gives an overall incidents per fault ratio of about 5.5 and with about 6.2 system failures or 1.1 faults expected per month, from Figures 9.2 and 9.3 the short term system failures become approximately:

	System failures/ month	System failures/ 1000 hours
10% of months worse than	15	60
1% of months worse than	30	120

Spoilt Work Time

For the above, spoilt work time could have been included in the calculations of the various recovery factors but, assuming that this only applies to system failures, a separate series spoilt work factor can be calculated:

System failures/1000 hours   24.835
Mean spoilt work time   0.25
Spoilt work factor   0.99383

This gives an overall serviceability, including spoilt work, of $0.99383 \times 0.97781 = 0.97178$.

Weighting Factor Serviceability Calculations

Chapter 8 showed a method of calculating serviceability ratios, using a weighting factor scheme, where the ratio is intended to reflect the loss in throughput due to faults. For example, the five disk units, shown in Figure 12.5, would all be used, and throughput would drop with one unit out of service, but could continue with limited working capabilities with 2 or more units faulty. The following weighting factors might apply.

No of units out of service	Weighting factor	
1	0.2	the down time is multiplied
2	0.5	by this factor when the given
3	0.8	number of units are out of service.
4	1.0	
5	1.0	

Estimations of weighted serviceability can be made using an extension of the binomial distribution, as shown in Table 12.2. The minimum configuration serviceability predictions, shown earlier in this chapter, are equivalent to having weighting factors of 0 and 1, so, for comparison purposes, these calculations are also shown in Table 12.2, for the five disk units. The table shows that there can be a considerable reduction in serviceability of subsystems with standby units, when the weighting factor scheme is applied.

The program for calculating serviceability, given in Appendix 2, also has provision for the inclusion of weighting factors.

Table 12.2   Prediction of serviceability using weighting factors (unit serviceability = 0.99721)

No of units working	No of units not working	Probability	Minimum configuration Weighting factor	Minimum configuration Unserviceability	Weighted calculations Weighting factor	Weighted calculations Unserviceability
5	0	0.9861276	–	–	–	–
4	1	0.0137950	0	0	0.2	0.0027590
3	2	0.0000772	1	0.0000772	0.5	0.0000386
2	3	0.0000002	1	0.0000002	0.8	0.0000002
1	4	–	1	–	1	–
0	5	–	1	–	1	–
Total				0.0000774		0.0027978
Overall serviceability				0.9999226		0.9972022

Note that the program given in Appendix 2 accumulates serviceability rather than unserviceability as used in the above table.

Scheduled Maintenance

On a system requiring continuous operation, scheduled or supplementary maintenance may have to be taken into account. In this case the availability ratios could be used instead of the serviceability ratios; however, as this type of maintenance can often be curtailed or deferred, it is better left to engineering judgement as the calculations are being made. On new types of system, as indicated in Chapters 3, 5 and 7, supplementary maintenance time, for the incorporation of hardware modifications or software changes, can be excessive and cannot be ignored.

MULTI PROCESSOR SYSTEMS

When standby processors are provided, it is often suggested that high serviceability ratios will be obtained but, because of the recovery factors, this may not be the case. Considering the worst case, where one computer is carrying out the live work, a second one running development work, using a variation of the operating system, and peripherals switchable to either system, the overall serviceability could be calculated as shown in Figure 12.7 (using the same systems considered earlier). The peripheral switch calculation assumes 5 active switches each giving 0.1 incidents per 1000 hours, 1 hour mean down time and a serviceability ratio of 0.9999.

This time, the overall unserviceability is 1.52%, compared with 2.22% for the single processor system, that is not too much of an improvement for the extra expense of a second mainframe. The limiting factors are, of course, the software reliability and other recovery actions.

There are many forms of multiprocessor which could give somewhat better serviceability than the foregoing. For example, twin processors may be provided, working in a master slave relationship, where each runs its

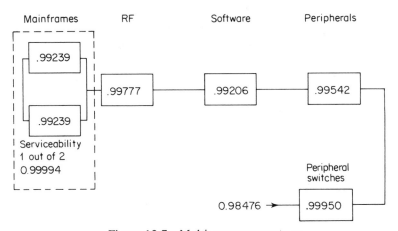

Figure 12.7   Multi-processor systems

own operating system, but the master is responsible for scheduling jobs for the slave. In this case the slave may have system failures without affecting the master, but in the event of the master failing, both systems may be effectively out of service, until the recovery action is complete. If the slave is running the same operating system as the master, recovery can be much faster than in the above example. In other systems, the two processors may have equal status and one version of the operating system may run on either processor, as is required. In this case, it may be possible to arrange that hardware failures on one processor do not give rise to a complete system stoppage. It is also possible to arrange that certain types of software failure do not bring the whole system to a halt, but there are likely to be many others which have the same disastrous effects as described earlier. Other limiting factors are the main and backing stores which contain the software, where incidents are likely to lead to system failures, thus making it difficult for the theoretical 99.9% plus system serviceabilities from being obtained.

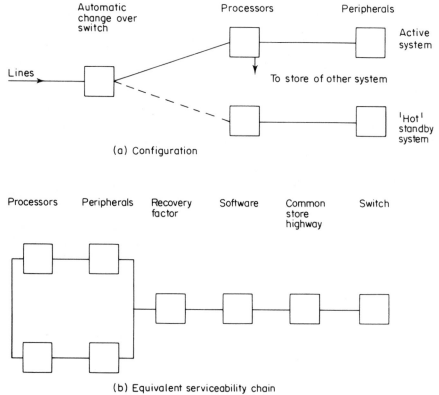

(a) Configuration

(b) Equivalent serviceability chain

Figure 12.8   Message switching system

Message Switching Systems

One of the most reliable forms of computer system is the type used for military message switching applications, which may have typical arrangements shown in Figure 12.8a.

In this case, both processors receive messages, store them on both magnetic tape and disk, process them, generate output route queues, but only one transmits the messages to the required destinations. The equivalent serviceability chain is shown in Figure 12.8b.

This system has very good file security, with little chance of files being lost but, in the event of a system failure, incoming messages may be lost. To overcome this problem, the usual recovery action is for all terminals to retransmit their last message. As each processor is operating in an almost identical manner, software errors are likely to cause a stoppage on both processors but recovery time should be quite fast. The switching arrangements and common store highway are other critical areas but these should normally be very reliable.

Multi–mini System

There are many applications where a user is considering the provision of a multi-mini system, instead of a mainframe, so it is useful to consider reliability in relation to the mainframe.

Figure 12.9a shows a multi–mini configuration, which could be considered for the same application as the system shown in Figure 12.5, and Figure 12.9b shows the approximate serviceability chains. This time, three mini processors of 300 KIPS and 2 megabits of store are used, where 2 out of 3 are required to carry out the work. The disk controller is a 200 KIPS mini with $\frac{1}{2}$ megabit of store. It is assumed that the systems are again delivered three years after introduction of the products and the calculations are based on a 2-year period, using average hardware figures. Each processor has its own system disk and runs using its own copy of the software. It is also assumed that new software has to be written to control the multiprocessor system, to suit the particular application and the reliability figures are for years 2 and 3 of this software, but this has a bad frequency of change factor over the period. The hardware has factors for good environment, good maintainability, medium quality, medium to low utilization, medium to low speed, on-site maintenance, electronics medium down time distribution and peripherals the higher down time figures.

The calculations for frequency of incidents, system failures and serviceabilities are shown in Table 12.3. Compared with the mainframe system, the total number of incidents on the minis is higher, due to the lower quality peripherals, but system failures are less, because of the simpler electronics and software of smaller size. Overall unserviceability of the mini system is 1.04% against 2.22% for the single processor mainframe

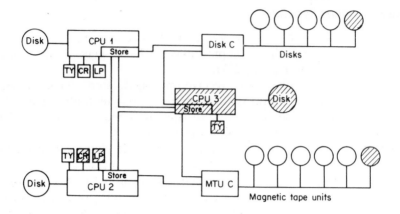

(a) Configuration

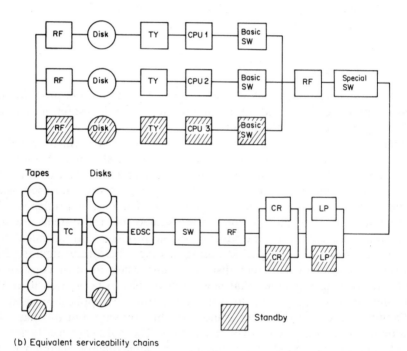

(b) Equivalent serviceability chains

Figure 12.9   Multi-mini system

system and 1.52% for the dual processor system, this again being influenced by the simpler hardware and software but mainly because it is assumed that the mini recovery time is shorter, which is not necessarily the case.

The overall serviceability for the mini system can be further degraded considerably by the lack of on-line engineering test programs for the peripherals, which is often the case. Because special software has to be written for a one off configuration, there could be considerable delays in implementation and it may be necessary to frequently take over the whole configuration for testing purposes and for fault finding. The overall engineering investigation rate for the system comes out at about 24 investigations per 1000 hours, or 1.44 per week of 60 hours. With an average of about 3 hours per investigation, even when preventative maintenance time is added, reliability of the system could not really justify on-site engineers: on-call maintenance could further degrade the serviceability. If 2, instead of 3, processors were provided, the overall serviceability would be approximately 96.2% or unserviceability 3.8%; that is much worse than the mainframe, this being due to each of the mini systems being dependent on their own typewriter and system disk, but the serviceability could be improved by about 1.8% by the provision of standby peripherals.

COMMUNICATIONS SUBSYSTEMS

Communications subsystems can also be considered as serviceability chains, for evaluation of reliability from a remote user's point of view. At the same time, it is useful to consider user impressions and user satisfaction, human factors which may be more important than actual reliability; for example, because of the feeling of remoteness, a user may not tolerate a failure rate, which would normally be considered to be quite good; alternatively, he may tolerate a high failure rate if he is constantly informed of the status of the system, under failure conditions. In considering a total system, designed to give the highest satisfaction to users and the least headaches for the computer manager, it is useful to consider reliability in terms such as 'potential complaints per 1000 hours': for example, with 400 terminals connected to a system which suffers from 50 system failures per 1000 hours, there are 20,000 potential complaints per 1000 hours.

Line Reliability

There are two factors to be taken into account when considering line reliability; the first is random errors, which are likely to be present when the line is considered to be working and the second, breakdowns of the line, necessitating unscheduled maintenance.

Random Errors

The performance of a line under normal working conditions with the presence of random errors is dependent on type and length of line, speed, block lengths, error correction and detection facilities, line error rate and error distribution, line delay time etc. The first effect of random errors is

Table 12.3 Calculations for multi-mini system (see Figures 11.4, 11.5 and Tables 11.3 and 11.6)

Unit	Basic	Derating factors	Incidents per 1000 hours		Mean down time	Serviceability
			Overall	System failures		
CPU	0.28	× 2	0.56	0.56	1.25	0.99930
Store	0.49 × 2	× 2	1.96	1.96	1.25	0.99756
Disk	1.2	× 2 × 0.7	1.68	1.68	2.33	0.99610
Typewriter	3.9	× 0.5 × 2 × 0.7	2.73	0.68	2.0	0.99457
1 System HW			6.93	4.88		0.98758
Recovery				4.88	0.3	0.99854
Basic SW	25	× 0.04	1.0	1.0	0.3	0.99970
1 System			7.93	5.88		0.98584
2 out of 3			23.79	11.76		0.99940
Recovery				11.76	0.3	0.99648
Special SW	25	× 0.15 × 2	7.5	7.5	0.3	0.99776
Printer	5.4	× 2	10.8		2.33	0.97545
1 out of 2			10.8			0.99940

1 out of 2			**5.1**			**0.99986**
Disk cont.	0.22	× 2	0.44		1.25	0.99945
Store	0.49 × ½	× 2	0.49		1.25	0.99939
Recovery	6		0.93	0.46	0.2	0.99981
Software		× 0.04	0.24		0.2	0.99995
Overall DC			**1.17**	**0.46**		**0.99860**
Disks	1.2	× 2	2.4		2.33	0.99444
4 out of 5			**9.6**			**0.99969**
Tape cont.	0.085	× 2	0.17		1.25	0.99979
Recovery				**0.085**	0.2	0.99998
Overall TC						**0.99977**
Mag. tapes	2.1	× 2	4.2		2.33	0.99031
5 out of 6			**21.0**			**0.99863**
Overall system			**79.13**	**19.805**		**0.98963**

Add for overall system incident rates, multiply for overall system serviceability

232

to reduce the throughput on the line due to retransmissions of faulty blocks and the second to give unexpected stoppages or undetected errors, necessitating in operator intervention and retransmission of data for a complete job.

An example of line errors for a 2400 baud line could be:

Bit error rate	1 in 10^5
5000 bit block error rate	2%
Blocks transferred in 1000 hours	10^6
Blocks in error (mainly retransmitted successfully)	2×10^4
Incidents causing terminal stoppage or undetected error	20/1000 hours

Although the block retransmissions degrade the throughput to 98% of the nominal rate at the given block length, the user may not complain (he may not even notice them) as no operator intervention is required.

Line Breakdowns

From information available in the UK, it appears that, typically, lines break down at an average rate of at least twice per year and are out of service from 2 hours to 2 days. Also, when the breakdown is imminent, the line may suffer from intermittent failures, giving rise to excessive retransmissions or periodic disconnections. For the latter type of problem, requiring operator intervention, at least 2 incidents per breakdown could be expected.

Overall Line Reliability

In the UK, if more accurate information is not available from the Post Office, in order to help in reliability sizing, one could use figures similar to those given in the following examples, e.g. 0.998 serviceability ratio and 10 incidents/1000 hour for a local line.

Switched Network Telephone Lines

Typical bit error rates quoted for switched network telephone lines are 1 in 10^3 to 10^4. Most plant failures seem to delay connection in the first place but some cause the line to be disconnected when in use; these problems are usually overcome by redialling. The overall serviceability of the local line is probably as good as the 0.998 figure indicated above, but the incident rate is likely to be greater, especially if efficient error detection/correction facilities are not provided.

Modems

Manufacturers typically claim mtbfs of around 15,000 hours for modems, or about one fault per 2 years of continuous use. Experience indicates about 1 fault per 2 years, but with less frequent use. The modem faults may be intermittent, giving periodic interruptions to service; hence, the incident rate may average about 1 per 1000 hours and serviceability 0.999 or 0.997 including waiting time for maintenance.

Terminals

The following sections give examples of calculations of serviceability and incident rates for various types of terminals. The central site equipment is assumed to have a serviceability ratio of 0.978 and system failure rate of 25 per 1000 hours, including a line multiplexor, whereby transmissions are disconnected for each incident and the complete job usually needs to be resubmitted from the terminals.

Remote Batch Terminal

Remote batch terminals often have low cost peripherals and are covered by on-call maintenance. When connected they tend to have continuous stop/start utilization. Therefore serviceability of the peripherals can be expected to be fairly low. The calculations, given in Figure 12.10, are based on the reliability information given in Chapter 11 and assume medium environment, good maintainability, medium utilization (typewriter very low), low speed and medium quality. For the terminal recovery factor it is assumed that the mean recovery time, to sort out the cards and resubmit the failing jobs, where required, is 0.2 hours.

The overall serviceability and reliability is:

	Serviceability	Incidents/1000 hours
Terminal	0.89891	32.3
Line and modems	0.99000	22.0
Central site	0.97800	25.0
Overall	0.87034	79.3 @ 0.2 hours
Recovery factor	0.98439	
Overall including RF	0.85675	

This overall serviceability and reliability may not be considered to be satisfactory by the terminal user, especially when the short term figures are taken into account. A large proportion of user complaints about excessive incidents would probably be about the items outside his direct control, that is the line and central site equipment, although the terminal gives the highest unserviceability.

Assuming the remote batch terminal user accepts occasional slow turnaround of jobs, once entered in the system, his main requirement

234

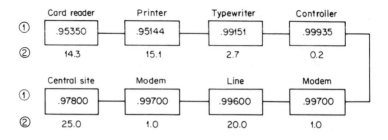

① Serviceability ② Incidents per 1000 hours

Figure 12.10 Remote batch terminal

could be to load jobs in the reader and expect correct results to be printed sometime later. This could be achieved by the configuration shown in Figure 12.11, where at the terminal, a copy of the job as sent to line is kept on the disk, until the user is satisfied that correct output has been received. The disk on the front end processor provides a buffer, such that for any central processor failures, transmissions are not interrupted. The two disks provide facilities for automatic recovery following any line failure.

With the revised configuration, the user may be satisfied, because of the reduced requirement for operator initiated recovery action, but overall serviceability may not be much better. However, major improvements in serviceability could be obtained by provision of standby peripherals at the terminal or by installing the terminal in a fully air conditioned room.

Transaction/Enquiry Terminal

Figure 12.12 shows the equivalent chain of a network which could be provided for transaction/enquiry applications. The terminals are polled from the central site and it is assumed that any transient incidents on the lines do not cause polling to cease.

As the terminal is not using the line for the whole period of a transaction, all transient incidents on the line will not affect the work flow

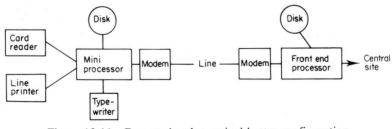

Figure 12.11 Remote batch terminal better configuration

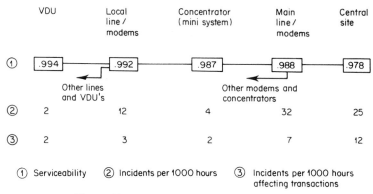

Figure 12.12   Transaction/enquiry terminal

in a given time. For example, assuming an enquiry of 100 characters and response of 500 characters, one transaction may take 5 minutes, most of the time being spent in keying in the data, correcting any errors and examining the response; the transmission time may be 5 seconds and response time of the processor 1–2 seconds. Hence, the number of incidents affecting transactions will depend on the duration of the fault conditions. Also, assuming that the standard recovery procedure is to transmit the enquiry stored at the VDU, except for VDU incidents, the recovery time will be a few seconds and recovery factor almost 1.0.

From Figure 12.12, the overall serviceability comes out at 94.0% and incident rate at 75 incidents per 1000 hours but, because of the relatively low utilization of the lines and central site, compared with the VDU, the overall incident rate indicated is 26 incidents per 1000 hours. On a total elapsed time basis, if the VDU utilization is low, the serviceability and incident rates will appear to be somewhat better.

Note that certain faults on the spur lines from the main line may cause the whole main line to be unusable. Hence, for a large number of spurs the main line serviceability may be less than indicated.

For this type of application, reliability improvements depend on the dispersion of terminals; e.g. if several are in the same building, spare VDUs may not be required; for others, a spare may be available, which can be delivered in a short time; duplicate or looped main lines may be provided or, for any lines, connection at various points to switched network alternatives may be made available. To ensure user satisfaction, front end processors are useful, with facilities to advise terminal users of reasons for delays at the central site.

Time Sharing Terminal

Figure 12.13 shows the equivalent chain of a terminal used in a time sharing application. Overall reliability will depend very much on the type

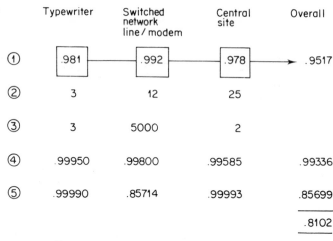

	Typewriter	Switched network line / modem	Central site	Overall
①	.981	.992	.978	.9517
②	3	12	25	
③	3	5000	2	
④	.99950	.99800	.99585	.99336
⑤	.99990	.85714	.99993	.85699
				.8102

① Serviceability
② Incidents per 1000 hours (disconnections)
③ Incidents per 1000 hours (corruptions)
④ Recovery factor (disconnections)
⑤ Recovery factor (corruptions)

Figure 12.13 Time sharing terminal

of work carried out. For example, the average job could consist of:

Job step	Time on line	Characters transmitted
Input	15 mins	1000
Edit	5 mins	100
Execute	5 mins	
Output (various steps)	5 mins	2500
	30 mins	3600

Assuming the program is saved on file at the central site after input and editing, the mean time spent by the operator in recovery after an unexpected disconnection could be about 10 minutes, including re-logging on etc.

With this type of terminal, error facilities comprise echoback on input, and check for illegal characters and commands, so a number of corrections are normally required for data corruptions; some will be corrected on input by retyping a line, others by editing and for those occurring on output, sometimes the job may be rerun and reprinted. Hence, recovery time for random corruptions could be 2 minutes.

An incident rate of 5 per hour is typical of personal experience in running jobs similar to the example given, on a time sharing system using the public switched network.

The overall serviceability, from Figure 12.13, is 81%, which is very bad and influenced mainly by the frequency of data corruptions.

The serviceability of the time sharing terminal can be made acceptable, by having spare typewriters available, but the major improvements required are associated with recoveries; again, a front end processor could buffer the user from central site failures, but other facilities required are improved error detection/correction, easy editing and automatic saving of jobs at all stages, to overcome disconnections.

Appendix 1

Exerciser Test Programs Written in FORTRAN

As described in Chapter 10, during acceptance trials, it is useful to exercise the processor and all peripherals under operating system control. To facilitate this, programs can be written in high level languages such as FORTRAN, COBOL, ALGOL and BASIC. This appendix gives brief descriptions, listings and typical outputs for a set of programs written in FORTRAN, which can be used to ensure a high and wide variety of utilization. The programs are in the following series:

FOPR	Processor tests	
FODK	Disk tests	} most of these can be used for testing
FOMT	Magnetic tape unit tests	either tapes or disks
FOLP	Line printer test	
FOCP	Card punch test	
FOCR	Card reader test	
FOTP	Paper tape punch test	
FOTR	Paper tape reader test	

It is useful to run the programs using each of the available compilers as they may give different instruction sequences, but for maximum utilization, the FOPR series should be run with non-optimizing compilers and the peripheral tests with maximum optimization, to reduce CPU time, which can be excessive with full checking.

Each program has variable parameters, which can be used to vary the time taken. The processor tests can be adjusted to take any time required, on even the largest processor, and generally give a wider variety of numbers as the parameters are made larger. The disk and tape tests can usually be arranged to write and read files of any size required. The slow peripheral tests carry out a more fixed amount of work, but this can be repeated to extend the time.

238

The program descriptions indicate a timing formula and give an example of running time for specific processor and peripheral speeds.

FOPR00 PROCESSOR TEST

To Test

Processors using a wide range of different floating point numbers.

Source

R. Longbottom, CCA.

Description

The Gamma Function $\Gamma(l) = \int_0^\infty e.^{-x}x.^{l-1}dx$

or $\int_0^\infty y.dx$

where l is a positive integer $\Gamma(l) = (l - 1)!$

The program calculates the functions twice and prints the results for 10 functions for $l = 1, 2, 3 \ldots 10$ by:

1. $(l - 1)!$
2. Integration using Simpson's formula.

Simpson's formula calculates the area of a strip of the curve by:

$$area = \frac{h}{3}(y_1 + 4y_2 + y_3)$$

where h is the width of the strip
and y_1 is calculated using x_1

y_2 is calculated using $x_1 + h$

y_3 is calculated using $x_1 + 2h$

The program also calculates a sumcheck based on the difference in value between adjacent strips.

Variables

MM – the integration is carried out from $X = 0$ to $X = 2$ MM

MS – h is set to $\dfrac{1}{MS}$

Note that different results are produced with different parameters.

Timing

Approximately proportional to MM × MS

Typical parameters for 15 minutes CPU time on a processor of speed 1000 KIPS:

$$MM = 50, MS = 4000$$

Modifications to run on Different Systems

To prevent underflow on some systems, the following adjustments may be necessary:

when MM = 50	minimum number used in multiplication is 0.37×10^{-43}
when MM = 40	minimum number used in multiplication is 1.8×10^{-35}
when MS = 1000	minimum number used in multiplication is 1.0×10^{-30}
when MS = 10000	minimum number used in multiplication is 1.0×10^{-40}
when MS = 100000	minimum number used in multiplication is 1.0×10^{-50}

However, even with underflow, the result produced is acceptable, except for underflow indications.

Program Listing FOPR00

```
C*********PARAMETERS*********
      MM=50
      MS=600
C*********PARAMETERS*********
      GF=1.0
      WRITE(6,50)
   50 FORMAT(5H     G,10X,14HGAMMA FUNCTION)
      AC=0.0
      AY=0.0
      YC=0.0
      DO 600 I=1,10
      IG=I+1
      GS=I
      A=0.0
      Y=0.0
      X=0.0
      GF=GF*GS
      WRITE(6,100)IG,GF
      AN=1.0/FLOAT(MS)
      DO 500 J=1,MM
      DO 500 K=1,MS
      XA=X+AN
```

```
      XB=XA+AN
      YA=EXP(-XA)*XA**GS
      YB=EXP(-XB)*XB**GS
      AY=(AN/3.0)*(Y+4.0*YA+YB)
      A=A+AY
      YC=YC+YA-YB
      X=XB
 500  Y=YB
      WRITE(6,100)IG,A
 100  FORMAT(I4,F35.24)
 600  CONTINUE
      WRITE(6,200)AC,YC
 200  FORMAT(8H SUMS = ,2E30.24)
      STOP
      END
```

Typical Correct Results

```
   G            GAMMA FUNCTION
   2      1.000000000000000000000000
   2      1.000000000000000000000000
   3      2.000000000000000000000000
   3      1.998812675476074000000000
   4      6.000000000000000000000000
   4      5.999705314636231000000000
   5      24.00000000000000000000000
   5      23.97731018066406000000000
   6      120.0000000000000000000000
   6      119.9982147216797000000000
   7      720.0000000000000000000000
   7      719.5979003906250000000000
   8      5040.000000000000000000000
   8      5033.710937500000000000000
   9      40320.00000000000000000000
   9      40322.09375000000000000000
  10      362880.0000000000000000000
  10      362822.3750000000000000000
  11      3628800.000000000000000000
  11      3627311.000000000000000000
SUMS =  0.0                0.109977798461914000000000E 03
```

FOPR01 PROCESSOR AND STORE TEST

To Test

Main stores—uses fixed point arithmetic only.

Source

R. Longbottom, CCA.

Description

The program is designed to produce specific patterns using 2's complement arithmetic but can easily be modified to produce the same patterns where 1's complement arithmetic is used. The program uses a 2 dimensional array

242

of any size and takes the computer word length into account. The program comprises three sections.

1. All 1s are written to each location of the whole array.
2. All 0s are written to each location, except one bit is set to 1 in each word of the array. (A different bit in adjacent locations.)
3. The pattern is read and checked. In the event of a miscompare, a print out is given, e.g. I21 J5 WAS 8191 EXPECTED 8192.

1–3 are then repeated until each bit of each word has been checked. Even passes of the program first write all 0s then all 1s except for one 0 bit.

With the listing shown, accesses to store are sequential, within limits of the array dimension. If the 3 loops, DO 1XO J and DO 1XO I are reversed the accesses are not sequential. For example, with the array dimension IA (256,256), the reversed loops access every 256th word: for virtual memory systems, this can be utilized to exercise the paging system, (assuming other programs are running to fill the physical memory) as the next (or next but 1, etc) page is likely to have been swopped out onto drum or disk.

Variables

Array size DIMENSIONS IA (A,A) governs size of store used.

IB determines the amount of store accessed and must be equal to A in dimension (or less).

IC = number of bits in word minus 1 (or less)

NB = number of times the program is repeated should normally be at least 2.

NA = number of times first and third sections repeated.

Timing

Approximately proportional to $NB \times IC \times IB^2 \times (1.25 \, NA + 1)$

Typical parameters for 15 minutes CPU time on a processor of speed 1000 **KIPS**:

IB = 256, Array (256,256), NB = 2

IC = 31, NA = 2

Note, where the I and J loops are reversed and cause swopping out to disk, parameters will have to be reduced so that the program finishes in a reasonable time.

Modifications to run on Different Systems

Vary parameter IC according to word size.

The program can use excessive CPU time, minimising time available for store accesses. The CPU time is dependent on the statement MM = 2∗∗M + 1. So where the function is available, the following alternative version can be run.

In DO 110 loop:

Replace MM = 2∗∗M + 1
            MM = MM∗ID
            IA (I,J) = MM + KK
By   MM = SHIFT (ID,M)
            IA (I,J) = MM

with similar changes in DO 120 loop.

Also replace 140 ID = − 1
by   140 ID = − 2

On certain systems, the above version has to be used, anyway, where exponentiation cannot embrace the whole word length.

This program can be optimized with a suitable compiler—in one case the 2∗∗M calculation is carried out by shifting. Optimization tends to increase the rate of accessing store, which is beneficial for this program.

There may be a limitation on the amount of store allowed in one program but, to fill the store, more than one version can be run concurrently.

Program Listing FOPR01

```
C********PARAMETERS********
       DIMENSION IA(64,64)
       IB=64
       IC=31
       NA=2
       NB=2
C********PARAMETERS********
       ID=1
       DO 200 K=1,NB
       KK=K/2*2-K
       WRITE(6,99)KK
    99 FORMAT(I6)
       IE=IC-1
       DO 120 N=1,IC
       M=N-1
       WRITE(6,99)M
       DO 100 JJ=1,NA
       DO 100 J=1,IB
       DO 100 I=1,IB
       IA(I,J)=KK
   100 CONTINUE
       DO 110 J=1,IB
       DO 110 I=1,IB
```

```
      MM=2**M+1
      MM=MM*ID
      IA(I,J)=MM+KK
      M=M+1
      IF(M—IE)110,110,105
105   M=0
110   CONTINUE
      DO 120 JJ=1,NA
      M=N—1
      DO 120 J=1,IB
      DO 120 I=1,IB
      MM=2**M+1
      MM=MM*ID+KK
      IF(IA(I,J)—MM)128,130,128
128   WRITE(6,129)I,J,IA(I,J),MM
129   FORMAT(2H I,I4,2H J,I4,2X,3HWAS,I10,2X,8HEXPECTED,I10)
130   M=M+1
      IF(M—IE)120,120,125
125   M=0
120   CONTINUE
      IF(ID)145,145,140
140   ID=—1
      GO TO 200
145   ID=1
200   CONTINUE
      STOP
      END
```

Typical Correct Results FOPR01
(for parameters shown on listing)

```
 −1
  0
  1
  2
  3
  4
  5
  6
  7
  8
  9
 10
 11
 12
 13
 14
 15
 16
 17
 18
 19
 20
 21
 22
 23
 24
 25
 26
 27
 28
 29
 30
```

```
0
0
1
2
3
4
5
6
7
8
9
10
11
12
13
14
15
16
17
18
etc. to
30
```

FOPR02 PROCESSOR TEST

To Test

Processors using a wide variety of different floating point numbers.

Source

R. Longbottom, CCA.

Description

The program calculates the binomial expansion $(Q + P)^N = 1$, where N is varied from 1 to IE and IE is set according to a processor's numerical capability, for each value of Q from $Q = 0.1$ to 0.9 in variable steps. Successive sums of the expansions are multiplied together and the final result should be approximately 1 (also gives an indication of potential accuracy—see typical results). Also, the last sums of the expansion for each value of IE are added, and the result should be approximately equal to IE. Note that if a bit is dropped in one calculation, this is likely to be carried forward to the final result.

Variables

IA—number of times whole program is repeated.

$\left.\begin{array}{l} \text{IB} \\ \\ \text{ID} \end{array}\right\}$ Number of values of Q is approximately $\dfrac{8\text{IB}}{\text{ID}}$

IE—maximum value of N

Note that result will be different if variables are changed.

Timing

Approximately proportional to $\dfrac{IA.IB}{ID} \left(\dfrac{IE}{77}\right)^2$

Typical parameters for 15 minutes CPU time on a processor of speed 1000 KIPS

$IA = 6$, $IB = 120$, $ID = 1$, $IE = 77$

Modifications to run on Different Systems

The maximum and minimum numbers generated are in the range 10^{22} and 10^{-IE}

So the variable IE should be adjusted for the particular system, e.g. IE = 77 for 32 bit word systems, IE=37 for 36 and 16 bit systems.

If IE is too large, a result of 0 is produced.

Program Listing FOPR02

```
      DIMENSION COMB(501)
      WRITE(6,250)
  250 FORMAT(8H1TSURL02)
C*********PARAMETERS*********
      IA=1
      IB=120
      ID=4
      IE=77
C*********PARAMETERS*********
      IC=9*IB
      AA=10*IB
      DO 600 M=1,IA
      BC=0.0
      BB=1.0
      DO 500 N=1,IE
      DO 400 K=IB,IC,ID
      AK=K
      L=N+1
      MM=L/2
      COMB(1)=1.0
      COMB(L)=1.0
      DO 120 I=2,MM
      AI=I−1
      L=L−1
      AN=L
      COMB(I)=AN/AI*COMB(I−1)
  120 COMB(L)=COMB(I)
      IF(N+1−MM*2)150,151,150
  150 COMB(L−1)=(AN−1.0)/(AI+1.0)*COMB(L)
  151 L=N+1
```

```
      Q=AK/AA
      P=1.0−Q
      BI=Q**N
      BII=BI
      DO 160 I=2,L
      BI=BI*COMB(I)/COMB(I−1)*P/Q
160   BII=BII+BI
400   BB=BB*BII
500   BC=BC+BII
      WRITE(6,200)M,BB,BC
200   FORMAT(I6,2F30.24)
600   CONTINUE
      STOP
      END
```

Typical Correct Results (parameters as shown in listing)

IBM 360
1   0.67963826656341550000000   76.99905395507812000000000

ICL 1900
1   0.99999825009581400081513   76.999999985090994414349552

FOPR03 PROCESSOR TEST

To Test

Processors—especially those which make assumptions on the result of a branch instruction.

Source

RHEL Rutherford benchmark—modified by CCA to indicate if wrong branch is taken.

Description

The program consists of all branching instructions, which, in effect, are translated as load and branch instructions. The second half of the program generally produces a sequence of different branching instructions to the first half.

Variables

N – the number of times the program is repeated is N^2.

Timing

Approximately proportional to N^2.

Typical parameters for 15 minutes CPU time on a processor of speed 1000 KIPS – $N = 4000$

Modifications to run on Different Systems

None

Program Listing FOPR03

```
C•••••••••PARAMETERS•••••••••
       N=4000
C•••••••••PARAMETERS•••••••••
       WRITE(6,1)N
     1 FORMAT(I10)
       I=−1
       J=0
       K=1
       DO 300 L=1,N
       DO 300 M=1,N
       GO TO 200
   100 IF(I)101,999,999
   101 IF(J)999,102,999
   102 IF(K)999,999,103
   103 IF(I)104,999,999
   104 IF(J)999,105,999
   105 IF(K)999,999,106
   106 IF(I)107,999,999
   107 IF(J)999,108,999
   108 IF(K)999,999,109
   109 IF(I)110,999,999
   110 IF(J)999,111,999
   111 IF(K)999,999,112
   112 CONTINUE
       GO TO 300
   200 IF(I)201,999,999
   202 IF(K)999,999,203
   201 IF(J)999,202,999
   203 IF(I)204,999,999
   205 IF(K)999,999,206
   204 IF(J)999,205,999
   206 IF(I)207,999,999
   208 IF(K)999,999,209
   207 IF(J)999,208,999
   209 IF(I)210,999,999
   211 IF(K)999,999,212
   210 IF(J)999,211,999
   212 CONTINUE
       GO TO 100
   999 WRITE(6,2)L,M
     2 FORMAT(8H RUBBISH,2I10)
       WRITE(6,3)I,J,K
   300 CONTINUE
       WRITE(6,3)I,J,K
     3 FORMAT(3I10)
       STOP
       END
```

Typical Correct Results

```
4000
  −1    0    1
```

FOPR04 PROCESSOR TEST

To Test

Processors using double precision working and to check that the various FORTRAN functions are provided.

Source

R. Longbottom, CCA.

Description

The program produces 1 from various formulae in 8 different routines for many values of the variables, multiplying subsequent results together to produce a printed answer, which should also be approximately 1. If a bit is dropped in one calculation this is likely to be carried forward to the final answer. For checking purposes, a sumcheck subroutine has been incorporated to check the complete double word by shifting and adding, the sumcheck total being printed along with the other answer. The various routines and formulae used are:

ROUTINE 1

Using $\qquad$ $\sin^2 A + \cos^2 A = 1$

for $\qquad$ $A = 0 \text{ to } \dfrac{\pi}{2}$

Functions used   DSIN, DCOS FLOAT, **

ROUTINE 2

Using $\dfrac{e^A - e^{-A}}{e^A + e^{-A}} (= \tanh A)$ divided by $\tanh A$

for $\qquad$ $A = 0.0033 \text{ to } 166.67$

Number range $2.4 \times 10^{72} \text{ to } 4.1 \times 10^{-73}$

Functions used DEXP, SNGL, FLOAT, TANH

ROUTINE 3

Using $\dfrac{\log (e^A)}{A} = 1$

A and number range as routine 2

Functions used DEXP, DLOG, FLOAT

ROUTINE 4

Using $\dfrac{\sqrt{10^{2.\log_{10}A}}}{A} = 1$

for $A = 1$ to 50,0001 × variable IC
Functions used FLOAT, DLOG10,∗∗, DSQRT

ROUTINE 5

Using $CA = e^{C + jC} = \cos C + j \sin C$

then $= (\cos C + j \sin C)(\cos C - j \sin C)(\cos^2 C - \sin^2 c + j2 \sin C \cos C)$

$\quad = (\cos^2 C + \sin^2 C) \times (\cos C + j \sin C)^2$

$\quad = 1 \times (\cos C + j \sin C)^2$

then square root $= \cos C + j \sin C$

then $\log_e (\cos C + j \sin C) = C + jC$

then $(|C| + |C|) \div 2C = 1$

for $C = 0.6 \times 10^{-5}$ to $> \dfrac{\pi}{2}$

Functions used FLOAT, SNGL, CEXP, CMPLX, CSQRT, CONJG, COS, SIN, CLOG, DABS, DBLE, REAL, ABS, AIMAG, ∗∗.

ROUTINE 6

Using $CA = a + jb$

and $\dfrac{CABS(CA)}{\sqrt{a^2 + b^2}} = 1$

for $a = 1$ to 50,001

and $b = 50,000$ to 0

Functions used CMPLX, FLOAT, CABS, SQRT, REAL, AIMAG, ∗∗.

ROUTINE 7

An array is filled with variables I.M. and another with 1/I.M. The minimum value of the first array is extracted and multiplied by the maximum value from the second array, (giving a result of 1), for each element of the arrays in turn.

for $M = 1$ to 10 and $I = 1$ to 50,001

Functions used AMIN0, AMAX0, FLOAT, MIN0, MAX0, DMIN1, DMAX1.

ROUTINE 8

Using $R = \left(\text{arctangent} \left(\dfrac{\sin C}{\cos C} \right) \middle/ C \right)^2 = \left(\dfrac{C}{C} \right)^2 = 1$

then negated and multiplied by $-R \times \left(\text{remainder of } \dfrac{5000 + I}{4999 + I} \right) \times$

largest integer of $(I + 0.5) \div I$

$\qquad = -R. - R.1. \dfrac{I}{I} = 1$

for $\qquad C = 1 \text{ to} > \pi$

Functions used   FLOAT, SNGL, DBLE, ATAN, SIN, COS, DATAN2,
DSIN, DCOS, DSIGN, AINT, MOD.

Variables

IA for number of outer loops

IC for number of inner loops

Note results will be different if variables are changed.

Timing

Approximately proportional to IA $\times$ (1 + 1.5IC)

Typical parameters for 15 minutes CPU time on a processor of 1000 KIPS
for double precision operations:

IA = 50000, IC = 4

Modifications to run on different Systems

On 16 bit machines the maximum integer is 32, 767 so:

change IB = 50000/IA to IB = 5000/IA

and DO loops for each routine to e.g. DO 100 I = 1,5001, IB

also routine 7 line labelled 688 to:

688 E(M) = 1.0/(FLOAT(MIN0(I,M))*FLOAT(MAX0(I,M)))

Routines 2 and 3 produce numbers in the range 2×10^{72} to 4×10^{-73} when
the DO loop values are 50001. On machines with maximum number range
10^{-38} to 10^{38}, either the DO loops should be reduced to say e.g. DO 100
I = 1,26000, IB or A = FLOAT(I)/300.0 changed to say A = FLOAT(I)/600.

Program Listing FOPR04

```
      REAL *8 RM,PII,A,R,B
      REAL *8 D(10),E(10)
      COMPLEX *8 CA
      COMMON RM
C********PARAMETERS********
      IA=5000
      IC=2
C********PARAMETERS********
      PI=3.14159265
      PII=DBLE(PI/100000.0)
      IB=50000/IA
      WRITE(6,1)
    1 FORMAT(10H1FUNCTIONS,18X,6HANSWER,15X,8HSUMCHECK)
C     ROUTINE 1
      RM=1.0
      DO 100 I=1,50001,IB
      A=DFLOAT(I-1)*PII
      DO 100 J=1,IC
      R=DSIN(A)**2+DCOS(A)**2
  100 RM=RM*R
      WRITE(6,11)
   11 FORMAT(8H SIN COS)
      CALL SUMCK
C     ROUTINE 2
      RM=1.0
      DO 200 I=1,50001,IB
      A=DFLOAT(I)/300.0
      DO 200 J=1,IC
      SA=SNGL(A)
      R=(DEXP(A)-DEXP(-A))/(DEXP(A)+DEXP(-A))/TANH(SA)
  200 RM=RM*R
      WRITE(6,12)
   12 FORMAT(9H EXP TANH)
      CALL SUMCK
C     ROUTINE 3
      RM=1.0
      DO 300 I=1,50001,IB
      A=DFLOAT(I)/300.0
      DO 300 J=1,IC
      B=DEXP(A)
      R=DLOG(B)/A
  300 RM=RM*R
      WRITE(6,13)
   13 FORMAT(8H LOG EXP)
      CALL SUMCK
C     ROUTINE 4
      RM=1.0
      DO 400 I=1,50001,IB
      DO 400 J=1,IC
      A=FLOAT(I)*FLOAT(J)
      B=2.0*DLOG10(A)
      B=10.0**B
      R=DSQRT(B)/A
  400 RM=RM*R
      WRITE(6,14)
   14 FORMAT(11H LOG10 SQRT)
      CALL SUMCK
C     ROUTINE 5
      RM=1.0
      DO 500 I=1,50001,IB
      C=(FLOAT(I)-0.8)*SNGL(PII)
      DO 500 J=1,IC
```

```
          CA=CEXP(CMPLX(C,C))
          CA=CSQRT(CA*CONJG(CA)*CMPLX(COS(C)**2-SIN(C)**2,
          12.0*SIN(C)*(COS(C)))
          CA=CLOG(CA)
          R=(DABS(DBLE(REAL(CA)))+ABS(AIMAG(CA)))/(2.0*C)
      500 RM=RM*R
          WRITE(6,15)
       15 FORMAT(11H CEXP CMPLX,5H CLOG/
          112H CONJG CSQRT)
          CALL SUMCK
C     ROUTINE 6
          RM=1.0
          DO 600 I=1,50001,IB
          CA=CMPLX(FLOAT(I),FLOAT(50001-I))
          DO 600 J=1,IC
          R=CABS(CA)/SQRT(REAL(CA)**2+AIMAG(CA)**2)
      600 RM=RM*R
          WRITE(6,16)
       16 FORMAT(5H CABS,5H REAL,6H AIMAG)
          CALL SUMCK
C     ROUTINE 7
          RM=1.0
          DO 700 I=1,50001,IB
          DO 688 M=1,10
          D(M)=AMIN0(I,M)*AMAX0(I,M)
      688 E(M)=1.0/DFLOAT(MIN0(I,M)*MAX0(I,M))
          DO 700 J=1,IC
          DO 699 N=1,10
          A=DMIN1(D(1),D(2),D(3),D(4),D(5),D(6),D(7),D(8),
          1D(9),D(10))
          D(N)=1000000.0
          R=A*DMAX1(E(1),E(2),E(3),E(4),E(5),E(6),E(7),E(8),
          1E(9),E(10))
          RM=RM*R
      699 E(N)=0.000001
      700 CONTINUE
          WRITE(6,17)
       17 FORMAT(12H DMIN1 DMAX1)
          CALL SUMCK
C     ROUTINE 8
          RM=1.0
          PII=3.142/1000000.0
          DO 800 I=1,50001,IB
          C=FLOAT(I)*SNGL(PII*2.0)
          DO 800 J=1,IC
          R=DBLE(ATAN(SIN(C)/COS(C))/C)
          1*DATAN2(DSIN(DBLE(C)),DCOS(DBLE(C)))/C
          R=-R*DSIGN(R,DBLE(-1.0))*FLOAT(MOD(I+5000,I+4999))
          1*AINT(SNGL(R)/2.0+FLOAT(I))/FLOAT(I)
      800 RM=RM*R
          WRITE(6,18)
       18 FORMAT(18H ATAN DATAN2 DSIGN/9H MOD AINT)
          CALL SUMCK
          STOP
          END

          SUBROUTINE SUMCK
          REAL*8 RM,V,VW
          COMMON RM
          V=RM
          VW=0.0
          IV=0
          DO 111 I=1,100
          V=(V-VW)*10.0
          VV=SNGL(V)
```

254

```
        IW=IFIX(VV)
        IV=IV+IW*I
   111  VW=DFLOAT(IW)
        WRITE(6,9)RM,IV
     9  FORMAT(1H+,15X,D28.20,I10)
        RETURN
        END
```

Typical Correct Results

FUNCTIONS	ANSWER	SUMCHECK
SIN COS	0.99999999999989990000D+00	6716
EXP TANH	0.10000061950621120000D+01	6301
LOG EXP	0.99999999999954110000D+00	6529
LOG10 SQRT	0.99999999999881233000D+00	7747
CEXP CMPLX CLOG		
CONJG CSQRT	0.98467964928105470000D+00	5904
CABS REAL AIMAG	0.99399552456004720000D+00	6622
DMIN1 DMAX1	0.97185013837173690000D+00	6707
ATAN DATAN2 DSIGN		
MOD AINT	0.98721262141963900000D+00	5229

FODK00 RANDOM DISK TEST

To Test

One or two disks (or drums) using indexed access methods and random head movements.

Source

R. Longbottom, CCA (based on a MOD program).

Description

The program comprises a main routine, a reading subroutine and a random number generator subroutine. The main routine writes a number of records to two files in serial mode, the records comprising random numbers preceded by the record number. The two files are read serially and data compared. A number of random record addresses are then produced and the appropriate records read and compared again. In both cases, the reading subroutine checks that the correct records have been read and that the data compares correctly, a print out being given of any discrepancies. Also, in the event of a miscomparison, 5 re-attempts are made to read the failing record. To check the error message print out and re-reading technique, two error routines are incorporated (see typical output). After the first record has been read, during the serial read, an error is forced and print out given—preceded by 'CHECK OF FAIL TEST'. On the 14th record read during the random read phase, a record count error and record content error is forced to check this failure mode. When the program is finished a print out is given of the random records read but this can be suppressed if a suitable printer is not available.

Variables

File definition—in the program listing shown this is in the DEFINE FILE statements, which define files comprising 1000 records each of 100 words, U for unformatted read and write and IA or IB as pointers to the records to be written or read. In other cases or in addition to the above the file is defined in the JCL (Job Control Language). The JCL also normally defines the physical location of the files—these can be both on one unit or diskpack or on two separate ones—the main point being to spread the files out sufficiently to ensure adequate head movement (on moving head devices), KA defines the number of records written to each file: this may be less than the number defined, again to ensure head movement.

KB defines the number of words written to each record—this should be small compared to the record size, to ensure that CPU time for checking is small compared with disk activity time. Arrays AA and AB should be equal to or greater than KB.

KD defines the number of random reads. Array MA should be equal to or greater than KD.

Timing

As there is no overlap on reading or writing and checking the total time can be assumed to be the sum of CPU time and disk access time. A general formula cannot be given for the CPU time as it is too system dependent, depending on the defined record size and the variables KA, KB and KD. The disk access time depends on the characteristics of the device, access methods and whether the files are on one disk or two. With indexed sequential access methods and files on different units, for serial read and write, the access time may be dependent on half revolution time. In all other cases, the average access time may be used.

Typical parameters for 15 minutes stand alone elapsed time on a processor of speed 1000 KIPS and disk with average access time of 38.3 millisecs (giving approximately 2 minutes CPU time and 13 minutes disk access time)

Files 6000 records of 500 words

KA = 6000, KB = 25, KD = 6000

On another system of equivalent processing power and disk speed, because of software inefficiency, with recorded job CPU time of about 2 minutes, the parameters might be:

KA = 700, KB = 5, KD = 700.

256

Modifications to run on Different System

File definition is likely to be different.

Reading and writing statements are likely to be different.

Additional arrays may be required for indexing purposes. Other COMMON statements may be required.

The pointer statements (IA=1, IB=1, IA=I, IB=I) may have to be changed or may be redundant.

To identify failing bit patterns, format statement at labels 80 and 94 use the hexadecimal Z format in the version shown. On many systems it will be necessary to change this to O or H format.

The random number subroutine will cause an integer overflow on 16 bit machines and should be replaced by an alternative.

Program Listing FODK00

```
C       THIS IS FODKOO — RANDOM DISK TEST
        DIMENSION AA(500),AB(500),MA(5000)
        COMMON AA,AB,II,KC,KB,MERR,I
        COMMON MA,J,MM
C••••••••PARAMETERS••••••••
        DEFINE FILE 1(1000,100,U,IA)
        DEFINE FILE 2(1000,100,U,IB)
        KA=500
        KB=25
        KD=1000
C••••••••PARAMETERS••••••••
        KC=KB+1
        MM=1
        WRITE(6,90)
    90  FORMAT(1H1,16HRANDOM DISK TEST//)
        IA=1
        IB=1
        IX=22
        DO 200 I=1,KA
        AA(1)=FLOAT(I)
        AB(KB)=FLOAT(I)
        DO 100 J=2,KB
        L=KC−J
        CALL RANDYB(IX,YFL)
        AA(J)=YFL
   100  AB(L)=AA(J)
        WRITE(1'IA)(AA(K),K=1,KB)
        WRITE(2'IB)(AB(K),K=1,KB)
   200  CONTINUE
        WRITE(6,250) KA,KB
   250  FORMAT(14H DISKS WRITTEN,I10,10H BLOCKS OF,I10,
        17H WORDS //)
        II=0
        MERR=0
        DO 300 I=1,KA
        J=I
        MA(J)=I
        CALL DSKC
   300  CONTINUE
        WRITE(6,350)
   350  FORMAT(19H END OF SERIAL READ///)
        IX=1
```

```
      MM=1
      II=-12
      DO 400 J=1,KD
      CALL RANDYB(IX,YFL)
      I=YFL*FLOAT(KA)
      MA(J)=I
      IF(I)400,400,390
390   CONTINUE
      CALL DSKC
400   CONTINUE
      WRITE(6,450)
450   FORMAT(19H0END OF RANDOM READ///7H BLOCKS)
      WRITE(6,500)(MA(J),J=1,KD)
500   FORMAT(1H ,10I6)
      STOP
      END


      SUBROUTINE DSKC
      DIMENSION AA(500),AB(500)
      DIMENSION MA(5000)
      COMMON AA,AB,II,KC,KB,MERR,I
      COMMON MA,JJ,MM
      IERR=0
255   II=II+1
      IA=I
      IB=IA
      READ(1'IA)(AA(K),K=1,KB)
      READ(2'IB)(AB(K),K=1,KB)
258   IG=0
      ABC=FLOAT(I)
      IF(AA(1).NE.ABC) IG=1
      IF(AB(KB).NE.ABC) IG=1
      IF(IG)285,290,285
285   WRITE(6,94) I,ABC,AA(1),AB(KB)
      IERR=IERR+1
      IF(IERR-1)290,287,290
287   WRITE(6,90)
      WRITE(6,95) (MA(M),M=MM,JJ)
      MM=JJ
290   DO 300 J=2,KB
      L=KC-J
      IF(AA(J).EQ.AB(L)) GO TO 300
      IERR=IERR+1
      WRITE(6,80) I,J,AA(J),AB(L)
      IF(IERR-1)300,299,300
299   WRITE(6,90)
      WRITE(6,95)(MA(M),M=MM,JJ)
      MM=JJ
300   CONTINUE
      IF(IERR)370,390,350
350   IERR=-1000
      LERR=1
      IAA=0
370   IAA=IAA+1
      WRITE(6,70)IAA,I
      IF(IAA-5)255,255,380
380   MERR=MERR+LERR
      IF(MERR-100)400,400,385
385   STOP 1
390   IF(II-1)400,395,400
395   WRITE(6,60)
      AA(1)=1.0
      AA(2)=AA(2)+1.0
      GO TO 258
```

```
 60  FORMAT(19H CHECK OF FAIL TEST)
 70  FORMAT(20H END OF READ ATTEMPT, I3,2X,5HBLOCK,I6//)
 80  FORMAT(19H COMPARISON FAILURE,6H BLOCK,I6,5H WORD,I4/
    111H DISK 1 WAS,Z20,5X,11H DISK 2 WAS,Z20/)
 90  FORMAT(19H BLOCKS READ SO FAR/)
 94  FORMAT(27H WRONG BLOCK READ SHOULD BE,I6,3H OR,Z20/
    111H DISK 1 WAS,Z20,5X,11H DISK 2 WAS,Z20/)
 95  FORMAT(10I6)
400  RETURN
     END

     SUBROUTINE RANDYB(I,X)
     J=125*I
     K=J/8192
     I=J-K*8192
     X=FLOAT(I)/8192.0
     RETURN
     END
```

Typical Correct Output

```
RANDOM DISK TEST

DISKS WRITTEN          500 BLOCKS OF          25 WORDS

CHECK OF FAIL TEST
COMPARISON FAILURE BLOCK       1 WORD   2
DISK 1 WAS                41155F00     DISK 2 WAS              4055F000

BLOCKS READ SO FAR

     1
END OF READ ATTEMPT  1  BLOCK      1

END OF READ ATTEMPT  2  BLOCK      1

END OF READ ATTEMPT  3  BLOCK      1

END OF READ ATTEMPT  4  BLOCK      1

END OF READ ATTEMPT  5  BLOCK      1

END OF READ ATTEMPT  6  BLOCK      1

END OF SERIAL READ

CHECK OF FAIL TEST
WRONG BLOCK READ SHOULD BE      166 OR          42A60000
DISK 1 WAS                41100000     DISK 2 WAS              42A60000

BLOCKS READ SO FAR

     7   453   209   161   149   153   233   212   118   369
   211   405   166
COMPARISON FAILURE BLOCK    166 WORD    2
DISK 1 WAS                411CFF00     DISK 2 WAS              40CFF000

END OF READ ATTEMPT  1  BLOCK      166

END OF READ ATTEMPT  2  BLOCK      166

END OF READ ATTEMPT  3  BLOCK      166
```

END OF READ ATTEMPT 4 BLOCK 166

END OF READ ATTEMPT 5 BLOCK 166

END OF READ ATTEMPT 6 BLOCK 166

END OF RANDOM READ

BLOCKS

7	453	209	161	149	153	233	212	118	369
211	405	166	351	391	488	42	348	25	211
496	110	362	326	279	389	152	81	139	433
145	226	327	492	92	12	94	317	241	189
189	158	344	6	362	265	149	214	363	387
408	63	442	274	370	302	349	178	285	182
334	347	403	453	148	31	474	364	39	481
249	166	259	447	476	108	57	179	407	441
183	426	291	415	387	439	378	279	419	467
418	284	30	261	161	179	468	70	357	215
485	146	257	142	329	236	109	210	252	93
165	168	3	465	174	266	332	103	386	255
490	256	51	385	225	175	419	406	288	109
240	67	430	310	264	119	400	25	242	311
448	7	423	394	324	4	56	118	278	267
393	232	60	45	183	487	420	89	177	132

etc.

FODK01 DISK TEST OR
FOMT01 MAGNETIC TAPE UNIT TEST

To Test

Disks or drums using up to 10 sequential unformatted binary files, or up to 10 magnetic tape units or any combination of 10 tapes or disk or drum files: also random selection of units.

Source

R. Longbottom, CCA.

Description

The program comprises four sections.

Section 1: Pattern generation—A series of patterns are generated comprising of a '1' in each bit position then patterns building up to '1010101', '11001100' etc, some of which are likely to represent worst case patterns. (See sample output with hexadecimal print out.) The number of patterns generated is dependent on the computer wordsize, e.g.

72 patterns for 16 bits 118 patterns for 24 bits
164 patterns for 32 bits 188 patterns for 36 bits
342 patterns for 60 bits (see modifications)

Section 2: Reading sequence generation—This section generates a series of randomized reading sequences, using the declared logical unit numbers (see example output). The number of reading sequences (and records written to each file) is a multiple of the number of patterns generated. The number of different sequencies depends on the number of files, e.g. 60 different combinations for six files.

Section 3: Writing files—This section writes the files one at a time. Each record contains the file number, reading sequence repeat number, pattern number and a variable number of words of the appropriate pattern.

Section 4: Reading files—This section reads a record from each file in turn, according to the random reading sequence, and checks the data against the expected pattern. A print out of any miscompares is given and, in this event, the file is backspaced and the failing record read a further five times. To check the error message print out and rereading procedures, an error is forced on reading the first record (see example output). The files can also be read a variable number of times.

Variables

NB—the number of bits in the computer word.
NF—the number of files written and read (1 to 10).
IFNN—the logical number of the first file, e.g. IFNN = 10, NF = 6 files used are 10, 11, 12, 13, 14, 15.
NR—the number of times patterns repeated (to write longer files, see reading sequence generation).
NWB—the number of words per block or record.
NRD—the number of times all files read.

The following array sizes may have to be changed in conjunction with these variables.

Arrays

MA contains patterns generated.
MAD and JF are used to contain the logical number of files during generation of reading sequences.
JA is used to contain the file reading sequences. (This has to be increased for longer files.)
LFA contains the records written or regenerated for comparison purposes
LIS is used for data read and is compared with LFA.
LERR is used to contain details of any words which fail to compare. (LFA, LIS and LERR dimensions should be equal to or greater than NWB + 3.)

Timing

As for FODK00, the timing is difficult to calculate from a general formula. On disks, where the files are written on different units, the time is likely to be approximately:

1. Writing NF.NBC.R where R is disk revolution time or a multiple of revolution times greater than the CPU time taken for 1 record and NBC is total blocks written.

2. Reading NF.NRD.NBC.HR + processor time where HR is half disk revolution time.

Where files are written on the same disk the time is:

1. Moving head disks – writing as above, reading NRD.NF. NBC.A + processor time where A is average access time.

2. Fixed disks writing + reading (NRD + 1).NF.NBC.R

On magnetic tape units, an estimate of time is

NF(NRD + 1) [NBC(T + S) + RW] + processor time where T is tape movement time for one block, S is start/stop time, RW is rewind time.

In all the above, it is assumed that the systems blocking factor used is the same as NWB.

CPU time used by the program is roughly proportional to (NRD+1).NWB.NF.NBC. This can be quite excessive, as indicated in the following example, so where possible, the program should be run using optimizing compilers, especially where the optimizer makes use of block transfers to the input/output area, rather than transfers of one word at a time. A good optimizing compiler, where block transfers can be arranged, can reduce CPU time by up to 10 times.

Typical parameters for 15 minutes stand alone elapsed time on a processor of speed 1000 KIPS, six disk units with revolution time of 16.7 ms and four magnetic tape units of 75 ips, 1600 bpi (giving approximately 7 minutes file activity and 8 minutes CPU time with a non-optimizing compiler):

NB = 32, NF = 10, NR = 4 (giving NBC = 656), NWB = 297, NRD = 3.

Modifications to run on Different Systems

The array dimensions (see earlier) will have to be varied in conjunction with the parameters. (The usual reason for not running correctly is the JA dimensions being too small.)

There may be a limit on the number of files, which can be handled by one program.

On some systems, the parameters cannot be generated to cover the whole word, using the ** function, but it may be posssible to use a SHIFT function as FOPR01.

The 17 FORMAT statement shown uses the hexadecimal Z format: where this is not recognized, it may be replaced by appropriate Octal O or Hollerith H formats. The BACKSPACE command cannot be used on certain systems but the backspace and reread facility can be omitted.

Program Listing FODK01/FOMT01

```
C*********PARAMETERS********
      DIMENSION MA(400),MAD(10),JF(10),JA(400.10)
      DIMENSION LFA(103),LIS(103),LERR(103)
      NB=32
C     NB=NUMBER OF BITS IN WORD
      NF=4
C     NF=NUMBER OF FILES WRITTEN AND READ
      IFNN=10
C     IFNN=LOGICAL NUMBER OF FIRST FILE
      NR=2
C     NR=NUMBER OF TIMES PATTERNS REPEATED
      NWB=10
C     NWB=NUMBER OF WORDS PER BLOCK
      NRD=2
C     NRD=NUMBER OF TIMES ALL SECTIONS READ
C*********PARAMETERS********
C
C*********PATTERN GENERATION
      NH=NB/2
      II=NB
      IFNM=IFNN-1
      NFI=NF+IFNM
      NC=NB+2
      MA(1)=0
      DO 10 I=2,NB
   10 MA(I)=2**(I-2)
      DO 13 M=1,NH
      IN=M-1
      IM=2*M
      IW=0
      NK=NC-IM
      DO 13 I=2,NK,IM
      IB=I+IN
      DO 12 J=I,IB
   12 IW=IW+MA(J)
      II=II+1
   13 MA(II)=IW
      DO 14 I=1,II
   14 MA(II+I)=-(MA(I)+1)
      IJ=2*II
      WRITE(6,15)
   15 FORMAT(19H1PATTERNS GENERATED//2(7H NUMBER,8X,
     18H PATTERN,5X,3H OR,2X))
      DO 16 I=1,IJ,2
      J=I+1
   16 WRITE(6,17)I,MA(I),MA(I),J,MA(J),MA(J)
   17 FORMAT(2(I7,I16,Z10))
C*********READING SEQUENCE GENERATION
      NBC=NR*IJ
      DO 30 I=1,NF
   30 JF(I)=I
      WRITE(6,66)
      DO 60 J=1,NBC
      DO 31 K=1,NF
   31 MAD(K)=K+IFNM
```

```
      DO 50 I=1,NF
      JFA=JF(I)
      JA(J,I)=MAD(JFA)
      IF(I.EQ.JFA) GO TO 40
      JFI=I+1
      DO 39 M=JFI,JFA
      MFI=JFA-M+JFI
   39 MAD(MFI)=MAD(MFI-1)
   40 IF(JFA-NF)42,41,41
   41 JF(I)=I
      GO TO 50
   42 JF(I)=JFA+1
   50 CONTINUE
   60 WRITE(6,65)J,(JA(J,JJ),JJ=1,NF)
   65 FORMAT(I5,6X,10I3)
   66 FORMAT(17H1READING SEQUENCE//7H NUMBER,10X,5HFILES)
C*********WRITING FILES
      NWC=NWB+3
      MERR=0
      INDE=0
      ICN=-1
      DO 210 I=IFNN,NFI
  210 REWIND I
      DO 805 I=IFNN,NFI
      LFA(1)=I
      DO 800 K=1,NR
      LFA(2)=K
      DO 800 J=1,IJ
      LFA(3)=J
      DO 701 M=4,NWC
  701 LFA(M)=MA(J)
  800 WRITE(I)(LFA(M),M=1,NWC)
      ENDFILE I
      WRITE(6,804)I
  804 FORMAT(5H0FILE,I3,2X,8H WRITTEN)
  805 REWIND I
C*********READING & COMPARING FILES
      DO 852 KK=1,NRD
      DO 850 K=1,NR
      LFA(2)=K
      DO 850 J=1,IJ
      LFA(3)=J
      KJ=J+IJ*(K-1)
      DO 810 M=4,NWC
  810 LFA(M)=MA(J)
      DO 850 L=1,NF
      I=JA(KJ,L)
      LFA(1)=I
      IRP=0
  813 IERR=0
      ICN=ICN+1
      READ(I)(LIS(M),M=1,NWC)
  814 DO 819 M=1,NWC
      IF(LFA(M)-LIS(M))815,819,815
  815 IERR=IERR+1
      LERR(IERR)=M
  819 CONTINUE
      IF(IERR)820,828,820
  820 WRITE(6,821)I,KJ,J,I,K,J,NWC,MA(J)
  821 FORMAT(5H0FILE,I3,2X,17H READING SEQUENCE,I4,2X,
     18H PATTERN,I4,/17H WORD 1 SHOULD BE,I4/
     217H WORD 2 SHOULD BE,I14/17H WORD 3 SHOULD BE,
     3I14/11H WORDS 4 TO,I4/10H SHOULD BE,I21//)
      MERR=MERR+IERR
```

K

```
      IF(MERR-8*NWB)822,860,860
822 DO 824 NN=1,IERR
      NM=LERR(NN)
      WRITE(6,823) NM,LIS(NM)
823 FORMAT(5H WORD,I4,2X,4H WAS,I16)
824 CONTINUE
825 IRP=IRP+1
      IF(IRP-5)826,826,840
826 WRITE(6,827)IRP
827 FORMAT(21H BACKSPACE AND REPEAT,I3)
      BACKSPACE I
      GO TO 813
828 IF(IRP)840,840,830
830 WRITE(6,831)
831 FORMAT(10H REPEAT OK)
      GO TO 825
840 IF(ICN)850,841,850
841 WRITE(6,842)
842 FORMAT(19H1CHECK OF FAIL TEST)
      LIS(4) = 1234
      LIS(6)=4321
      INDE=2
      GO TO 814
850 CONTINUE
      DO 851 IK=IFNN,NFI
851 REWIND IK
852 WRITE(6,853)KK
853 FORMAT(17H END OF READ PASS,I4)
      WRITE(6,855)
855 FORMAT(////12H END OF TEST)
      MERR=MERR-INDE
      IBC=(NWB+3)*NB*NBC
      WRITE(6,858)NF,IBC
      WRITE(6,859)NRD
858 FORMAT(I4,6H FILES,8H EACH OF,
     1I8,22H BITS WRITTEN AND READ)
859 FORMAT(11H FILES READ,I4,6H TIMES)
860 WRITE(6,865)MERR
865 FORMAT(I8,7H ERRORS)
      STOP
      END
```

Typical Correct Results FODK01/FOMT01
(NB = 32 NF = 10 IFNN = 10 NR = 4 NWB = 397 NRD = 4)

PATTERNS GENERATED

NUMBER	PATTERN	OR	NUMBER	PATTERN	OR
1	0	00000000	2	1	00000001
3	2	00000002	4	4	00000004
5	8	00000008	6	16	00000010
7	32	00000020	8	64	00000040
9	128	00000080	10	256	00000100
11	512	00000200	12	1024	00000400
13	2048	00000800	14	4096	00001000
15	8192	00002000	16	16384	00004000
17	32768	00008000	18	65536	00010000
19	131072	00020000	20	262144	00040000
21	524288	00080000	22	1048576	00100000
23	2097152	00200000	24	4194304	00400000
25	8388608	00800000	26	16777216	01000000
27	33554432	02000000	28	67108864	04000000

29	134217728	08000000		30	268435456	10000000
31	536870912	20000000		32	1073741824	40000000
33	1	00000001		34	5	00000005
35	21	00000015		36	85	00000055
37	341	00000155		38	1365	00000555
39	5461	00001555		40	21845	00005555
41	87381	00015555		42	349525	00055555
43	1398101	00155555		44	5592405	00555555
45	22369621	01555555		46	89478485	05555555
47	357913941	15555555		48	1431655765	55555555
49	3	00000003		50	51	00000033
51	819	00000333		52	13107	00003333
53	209715	00033333		54	3355443	00033333
55	53687091	03333333		56	858993459	33333333
57	7	00000007		58	455	000001C7
59	29127	000071C7		60	1864135	001C71C7
61	119304647	071C71C7		62	15	0000000F
63	3855	00000F0F		64	986895	000F0F0F
65	252645135	0F0F0F0F		66	31	0000001F
67	31775	00007C1F		68	32537631	01F07C1F
69	63	0000003F		70	258111	0003F03F
71	127	0000007F		72	2080895	001FC07F
73	255	000000FF		74	16711935	00FF00FF
75	511	000001FF		76	1023	000003FF
77	2047	000007FF		78	4095	00000FFF
79	8191	00001FFF		80	16383	00003FFF
81	32767	00007FFF		82	65535	0000FFFF
83	−1	FFFFFFFF		84	−2	FFFFFFFE
85	−3	FFFFFFFD		86	−5	FFFFFFFB
87	−9	FFFFFFF7		88	−17	FFFFFFEF
89	−33	FFFFFFDF		90	−65	FFFFFFBF
91	−129	FFFFFF7F		92	−257	FFFFFEFF
93	−513	FFFFFDFF		94	−1025	FFFFFBFF
95	−2049	FFFFF7FF		96	−4097	FFFFEFFF
97	−8193	FFFFDFFF		98	−16385	FFFFBFFF
99	−32769	FFFF7FFF		100	−65537	FFFEFFFF
101	−131073	FFFDFFFF		102	−262145	FFFBFFFF
103	−524289	FFF7FFFF		104	−1048577	FFEFFFFF
105	−2097153	FFDFFFFF		106	−4194305	FFBFFFFF
107	−8388609	FF7FFFFF		108	−16777217	FEFFFFFF
109	−33554433	FDFFFFFF		110	−67108865	FBFFFFFF
111	−134217729	F7FFFFFF		112	−268435457	EFFFFFFF
113	−536870913	DFFFFFFF		114	−1073741825	BFFFFFFF
115	−2	FFFFFFFE		116	−6	FFFFFFFA
117	−22	FFFFFFEA		118	−86	FFFFFFAA
119	−342	FFFFFEAA		120	−1366	FFFFFAAA
121	−5462	FFFFEAAA		122	−21846	FFFFAAAA
123	−87382	FFFEAAAA		124	−349526	FFFAAAAA
125	−1398102	FFEAAAAA		126	−5592406	FFAAAAAA
127	−22369622	FEAAAAAA		128	−89478486	FAAAAAAA
129	−357913942	EAAAAAAA		130	−1431655766	AAAAAAAA
131	−4	FFFFFFFC		132	−52	FFFFFFCC
133	−820	FFFFFCCC		134	−13108	FFFFCCCC
135	−209716	FFFCCCCC		136	−3355444	FFCCCCCC
137	−53687092	FCCCCCCC		138	−858993460	CCCCCCCC
139	−8	FFFFFFF8		140	−456	FFFFFE38
141	−29128	FFFF8E38		142	−1864136	FFE38E38
143	−119304648	F8E38E38		144	−16	FFFFFFF0
145	−3856	FFFFF0F0		146	−986896	FFF0F0F0
147	−252645136	F0F0F0F0		148	−32	FFFFFFE0
149	−31776	FFFF83E0		150	−32537632	FE0F83E0
151	−64	FFFFFFC0		152	−258112	FFFC0FC0
153	−128	FFFFFF80		154	−2080896	FFE03F80
155	−256	FFFFFF00		156	−16711936	FF00FF00

157	−512	FFFFFE00	158	−1024	FFFFFC00
159	−2048	FFFFF800	160	−4096	FFFFF000
161	−8192	FFFFE000	162	−16384	FFFFC000
163	−32768	FFFF8000	164	−65536	FFFF0000

READING SEQUENCE

NUMBER	FILES
1	10 11 12 13 14 15 16 17 18 19
2	11 12 13 14 15 16 17 18 19 10
3	12 13 14 15 16 17 18 19 10 11
4	13 14 15 16 17 18 19 10 12 11
5	14 15 16 17 18 19 10 12 11 13
6	15 16 17 18 19 10 12 14 13 11
7	16 17 18 19 10 12 14 11 13 15
8	17 18 19 10 12 14 16 13 15 11
9	18 19 10 12 14 16 11 17 13 15
10	19 10 12 14 16 18 13 11 17 15
11	10 12 14 16 18 11 17 15 13 19
12	11 13 15 17 19 12 18 16 14 10
13	12 14 16 18 10 15 11 13 17 19
14	13 15 17 19 11 16 12 14 18 10
15	14 16 18 10 13 19 15 17 11 12
16	15 17 19 11 14 10 18 12 16 13
17	16 18 10 13 17 12 11 15 14 19
18	17 19 11 14 18 13 12 16 15 10
19	18 10 13 16 11 17 15 12 14 19
20	19 11 14 17 12 18 16 13 15 10
21	10 13 16 19 14 11 12 18 15 17
22	11 14 17 10 16 13 15 12 19 18
23	12 15 18 11 17 14 16 13 10 19
24	13 16 19 12 18 15 17 14 11 10
25	14 17 10 15 11 19 12 13 16 18
26	15 18 11 16 12 10 14 17 19 13
27	16 19 12 17 13 11 15 18 10 14
28	17 10 14 19 15 13 18 11 16 12
29	18 11 15 10 17 16 12 14 13 19
30	19 12 16 11 18 17 13 15 14 10
31	10 14 18 13 11 12 17 15 16 19
32	11 15 19 14 12 13 18 16 17 10
33	12 16 10 17 14 15 11 19 13 18
34	13 17 11 18 15 16 12 10 19 14
35	14 18 12 19 16 17 13 11 10 15
36	15 19 13 10 18 11 17 16 14 12
37	16 10 15 12 11 14 13 17 18 19
38	17 11 16 13 12 15 14 18 19 10
39	18 12 17 14 13 16 15 19 10 11
40	19 13 18 15 14 17 16 10 12 11
41	10 15 11 18 17 12 13 16 14 19
42	11 16 12 19 18 13 14 17 15 10
43	12 17 13 10 11 16 18 14 15 19
44	13 18 14 11 12 17 19 15 16 10
45	14 19 15 12 13 18 10 17 11 16
46	15 10 17 14 16 11 13 12 19 18
47	16 11 18 15 17 12 14 13 10 19
48	17 12 19 16 18 13 15 14 11 10
49	18 13 10 19 11 16 12 14 15 17
50	19 14 11 10 13 18 15 16 17 12
51	10 16 13 12 15 11 18 19 14 17
52	11 17 14 13 16 12 19 10 18 15
53	12 18 15 14 17 13 10 16 11 19
54	13 19 16 15 18 14 11 17 12 10
55	14 10 18 17 11 19 15 12 13 16
56	15 11 19 18 12 10 17 14 16 13

```
57          16 12 10 11 15 14 13 19 17 18
58          17 13 11 12 16 15 14 10 19 18
59          18 14 12 13 17 16 15 11 10 19
 .
 .
 .
 .
 .
 .
 .
etc.
to
 .
 .
640         19 10 18 13 15 17 16 11 14 12
641         10 12 11 16 18 13 14 17 15 19
642         11 13 12 17 19 14 15 18 16 10
643         12 14 13 18 10 16 17 11 15 19
644         13 15 14 19 11 17 18 12 16 10
645         14 16 15 10 13 19 11 18 12 17
646         15 17 16 11 14 10 13 12 19 18
647         16 18 17 12 15 11 14 13 10 19
648         17 19 18 13 16 12 15 14 11 10
649         18 10 11 16 12 17 13 14 15 19
650         19 11 12 17 13 18 14 15 16 10
651         10 13 14 19 15 11 17 18 12 16
652         11 14 15 10 17 13 19 12 18 16
653         12 15 16 11 18 14 10 17 13 19
654         13 16 17 12 19 15 11 18 14 10
655         14 17 18 13 10 19 15 11 12 16
656         15 18 19 14 11 10 17 13 16 12
```

FILE 10   WRITTEN

FILE 11   WRITTEN

FILE 12   WRITTEN

FILE 13   WRITTEN

FILE 14   WRITTEN

FILE 15   WRITTEN

FILE 16   WRITTEN

FILE 17   WRITTEN

FILE 18   WRITTEN

FILE 19   WRITTEN

CHECK OF FAIL TEST

FILE 10   READING SEQUENCE   1   PATTERN   1
WORD 1 SHOULD BE   10
WORD 2 SHOULD BE   1
WORD 3 SHOULD BE   1
WORDS 4 TO 400
SHOULD BE   0

WORD   4   WAS   1234
WORD   6   WAS   4321

```
BACKSPACE AND REPEAT  1
REPEAT OK
BACKSPACE AND REPEAT  2
REPEAT OK
BACKSPACE AND REPEAT  3
REPEAT OK
BACKSPACE AND REPEAT  4
REPEAT OK
BACKSPACE AND REPEAT  5
REPEAT OK
END OF READ PASS   1
END OF READ PASS   2
END OF READ PASS   3
END OF READ PASS   4

END OF TEST
   10 FILES EACH OF 8396800 BITS WRITTEN AND READ
FILES READ    4 TIMES
       0 ERRORS
```

FODK02 DISK TEST OR FOMT00 MAGNETIC UNIT TEST

To Test

One disk, drum or magnetic tape unit using an unformatted binary file.

Source

R. Longbottom, CCA (based on a ULCC program).

Description

A variable number of fixed length blocks are written to one file, with different binary numbers in each block (e.g. with 500 word blocks—0 to 499 in the first block 500 to 999 in the second block). The tape is then rewound and read a variable number of times, a comparison being made with the expected data. In the event of a miscompare, a print out is given. Where 100 of these (normally undetectable) words in error are detected, the particular read pass is terminated. On subsequent passes it is terminated on encountering 1 error. To check the error message print out, an error is forced after reading the first block (see example output).

Variables

NB—the number of blocks written.
NC—the number of words per block.
NP—the number of reading passes.
Array IA must be equal to or greater than NC.

Timing

On disks, the time can be estimated as approximately
   (NP+1). NB.R

where R is the disk revolution or a multiple of the revolution time greater than the CPU time used for 1 record.

On magnetic tape units, an estimate of the time is

(NP + 1) [NB (T + S) + RW] + CPU time, where T is the tape movement time for one block, S is the start/stop time, RW is the rewind time.

In the above, it is assumed that the systems blocking factor is the same as NC.

CPU time used by the program is roughly proportional to (NP + 1).NC.NB. This can be quite excessive as for FODK01 and as indicated in the following example. Tape activity can be improved by using a good optimizing compiler, which can reduce CPU time considerably.

Typical parameters for 15 minutes stand alone elapsed time on a processor of speed 1000 KIPS and a disk with 16.7 ms revolution time:

NB = 3000, NC = 500, NP = 7 (12 mins CPU time)

or on a magnetic tape unit of 75 ips 1600 ipi:

NB = 6000, NC = 500, NP = 2 (9 mins CPU time).

Modifications to run on Different Systems

Where the word size is small it should be ensured that the integer value NC*NB does not cause an overflow.

Program Listing FOMT00/FODK02

```
      DIMENSION IA(500)
      REWIND 10
      IERR=0
      WRITE(6,10)
   10 FORMAT(1H1,23HMAGNETIC TAPE UNIT TEST)
C*********PARAMETERS********
      NB=1000
      NC=500
      NP=2
C*********PARAMETERS********
C*********WRITE
      DO 200 I=1,NB
      JJ=I*NC-NC
      DO 100 J=1,NC
  100 IA(J)=J+JJ
  200 WRITE(10) (IA(K),K=1,NC)
      WRITE(6,300)
  300 FORMAT(13H TAPE WRITTEN)
      END FILE 10
      REWIND 10
C*********READ & COMPARE
      DO 700 I=1,NP
      DO 600 J=1,NB
      JJ=J*NC-NC
      READ(10) (IA(K),K=1,NC)
  400 DO 570 L=1,NC
      IB=L+JJ
      IF(IA(L).EQ.IB) GO TO 570
      WRITE(6,550)I,J,L,IA(L),IB
  550 FORMAT(10H READ PASS,I4,2X,5HBLOCK,I4,2X,4HWORD,
```

```
        1I4,2X,3HWAS,I10,2X,9HSHOULD BE,I10)
        IERR=IERR+1
        IF(IERR-100)570,560,560
   560  REWIND 10
        GO TO 700
   570  CONTINUE
        IF(IB+I+IERR-NC-1)600,580,600
   580  WRITE(6,585)
   585  FORMAT(19H CHECK OF FAIL TEST)
        IA(1)=999
        GO TO 400
   600  CONTINUE
        REWIND 10
        WRITE(6,650)I
   650  FORMAT(1H ,16HEND OF READ PASS,I4)
   700  CONTINUE
        STOP
        END
```

Typical Correct Results

```
MAGNETIC TAPE UNIT TEST
TAPE WRITTEN
CHECK OF FAIL TEST
READ PASS   1   BLOCK   1   WORD   1   WAS      999   SHOULD BE
END OF READ PASS    1
END OF READ PASS    2
```

FODK03 DISK TEST or FOMT02
MAGNETIC TAPE UNIT TEST

To Test

One disk or magnetic tape unit, with a formatted file using all characters. The program is specifically designed for testing magnetic tape unit drive actuators or servos.

Source

R. Longbottom, CCA (based on an ICL magnetic tape unit test used on 1900 systems).

Description

This program generates various patterns for testing purposes consisting of the following:

1. Ripple (as printer wallpaper pattern).
2. Full record of each character.
3. One character record of each character.
4. Increasing ripple—as 1 but increasing from 1 character to full record length.

The program sequence consists of writing three records, backspacing three records, then reading and checking three records, writing three records and so on, until all the patterns have been written and checked. The tape is then rewound and can be read a variable number of times, without backspacing. On reading, the records are compared with the expected patterns and a print out given of any discrepancies. To check the error message print out, an error is forced on reading the first record (see example output).

The parameters and character set for this program are read from data cards.

Variables

Read from data card 1:

Column

1–2	NCH	number of characters in character set to be read from data card 2 (e.g. 64).
3–5	NCHBL	maximum record length (e.g. 160). If greater than 160 characters, format statements and array sizes will have to be changed.
6–7	NWRP	number of times all patterns written/read (e.g. 02).
8–9	NMTU	logical number of tape unit or disk (e.g. 10).
10–11	NRD	number of read passes (e.g. 02): if 02, the tape ie read once after the write/read pass.

Read from data card 2:
All characters available—number specified on data card 1.

Timing

The timing for this program is best established by experiment as the backspacing on writing usually leads to high system overheads in closing and opening files. Sometimes this gives a good test of the system disk.

The number of records written is as follows (printed as BLOCKS WRITTEN at the end of the program):

$$3 \times (3 \times NCH + NCHBL) \times NWRP$$

On disks the time taken is likely to be approximately:

$(NRD+1) \times$ number of records written $\times$ R + overheads

where R is a multiple of disk revolution times greater than the CPU time taken for 1 record.

On magnetic tape units the time taken depends on tape speed, start/stop time, turn around time, average block length, rewind time, CPU time and overheads; experience indicates that an accurate time can only be established by running the program.

Typical parameters for 15 minutes stand alone elapsed time on a processor of 1000 KIPS and a 75 ips 1600 bpi magnetic tape unit: NCH=64, NCHBL=100, NWRP=10, NRD=2 (3 mins CPU time).

Modifications to run on Different Systems

On certain systems the BACKSPACE command cannot be used so the program will not run. On other systems, as the backspace on writing may close the file, there may be an upper limit of files allowed (e.g. 32) so the program may abort with a execution error. To overcome this, a second version of the program has been written (see example of changes given later), which writes the file completely then backspaces on reading.

Note that some computer suppliers may refuse to run this program as it tends to break the units.

Program Listing FOMT02/FODK03

```
C       THIS IS FOMT02
        DIMENSION LSB(300),LSC(160)
C******READ PARAMETERS FROM DATA CARDS
        READ(5,100)NCH,NCHBL,NWRP,NMTU,NRD
100 FORMAT(I2,I3,3I2)
        READ(5,101)(LSB(J),J=1,NCH)
101 FORMAT(80A1)
C******READ PARAMETERS FROM DATA CARDS
        WRITE(6,110)
110 FORMAT(24H1MAGNETIC TAPE UNIT TEST)
        REWIND NMTU
        IERR=0
        IM=300-NCH
120 FORMAT(160A1)
        DO 150 I=1,IM
150 LSB(NCH+I)=LSB(I)
        DO 750 M=1,NRD
        NCT=0
        DO 700 MM=1,NWRP
        II=NCHBL
C       RIPPLE PATTERN
        N=NCHBL-1
        DO 200 J=1,NCH
        N=N+1
        IF(M.GT.1) GO TO 180
        WRITE(NMTU,120)(LSB(K),K=J,N)
        WRITE(NMTU,120)(LSB(K),K=J,N)
        WRITE(NMTU,120)(LSB(K),K=J,N)
        BACKSPACE NMTU
        BACKSPACE NMTU
        BACKSPACE NMTU
180 NCT=NCT+3
        CALL RDMT(NMTU,NCT,LSB,J,N,IERR,M,NCHBL,II)
200 CONTINUE
C       BLOCKS SAME CHARA.
        DO 300 J=1,NCH
        DO 250 I=1,NCHBL
250 LSC(I)=LSB(J)
        IF(M.GT.1) GO TO 280
        WRITE(NMTU,120)(LSC(K),K=1,NCHBL)
```

```
      WRITE(NMTU,120)(LSC(K),K=1,NCHBL)
      WRITE(NMTU,120)(LSC(K),K=1,NCHBL)
      BACKSPACE NMTU
      BACKSPACE NMTU
      BACKSPACE NMTU
  280 NCT=NCT+3
      CALL RDMT(NMTU,NCT,LSC,1,NCHBL,IERR,M,NCHBL,II)
  300 CONTINUE
C     1 CHARA BLOCKS
      II=1
      DO 400 J=1,NCH
      LSC(1)=LSB(J)
      IF(M.GT.1) GO TO 380
      WRITE(NMTU,330) LSB(J)
      WRITE(NMTU,330) LSB(J)
      WRITE(NMTU,330) LSB(J)
  330 FORMAT(1A1)
      BACKSPACE NMTU
      BACKSPACE NMTU
      BACKSPACE NMTU
  380 NCT=NCT+3
      CALL RDMT(NMTU,NCT,LSC,1,NCHBL,IERR,M,NCHBL,II)
  400 CONTINUE
C     INCREASING RIPPLE
      DO 500 J=1,NCHBL
      II=J
      LSC(J)=LSB(J)
      IF(M.GT.1) GO TO 480
      WRITE(NMTU,120)(LSC(K),K=1,J)
      WRITE(NMTU,120)(LSC(K),K=1,J)
      WRITE(NMTU,120)(LSC(K),K=1,J)
      BACKSPACE NMTU
      BACKSPACE NMTU
      BACKSPACE NMTU
  480 NCT=NCT+3
      CALL RDMT(NMTU,NCT,LSC,1,NCHBL,IERR,M,NCHBL,II)
  500 CONTINUE
  700 CONTINUE
      ENDFILE NMTU
      REWIND NMTU
      WRITE(6,720)M
  720 FORMAT(12H0END OF PASS,I4)
  750 CONTINUE
      WRITE(6,800)
  800 FORMAT(12H0END OF TEST)
      WRITE(6,801)NCT,M,IERR
  801 FORMAT(8H0TAPE OF,I12,24H BLOCKS WRITTEN AND READ,I4,6H TIMES/
     1I10,2X,6HERRORS)
      STOP
      END

      SUBROUTINE RDMT(I,NB,LS,J,K,IERR,M,NCHBL,II)
      DIMENSION LS(300),LIS(160)
      NB=NB-3
      DO 300 IR=1,3
      NB=NB+1
      READ(I,100)(LIS(L),L=1,II)
  100 FORMAT(160A1)
  199 JJ=J-1
      DO 220 L=1,NCHBL
      JJ=JJ+1
      IF(LS(JJ).EQ.LIS(L)) GO TO 220
      WRITE(6,201) M,NB
  201 FORMAT(29H0COMPARISON FAILURE READ PASS,I4,3X,5HBLOCK,I10//)
```

```
      WRITE(6,202)(LS(N),N=J,K)
  202 FORMAT(10H SHOULD BE,2X,100A1)
      WRITE(6,203)(LIS(N),N=1,NCHBL)
  203 FORMAT(4H WAS,8X,100A1)
      IERR=IERR+1
      GO TO 300
  220 CONTINUE
      NN=1
      IF(NB.NE.NN) GO TO 300
      WRITE(6,250)
  250 FORMAT(19H0CHECK OF FAIL TEST)
      LIS(1)=LS(2)
      IERR=IERR−1
      GO TO 199
  300 CONTINUE
      RETURN
      END
```

Changes Required for Different Systems

Modifications have been made to the program in a second version
such that problems encountered in closing files after backspacing
on writing have been overcome. In this version records are written
without backspacing but on reading the sequence is:

```
READ
READ
READ
BACKSPACE
BACKSPACE
BACKSPACE
READ
READ
READ
```

1 is added to the number of read passes NRD so that if NRD=1 the file
is read twice. The modifications are:

After card 8 add
        NRD=NRD+1
DO 200 loop replace 3 BACKSPACE commands by
        GO TO 200
DO 300 loop replace 3 BACKSPACE commands by
        GO TO 300
DO 400 loop replace 3 BACKSPACE commands by
        GO TO 400
DO 500 loop replace 3 BACKSPACE commands by
        GO TO 500

RDMT subroutine
After DIMENSION statement add
        ICV=M
     99 CONTINUE
After   300 CONTINUE add
        ICV=ICV−2
        IF(ICV.NE.0) GO TO 400
        BACKSPACE I
        BACKSPACE I
        BACKSPACE I
        GO TO 99
  400 CONTINUE
```
```

Typical Correct Results

MAGNETIC TAPE UNIT TEST

CHECK OF FAIL TEST

COMPARISON FAILURE READ PASS   1   BLOCK   1

SHOULD BE   1234567890QWERTYUIOPASDFGHJKLZXCVBNM,.
WAS   2234567890QWERTYUIOPASDFGHJKLZXCVBNM,.

END OF PASS   1

etc.

END OF TEST

TAPE OF   1006 BLOCKS WRITTEN AND READ   2 TIMES
               0 ERRORS

FOLP00 LINE PRINTER TEST

To Test

Line printers or with slight modification, typewriters. The program is also extremely useful for testing remote batch terminal printers, enabling tests to be carried out concurrently with normal user operations. Selected routines can also be used for testing VDUs and typewriters in a multi access environment.

Source

R. Longbottom, CCA (based on line printer tests used by various computer suppliers)

Description

This program generates various patterns of characters and prints them. An example of output is given later to clarify the patterns:

Preface   This reads the variable parameters from data cards. The program then prints the column number to make it easy to check that all print positions are covered.

Routine 1   Wallpaper pattern from data card 2— checks all characters in all print positions and, with suitable data card format, can be arranged to fire all hammers simultaneously on a chain printer.

Routine 2 Wallpaper pattern from data card 2—double line spacing.

Routine 3 Wallpaper pattern from data card 3.

Routine 4 One full line of each character from data card 2—on barrel printers this should fire all hammers simultaneously.

Routine 5 Decreasing then increasing wallpaper pattern from data card 2—this routine checks for buffer pick-up and tests variable speed printing, where the printing speed is dependent on the number of columns printed.

Routine 6 One full line of each character in odd columns then even columns, characters from data card 2. This routine is for checking pick-up between adjacent hammers or 'ghosting' on barrel printers.

Routine 7 Throws to top of page, line spacing suppressed and various line spaces—the paper throws are normally a good test of paper stacking.

Routine 8 Find the spacing control characters and printing short lines—this uses each of the characters from data card 2 as the carriage control characters. The following are FORTRAN standard control characters:

1 Throw to head of form
0 Double line spacing
+ Suppress line feed

but, sometimes, some remarkable effects are also found.

Variables

The variables are read from three data cards.

Data card 1:

Columns
1–2 NCH number of characters in character set to be read from other cards

3–5 NCOL number of columns to be printed, maximum 160

6–7 NPAGE number of lines per page, usually NCH to cover all patterns fully

8–9 NLOOPS number of times all sections repeated

Data card 2: Any 80 characters or less; number specified by NCH. Normally the characters should be in the same sequence as on the print barrel or chain.

Data card 3: Any 80 characters or less; number specified by NCH. This sequence of characters should represent some worst case pattern, e.g. a line of spaces and zeros for checking blank and zero suppression facilities on a data transmission system, or /*/*/*/* etc, for example, where this is a worst case noise pattern.

Timing

The timing can be estimated as printing time + CPU time. An estimate of printing time can be derived from NLOOPS × lines printed ÷ printing speed, where the lines printed is 46 + 8 × NPAGE + 2 × NCOL + 2 × NCH. More accurate estimates can be made by considering the time taken for the individual test patterns. The CPU time is also approximately proportional to the number of lines printed and 1000 lines on a CPU of speed 1000 KIPS requires about 10 seconds CPU time.

Modifications to run on Different Systems

The version of the program given in the listing is for printers where the carriage control character is included in the specified number of print positions. For printers where the specified number of print positions excludes the carriage control character, the following changes are required:

Remove NCOL = NCOL−1 (card 25 before 218 FORMAT) and NCOL = NCOL + 1 (card 119 after 627 FORMAT). Change card 24 to 215 WRITE (6,218) (LFC(N), N=1, NCOL).

Where the character set is greater than 80 characters, the data cards, initial reading statements and final printing statements can easily be changed to accommodate full testing. Arrays LFA and LFB should be increased in size to 4 × number of characters read in.

On some systems, it may be necessary to reduce the number in format statements at labels 218, 350 and 351 from 160 to the actual number of print positions available (e.g. 132); also at labels 451 and 471 to the number of print positions divided by 2.

Program Listing FOLP00

```
      DIMENSION LFA(320),LFB(320),LFC(161)
C*****PARAMETERS
      READ(5,100)NCH,NCOL,NPAGE,NLOOPS
  100 FORMAT(I2,I3,I2,I2)
      READ(5,200)(LFA(J),J=1,NCH)
```

```
        READ(5,200)(LFB(J),J=1,NCH)
  200   FORMAT(80A1)
C*****PARAMETERS
        IM=NCH*3
        DO 250 I=1,IM
        LFA(NCH+I)=LFA(I)
  250   LFB(NCH+I)=LFB(I)
  260   FORMAT(1H1,12HPRINTER TEST)
        DO 750 M=1,NLOOPS
        WRITE(6,260)
        WRITE(6,210)
  210   FORMAT(18H NUMBER OF COLUMNS)
        II=1000
        DO 215 I=1,3
        II=II/10
        DO 216 J=1,NCOL
        IJ=J/II
        IM=IJ/10
        IJ=IJ-IM*10
  216   LFC(J)=IJ
  215   WRITE(6,218)(LFC(N),N=2,NCOL)
        NCOL=NCOL-1
  218   FORMAT(1X,160I1)
  350   FORMAT(1H ,160A1)
C       WALLPAPER PATTERN FROM DATA CARD 2
        WRITE(6,260)
        N=NCOL-1
        DO 275 I=1,NPAGE
        N=N+1
  275   WRITE(6,350)(LFA(J),J=I,N)
        WRITE(6,260)
        N=N+1
        DO 277 I=1,NPAGE
        N=N-1
        NN=NPAGE+1-I
  277   WRITE(6,350)(LFA(J),J=NN,N)
C       WALLPAPER PATTERN FROM DATA CARD 2 - DOUBLE LINE SPACING
        WRITE(6,260)
        N=NCOL-1
        DO 273 I=1,NPAGE
        N=N+1
  273   WRITE(6,351)(LFA(J),J=I,N)
  351   FORMAT(1H0,160A1)
C       WALLPAPER PATTERN FROM DATA CARD 3
        WRITE(6,260)
        N=NCOL-1
        DO 278 I=1,NPAGE
        N=N+1
  278   WRITE(6,350)(LFB(J),J=I,N)
        WRITE(6,260)
        N=N+1
        DO 279 I=1,NPAGE
        N=N-1
        NN=NPAGE+1-I
  279   WRITE(6,350)(LFB(J),J=NN,N)
C       ONE FULL LINE EACH CHARACTER FROM DATA CARD 2
        WRITE(6,260)
        DO 355 J=1,NPAGE
        DO 400 I=1,NCOL
  400   LFC(I)=LFA(J)
  355   WRITE(6,350)(LFC(N),N=1,NCOL)
C       DECREASING THEN INCREASING WALLPAPER PATTERN FROM DATA CARD 2
        WRITE(6,260)
        DO 500 I=1,NCOL
  500   WRITE(6,350)(LFA(J),J=I,NCOL)
```

```
      NM=NCOL+1
      DO 501 I=1,NCOL
      NM=NM-1
 501  WRITE(6,350)(LFA(J),J=NM,NCOL)
C     ONE FULL LINE OF EACH CHARACTER IN ODD COLS. THEN EVEN COLS.
C     FROM DATA CARD 2
      WRITE(6,260)
      NCL=NCOL/2
      DO 450 J=1,NPAGE
      DO 460 I=1,NCL
 460  LFC(I)=LFA(J)
 450  WRITE(6,451)(LFC(N),N=1,NCL)
 451  FORMAT(1H ,80(1X,1A1))
      DO 470 J=1,NPAGE
      DO 480 I=1,NCL
 480  LFC(I)=LFA(J)
 470  WRITE(6,471)(LFC(N),N=1,NCL)
 471  FORMAT(80(1X,1A1))
C     THROWS TO TOP OF FORM AND VARIOUS LINE SPACES
      DO 560 I=1,5
      WRITE(6,260)
      WRITE(6,561)
 561  FORMAT(1H+,13X,26H LONG THROW TO HEAD OF FORM,1X,
     127HAND L N  S A I G S P R S E )
 560  WRITE(6,562)
 562  FORMAT(1H+,45X,22HI  E   P C N   U P E S D)
      DO 570 I=1,4
 570  WRITE(6,571)
 571  FORMAT(15H ONE LINE SPACE)
      WRITE(6,580)
 580  FORMAT(16H0TWO LINE SPACES//16H TWO LINE SPACES//16H TWO LINE SPAC
     1ES//16H TWO LINE SPACES)
      DO 590 I=1,4
 590  WRITE(6,591)
 591  FORMAT(//18H THREE LINE SPACES)
      DO 600 I=1,4
 600  WRITE(6,601)
 601  FORMAT(///17H FOUR LINE SPACES)
      DO 610 I=1,2
 610  WRITE(6,611)
 611  FORMAT(////17H FIVE LINE SPACES/////17H FIVE LINE SPACES)
C     FIND THE SPACING CONTROL CHARS AND PRINTING IN COL 1
      DO 620 J=1,NCH
      DO 625 I=1,10
 625  LFC(I)=LFA(J)
      DO 620 K=1,2
      WRITE(6,626)
 620  WRITE(6,627)(LFC(N),N=1,10)
 626  FORMAT(2H00)
 627  FORMAT(10A1)
      NCOL=NCOL+1
      WRITE(6,630)NCH,NCOL,NPAGE,NLOOPS
 630  FORMAT(25H1NUMBER OF CHARACTERS WAS,I3/22H NUMBER OF COLUMNS WAS,I
     16/25H NUMBER OF LINES/PAGE WAS,I3/20H NUMBER OF LOOPS WAS,I5)
      WRITE(6,640)(LFA(J),J=1,NCH)
      WRITE(6,641)(LFB(J),J=1,NCH)
 640  FORMAT(22H0DATA INPUT TO LFA WAS/1H ,80A1)
 641  FORMAT(22H0DATA INPUT TO LFB WAS/1H ,80A1)
 643  FORMAT(///7H END OF,I4,24H LOOP(S) OF PRINTER TEST)
      WRITE(6,643) M
 750  CONTINUE
      WRITE(6,650)
 650  FORMAT(//20H END OF PRINTER TEST)
      STOP
      END
```

Example of Output (NCH=25, NCOL=30, NPAGE=10, NLOOPS=1)

```
PRINTER TEST
NUMBER OF COLUMNS
000000000000000000000000000000
000000001111111111222222222223
234567890123456789012345678901
```

ROUTINE 1 – WALLPAPER PATTERN

```
PRINTER TEST
1234567890 ABCDEFGHIJKLMN1234
234567890 ABCDEFGHIJKLMN12345
34567890 ABCDEFGHIJKLMN123456
4567890 ABCDEFGHIJKLMN1234567
567890 ABCDEFGHIJKLMN12345678
67890 ABCDEFGHIJKLMN123456789
7890 ABCDEFGHIJKLMN1234567890
890 ABCDEFGHIJKLMN1234567890
90 ABCDEFGHIJKLMN1234567890 A
0 ABCDEFGHIJKLMN1234567890 AB
```

```
PRINTER TEST
0 ABCDEFGHIJKLMN1234567890 AB
90 ABCDEFGHIJKLMN1234567890 A
890 ABCDEFGHIJKLMN1234567890
7890 ABCDEFGHIJKLMN1234567890
67890 ABCDEFGHIJKLMN123456789
567890 ABCDEFGHIJKLMN12345678
4567890 ABCDEFGHIJKLMN1234567
34567890 ABCDEFGHIJKLMN123456
234567890 ABCDEFGHIJKLMN12345
1234567890 ABCDEFGHIJKLMN1234
```

ROUTINE 2 – WALLPAPER PATTERN – DOUBLE LINE SPACING

```
PRINTER TEST

1234567890 ABCDEFGHIJKLMN1234

234567890 ABCDEFGHIJKLMN12345

34567890 ABCDEFGHIJKLMN123456

4567890 ABCDEFGHIJKLMN1234567

567890 ABCDEFGHIJKLMN12345678

67890 ABCDEFGHIJKLMN123456789

7890 ABCDEFGHIJKLMN1234567890

890 ABCDEFGHIJKLMN1234567890

90 ABCDEFGHIJKLMN1234567890 A

0 ABCDEFGHIJKLMN1234567890 AB
```

ROUTINE 3 – WALLPAPER PATTERN FROM DATA CARD 3

```
PRINTER TEST
THIS IS A FUNNY PATTERN  THIS
HIS IS A FUNNY PATTERN  THIS
IS IS A FUNNY PATTERN  THIS I
S IS A FUNNY PATTERN  THIS IS
```

```
IS A FUNNY PATTERN  THIS IS
IS A FUNNY PATTERN  THIS IS A
S A FUNNY PATTERN  THIS IS A
A FUNNY PATTERN  THIS IS A F
A FUNNY PATTERN  THIS IS A FU
FUNNY PATTERN  THIS IS A FUN
```

```
PRINTER TEST
FUNNY PATTERN  THIS IS A FUN
A FUNNY PATTERN  THIS IS A FU
A FUNNY PATTERN  THIS IS A F
S A FUNNY PATTERN  THIS IS A
IS A FUNNY PATTERN  THIS IS A
IS A FUNNY PATTERN  THIS IS
S IS A FUNNY PATTERN  THIS IS
IS IS A FUNNY PATTERN  THIS I
HIS IS A FUNNY PATTERN  THIS
THIS IS A FUNNY PATTERN  THIS
```

ROUTINE 4 – ONE LINE OF EACH CHARACTER

```
PRINTER TEST
1111111111111111111111111111
2222222222222222222222222222
3333333333333333333333333333
4444444444444444444444444444
5555555555555555555555555555
6666666666666666666666666666
7777777777777777777777777777
8888888888888888888888888888
9999999999999999999999999999
0000000000000000000000000000
```

ROUTINE 5 – DECREASING THEN INCREASING WALLPAPER PATTERN

```
PRINTER TEST
1234567890 ABCDEFGHIJKLMN1234
234567890 ABCDEFGHIJKLMN1234
34567890 ABCDEFGHIJKLMN1234
4567890 ABCDEFGHIJKLMN1234
567890 ABCDEFGHIJKLMN1234
67890 ABCDEFGHIJKLMN1234
7890 ABCDEFGHIJKLMN1234
890 ABCDEFGHIJKLMN1234
90 ABCDEFGHIJKLMN1234
0 ABCDEFGHIJKLMN1234
 ABCDEFGHIJKLMN1234
ABCDEFGHIJKLMN1234
BCDEFGHIJKLMN1234
CDEFGHIJKLMN1234
DEFGHIJKLMN1234
EFGHIJKLMN1234
FGHIJKLMN1234
GHIJKLMN1234
HIJKLMN1234
IJKLMN1234
JKLMN1234
KLMN1234
LMN1234
MN1234
N1234
1234
234
34
4
```

```
4
34
234
1234
N1234
MN1234
LMN1234
KLMN1234
JKLMN1234
IJKLMN1234
HIJKLMN1234
GHIJKLMN1234
FGHIJKLMN1234
EFGHIJKLMN1234
DEFGHIJKLMN1234
CDEFGHIJKLMN1234
BCDEFGHIJKLMN1234
ABCDEFGHIJKLMN1234
 ABCDEFGHIJKLMN1234
0 ABCDEFGHIJKLMN1234
90 ABCDEFGHIJKLMN1234
890 ABCDEFGHIJKLMN1234
7890 ABCDEFGHIJKLMN1234
67890 ABCDEFGHIJKLMN1234
567890 ABCDEFGHIJKLMN1234
4567890 ABCDEFGHIJKLMN1234
34567890 ABCDEFGHIJKLMN1234
234567890 ABCDEFGHIJKLMN1234
1234567890 ABCDEFGHIJKLMN1234
```

ROUTINE 6 – EACH CHARACTER ODD THEN EVEN COLUMNS

PRINTER TEST
```
1 1 1 1 1 1 1 1 1 1 1 1 1
2 2 2 2 2 2 2 2 2 2 2 2 2
3 3 3 3 3 3 3 3 3 3 3 3 3
4 4 4 4 4 4 4 4 4 4 4 4 4
5 5 5 5 5 5 5 5 5 5 5 5 5
6 6 6 6 6 6 6 6 6 6 6 6 6
7 7 7 7 7 7 7 7 7 7 7 7 7
8 8 8 8 8 8 8 8 8 8 8 8 8
9 9 9 9 9 9 9 9 9 9 9 9 9
0 0 0 0 0 0 0 0 0 0 0 0 0
1 1 1 1 1 1 1 1 1 1 1 1 1
2 2 2 2 2 2 2 2 2 2 2 2 2
3 3 3 3 3 3 3 3 3 3 3 3 3
4 4 4 4 4 4 4 4 4 4 4 4 4
5 5 5 5 5 5 5 5 5 5 5 5 5
6 6 6 6 6 6 6 6 6 6 6 6 6
7 7 7 7 7 7 7 7 7 7 7 7 7
8 8 8 8 8 8 8 8 8 8 8 8 8
9 9 9 9 9 9 9 9 9 9 9 9 9
```

ROUTINE 7 – LINE SPACING
(EACH REPEATED 4 OR 5 TIMES)

PRINTER TEST LONG THROW TO HEAD OF FORM AND LINE SPACING SUPPRESSED

ONE LINE SPACE
ONE LINE SPACE

TWO LINE SPACES

THREE LINE SPACES

FOUR LINE SPACES

FIVE LINE SPACES

ROUTINE 8 – CONTROL CHARACTERS

0

111111111

0

111111111
0
222222222

0
222222222

0
333333333

0
333333333

0
444444444

0
444444444

etc.

NUMBER OF CHARACTERS WAS   25
NUMBER OF COLUMNS WAS   30
NUMBER OF LINES/PAGE WAS   10
NUMBER OF LOOPS WAS   1

DATA INPUT TO LFA WAS
1234567890 ABCDEFGHIJKLMN

DATA INPUT TO LFB WAS
THIS IS A FUNNY PATTERN

END OF   1 LOOP(S) OF PRINTER TEST

END OF PRINTER TEST

FOCP00 CARD PUNCH TEST

To Test

Card punches—cards are read by FOCR00 card reader test.

284

Source

R. Longbottom, CCA (based on card reader/punch tests used by various computer suppliers).

Description

The program generates various patterns of characters, using five routines; and outputs them to the card punch (Unit 7).

Preface   This reads the variable parameters from two data cards and fills an array in preparation for punching.

Routine 1:   Ripple punch (see FOLP00 wallpaper pattern). Two batches of cards are punched, such that each character is punched in each card column twice.

Routine 2:   Full card of each character.

Routine 3:   Each character in last column then first column, remainder blank. These are punched in two separate batches.

Routine 4:   Full card each character in odd then even columns. These are punched alternately.

Routine 5:   Decreasing then increasing ripple. This is the same pattern as routine 1, but 160 cards are punched, starting at 80 columns, reducing to 1 then increasing from 1 to 80.

At the end, the program prints the character set used and the number of cards punched.

Variables

The variables are read from two data cards.

Data card 1:
    Columns
        1–2   NCH number of characters in character set read from data card 2
        3–4   NLOOPS number of times all sections to be repeated

Data card 2: Starting at column 1, all characters in character set, number specified by NCH. (See restrictions given under 'Modifications to run on different systems'.)

Timing

The timing can be estimated as punching time + CPU time. An estimate of punching time can be derived from NLOOPS × cards punched ÷ punching speed, where cards punched is 160 + 7 × NCH (608 cards for a 64 character set). The CPU time is approximately proportional to the number of cards punched and 600 cards on a CPU of speed 1000 KIPS requires approximately 6 seconds CPU time.

Modifications to run on Different Systems

There may be some restrictions on the sequence of characters which can be read, for example an end of file (e.g. *****) or job control (e.g. //). These are usually punched by routine 2: the offending character should be omitted from the character set.

Program Listing FOCP00

```
C      PUNCH TEST
       DIMENSION LFA(400),LFC(80)
C*****PARAMETERS
       READ(5,100)NCH,NLOOPS
100    FORMAT(2I2)
       READ(5,200)(LFA(J),J=1,NCH)
200    FORMAT(80A1)
C*****PARAMETERS
       IM=NCH*3
       NCOL=80
       NCOM=NCOL+1
       NCOK=NCOL-1
       DO 250 I=1,IM
250    LFA(NCH+I)=LFA(I)
       LL=0
       DO 750 M=1,NLOOPS
C      RIPPLE PUNCH
       N=NCOK
       DO 275 I=1,NCH
       N=N+1
275    WRITE(7,200)(LFA(J),J=I,N)
       N=N+1
       DO 277 I=1,NCH
       N=N-1
       NN=NCH+1-I
277    WRITE(7,200)(LFA(J),J=NN,N)
C      FULL CARD EACH CHARACTER
       DO 355 J=1,NCH
       DO 400 I=1,NCOL
400    LFC(I)=LFA(J)
355    WRITE(7,200)(LFC(N),N=1,NCOL)
C      EACH CHARA. IN LAST THEN FIRST COLUMN REMAINDER BLANK
       DO 450 I=1,NCH
450    WRITE(7,451) LFA(I)
```

```
  451 FORMAT(79X,1A1)
      DO 460 I=1,NCH
  460 WRITE(7,461) LFA(I)
  461 FORMAT(1A1,79X)
C     FULL CARD EACH CHARA. ODD THEN EVEN COLUMNS
      NT=NCOL/2
      DO 480 J=1,NCH
      DO 470 I=1,NT
  470 LFC(I)=LFA(J)
      WRITE(7,481)(LFC(N),N=1,NT)
  481 FORMAT(40(1A1,1X))
  480 WRITE(7,482)(LFC(N),N=1,NT)
  482 FORMAT(40(1X,1A1))
C     DECREASING THEN INCREASING RIPPLE
      DO 500 I=1,NCOL
  500 WRITE(7,200)(LFA(J),J=I,NCOL)
      NM=NCOM
      DO 501 I=1,NCOL
      NM=NM-1
  501 WRITE(7,200)(LFA(J),J=NM,NCOL)
  750 LL=LL+1
      LM=LL*(2*NCOL+7*NCH)
      WRITE(6,800)(LFA(I),I=1,NCH)
  800 FORMAT(1H1,10HPUNCH TEST//15H DATA INPUT WAS//
     11X,80A1)
      WRITE(6,900)LM
  900 FORMAT(I10,14H CARDS PUNCHED)
      STOP
      END
```

FOCR00 CARD READER TEST

To Test

Card readers—cards are punched by FOCP00 card punch test. The program is useful for testing card readers on remote batch terminals.

Source

R. Longbottom, CCA (based on card reader/punch tests used by various computer suppliers).

Description

The program regenerates the patterns produced by the card punch test.

Routine 1: Ripple punch.

Routine 2: Full card of each character.

Routine 3: Each character in last column, then first column, remainder blank.

Routine 4: Full card of each character in odd and even columns.

Routine 5: Decreasing then increasing ripple.

The regenerated patterns are compared with the data read from the cards in subroutine RDCK and a print out is given of any miscompares of the form:

```
CARD 2
SHOULD BE   BCDEFGH ----etc
WAS         CDEFGH ----etc.
```

The most usual reasons for failure indications in a card reader test (more usual than machine faults) are cards transposed, blank cards in the pack, missing cards or extra cards with spurious data. For each of the foregoing an attempt is made at recovery. With transposed cards, the comparison failure print outs indicate the reason. After a miscompare a check is made to see if the card is blank and if it is the following is printed, e.g.

CARD NO 550 BLANK IGNORED

The next card is then read and compared with the same pattern. If a card is missing or extra cards are in the pack, failure messages are reported until the end of routine 1, then others printed out without a comparison being made, preceded by:

TOO MANY ERRORS FOLLOWING CARDS READ NOT CHECKED

An attempt is made to re-establish the correct sequence and if successful indicates:

CARRY ON READING AND CHECKING

At the end of each batch the number of cards read and errors are printed: e.g.

CARDS READ 601 0 ERRORS

After all batches have been read the following is printed:

END OF TEST

If any errors were detected during the last batch, the program attempts to read a further 1000 cards, preceded by the print out:

EXTRA CARDS FOLLOW

Any extra cards are then printed

Variables

The variables are read from two data cards—same as card punch test.

Data card 1:
columns

1–2 NCH number of characters in character set read from data card 2

3–4 NLOOPS number of times all sections repeated

5 IBLK this is read as a standard 'blank column'.

Data card 2: Starting in column 1, all characters in character set, number specified by NCH. If this card is not available, the first card of the following data cards can be reproduced and used in its place - the first NCH characters will be read.

Following data cards, the number of batches is specified by NLOOPS.

Timing

The timing can be estimated as reading time + CPU time. The reading time can be estimated from the number of cards to be read and the specified reading speed. The CPU time is approximately proportional to the number of cards read and 600 cards on a CPU of speed 1000 KIPS requires approximately 20 seconds CPU time.

Modifications to run on Different Systems

It should be ensured that the card punch does not generate a sequence of characters which cause false termination, for example, for end of file (e.g. ******) or job control (e.g. //). These are usually produced in routine 2. In the event of an unknown pack of cards being read (see data card 2 above) the offending cards can be replaced with a card containing e.g. THIS IS A DELIBERATE ERROR.

Program Listing FOCR00

```
C     CARD READER TEST
      COMMON LSB,IBLK,ICD,IERR,NCOL
      DIMENSION LFA(400),LSB(81)
      DIMENSION LCK(80)
C*****PARAMETERS
      READ(5,100)NCH,NLOOPS,IBLK
100   FORMAT(2I2,1A1)
      READ(5,200)(LFA(J),J=1,NCH)
200   FORMAT(80A1)
C*****PARAMETERS
```

```
  201 FORMAT(1X,80A1)
      IM=NCH*3
      NCOL=80
      NCOM=NCOL+1
      NCOK=NCOL-1
      DO 250 I=1,IM
  250 LFA(NCH+I)=LFA(I)
      WRITE(6,255)
  255 FORMAT(1H1,11HREADER TEST)
      DO 750 M=1,NLOOPS
      ICD=0
      IERR=0
C     RIPPLE READ
      DO 275 I=1,NCH
      ICD=ICD+1
      DO 274 J=1,NCOL
  274 LSB(J)=LFA(I+J-1)
      CALL RDCK
  275 CONTINUE
      DO 277 I=1,NCH
      ICD=ICD+1
      DO 276 J=1,NCOL
  276 LSB(J)=LFA(NCH+J-1)
      CALL RDCK
  277 CONTINUE
C     OUT OF SEQUENCE RECOVERY
      IF(IERR+5-2*NCH)399,300,300
  300 WRITE(6,301)
  301 FORMAT(26H TOO MANY ERRORS FOLLOWING,
     123H CARDS READ NOT CHECKED)
      DO 305 I=1,NCOL,2
      LSB(I)=IBLK
  305 LSB(I+1)=LFA(NCH)
      NN=1001
  306 DO 310 I=1,NN
      READ(5,200)(LCK(J),J=1,NCOL)
      WRITE(6,201)(LCK(J),J=1,NCOL)
      ICD=ICD+1
      DO 320 J=1,NCOL
      IF(LCK(J)-LSB(J))310,320,310
  320 CONTINUE
      GO TO 321
  310 CONTINUE
  321 IF(NN-1001)323,322,323
  322 NN=2*NCOL
      GO TO 306
  323 WRITE(6,333)
  333 FORMAT(30H CARRY ON READING AND CHECKING)
      GO TO 749
  399 CONTINUE
C     FULL CARD EACH CHARACTER
      DO 355 J=1,NCH
      ICD=ICD+1
      DO 400 I=1,NCOL
  400 LSB(I)=LFA(J)
      CALL RDCK
  355 CONTINUE
C     79 BLANKS EACH CHARA IN LAST OR FIRST COLUMN
      DO 450 I=1,NCH
      ICD=ICD+1
      DO 449 J=1,NCOK
  449 LSB(J)=IBLK
      LSB(NCOL)=LFA(I)
      CALL RDCK
```

```
 450 CONTINUE
     DO 460 I=1,NCH
     ICD=ICD+1
     LSB(1)=LFA(I)
     DO 459 J=2,NCOL
 459 LSB(J)=IBLK
     CALL RDCK
 460 CONTINUE
C    FULL CARD EACH CHARA ODD THEN EVEN COLUMNS
     DO 480 I=1,NCH
     ICD=ICD+1
     DO 478 J=1,NCOL,2
     LSB(J)=LFA(I)
 478 LSB(J+1)=IBLK
     CALL RDCK
     ICD=ICD+1
     DO 479 J=1,NCOL,2
     LSB(J)=IBLK
 479 LSB(J+1)=LFA(I)
     CALL RDCK
 480 CONTINUE
C    DECREASING THEN INCREASING RIPPLE
     DO 500 I=1,NCOL
     ICD=ICD+1
     NN=NCOM-1
     DO 498 J=1,NN
 498 LSB(J)=LFA(I+J-1)
     NM=NN+1
     DO 499 J=NM,NCOM
 499 LSB(J)=IBLK
     CALL RDCK
 500 CONTINUE
     DO 501 I=1,NCOL
     ICD=ICD+1
     NN=NCOM-I
     DO 503 J=1,I
 503 LSB(J)=LFA(J+NN-1)
     NM=I+1
     DO 550 J=NM,NCOM
 550 LSB(J)=IBLK
     CALL RDCK
 501 CONTINUE
 749 CONTINUE
     WRITE(6,810)ICD,IERR
 810 FORMAT(I6,11H CARDS READ,I6,7H ERRORS)
 750 CONTINUE
     WRITE(6,772)
 772 FORMAT(///12H END OF TEST)
     IF(IERR)770,770,771
 771 WRITE(6,773)
 773 FORMAT(///19H EXTRA CARDS FOLLOW///)
     DO 775 I=1,1000
     READ(5,200)(LSB(J),J=1,NCOL)
 775 WRITE(6,201)(LSB(J),J=1,NCOL)
 770 STOP
     END


     SUBROUTINE RDCK
C    READ CARD AND CHECK
     COMMON LSB,IBLK,ICD,IERR,NCOL
     DIMENSION LIS(80),LSB(81)
 100 READ(5,200)(LIS(I),I=1,NCOL)
 200 FORMAT(80A1)
     DO 300 J=1,NCOL
```

```
     IF(LSB(J)−LIS(J))997,300,997
300  CONTINUE
     GO TO 400
997  DO 350 J=1,NCOL
     IF(LIS(J)−IBLK)999,350,999
350  CONTINUE
993  WRITE(6,992) ICD
992  FORMAT(12H CARD NUMBER,I6,14H BLANK IGNORED)
     ICD=ICD+1
     GO TO 100
999  WRITE(6,998)ICD,(LSB(I),I=1,NCOL)
998  FORMAT(5H CARD,I6/10H SHOULD BE,2X,80A1)
     WRITE(6,888)(LIS(I),I=1,NCOL)
888  FORMAT(4H WAS,8X,80A1)
     IERR=IERR+1
400  RETURN
     END
```

FOTP00 PAPER TAPE PUNCH TEST

To Test

Paper tape punches—the tape is read by FOTR00 paper tape reader test.

Source

R. Longbottom, CCA (based on card reader/punch test).

Description

The program generates various patterns of characters, using four routines and outputs them to the paper tape punch (Unit 7).

Preface　　This reads the variable parameters from two data cards (or a data tape) and fills an array in preparation for punching. The parameters are also output to the paper tape punch.

Routine 1: Ripple punch (see FOLP00 wallpaper pattern) 80 character blocks.

Routine 2: 80 character block of each character.

Routine 3: 1 character block of each character.

Routine 4: Decreasing then increasing ripple, variable block length between 80 to 1 to 80 characters.

292

Variables

The variables are read from two data cards.

Data card 1:
    columns
        1–2 NCH number of characters in character set read from data card 2
        3–4 NLOOPS number of times all sections to be repeated
        5 IBLK space character or blank on card.

Data card 2: all characters in character set, number specified by NCH. (see restrictions given under 'Modifications to run on different systems').

Timing

The timing can be estimated as punching speed + CPU time. The approximate punching time can be derived from the rated punch speed and the total characters punched—NLOOPS (241.NCH + 6480)—e.g. 21904 for a 64 character set. The CPU time is roughly proportional to the characters punched and 22000 characters punched on a CPU of speed 1000 KIPS requires approximately 4 seconds CPU time.

Modifications to run on Different Systems

There may be some restriction on the sequence of characters that can be read, for example, end of file (e.g. ******) or job control (e.g. //). These are usually punched in routine 2: the offending character should be omitted from the character set.

Program Listing FOTP00

```
C       PUNCH TEST
        DIMENSION LFA(400),LFC(80)
C*****PARAMETERS
        READ(5,100)NCH,NLOOPS,IBLK
    100 FORMAT(2I2,1A1)
        WRITE(7,100)NCH,NLOOPS,IBLK
        READ(5,200)(LFA(J),J=1,NCH)
    200 FORMAT(80A1)
        WRITE(7,200)(LFA(J),J=1,NCH)
C*****PARAMETERS
        IM=NCH*3
        NCOL=80
        NCOM=NCOL+1
        NCOK=NCOL-1
        DO 250 I=1,IM
    250 LFA(NCH+I)=LFA(I)
        LL=0
        DO 750 M=1,NLOOPS
```

```
C       RIPPLE PUNCH
        N=NCOK
        DO 275 I=1,NCH
        N=N+1
  275   WRITE(7,200)(LFA(J),J=I,N)
        N=N+1
        DO 277 I=1,NCH
        N=N-1
        NN=NCH+1-I
  277   WRITE(7,200)(LFA(J),J=NN,N)
C       80 CHARA BLOCK OF EACH CHARA
        DO 355 J=1,NCH
        DO 400 I=1,NCOL
  400   LFC(I)=LFA(J)
  355   WRITE(7,200)(LFC(N),N=1,NCOL)
C       1 CHARA BLOCKS OF EACH CHARA
        DO 450 I=1,NCH
  450   WRITE(7,451) LFA(I)
  451   FORMAT(1A1)
C       DECREASING THEN INCREASING RIPPLE
        DO 500 I=1,NCOL
  500   WRITE(7,200)(LFA(J),J=I,NCOL)
        NM=NCOM
        DO 501 I=1,NCOL
        NM=NM-1
  501   WRITE(7,200)(LFA(J),J=NM,NCOL)
  750   LL=LL+1
        LM=LL*(2*NCOL+4*NCH)
        WRITE(6,800)(LFA(I),I=1,NCH)
  800   FORMAT(1H1,10HPUNCH TEST//15H DATA INPUT WAS//1X,80A1)
        WRITE(6,900)LM
  900   FORMAT(I10,15H BLOCKS PUNCHED)
        STOP
        END
```

FOTR00 PAPER TAPE READER TEST

To Test

Paper tape readers—the tape is punched by FOTP00 paper tape punch test.

Source

R. Longbottom, CCA (based on card reader/punch tests).

Description

The program regenerates the patterns produced by the tape punch test and checks them against the data read from the tape (Unit 4).

Routine 1: Ripple punch.

Routine 2: 80 character blocks of each character.

Routine 3: 1 character blocks of each character.

Routine 4: Decreasing then increasing ripple.

Reading Subroutine: Compares the tape read with the expected pattern and in the event of miscompare, gives the following print out, e.g.

> BLOCK 17
> SHOULD BE ABCDEF
> WAS   BBCDEF

At the end of each pass of the program an indication is given of the number of blocks read and the number of errors.

Variables

The variables used are the same as the paper tape punch test and should be punched by the punch test at the beginning of the tape.

Block 1:

    characters

    1–2 NCH number of characters in character set read from block 2

    3–4 NLOOPS number of times program repeated

    5 IBLK space character

Block 2: All characters in character set, number specified in NCH. (This should be identical to the first NCH characters of the first block to be read from the remaining tapes.)

Following data tapes, the number of times all routines are repeated are specified by NLOOPS.

Timing

The timing can be estimated as reading time + CPU time. The approximate reading time can be derived from the total characters read and rated speed of the reader, but stop/start time may have to be taken into account if the tape is read on-line with the program (this gives a better reader test). The total characters read is approximately NLOOPS (241.NCH + 6480) - e.g. 21904 for a 64 character set. The CPU time is roughly proportional to the characters read and 22000 read on a CPU of speed 1000 KIPS requires approximately 15 seconds CPU time.

Modifications to run on Different Systems

There may be some restrictions in the sequence of characters that can be read (see program FOTP00).

Program Listing FOTR00

```
C       PAPER TAPE READER TEST
        DIMENSION LFA(400),LSB(81)
        COMMON LSB,IBLK,ICD,IERR,NCOL
C*****PARAMETERS
        READ(4,100)NCH,NLOOPS,IBLK
100  FORMAT(2I2,1A1)
        READ(4,200)(LFA(J),J=1,NCH)
200  FORMAT(80A1)
C*****PARAMETERS
201  FORMAT(1X,80A1)
        IM=NCH*3
        NCOL=80
        NCOM=NCOL+1
        DO 250 I=1,IM
250  LFA(NCH+I)=LFA(I)
        WRITE(6,255)
255  FORMAT(1H1,11HREADER TEST)
        DO 750 M=1,NLOOPS
        ICD=0
        IERR=0
C       RIPPLE READ
        DO 275 I=1,NCH
        ICD=ICD+1
        DO 274 J=1,NCOL
274  LSB(J)=LFA(I+J-1)
        CALL RDCK
275  CONTINUE
        DO 277 I=1,NCH
        ICD=ICD+1
        DO 276 J=1,NCOL
276  LSB(J)=LFA(NCH+J-I)
        CALL RDCK
277  CONTINUE
C       80 CHARA BLOCK OF EACH CHARACTER
        DO 355 J=1,NCH
        ICD=ICD+1
        DO 400 I=1,NCOL
400  LSB(I)=LFA(J)
        CALL RDCK
355  CONTINUE
C       1 CHARA BLOCK OF EACH CHARA
        DO 460 I=1,NCH
        ICD=ICD+1
        LSB(1)=LFA(I)
        DO 459 J=2,NCOL
459  LSB(J)=IBLK
        CALL RDCK
460  CONTINUE
C       DECREASING THEN INCREASING RIPPLE
        DO 500 I=1,NCOL
        ICD=ICD+1
        NN=NCOM-I
        DO 498 J=1,NN
```

L

```
498 LSB(J)=LFA(I+J−1)
    NM=NN+1
    DO 499 J=NM,NCOM
499 LSB(J)=IBLK
    CALL RDCK
500 CONTINUE
    DO 501 I=1,NCOL
    ICD=ICD+1
    NN=NCOM−I
    DO 503 J=1,I
503 LSB(J)=LFA(J+NN−1)
    NM=I+1
    DO 550 J=NM,NCOM
550 LSB(J)=IBLK
    CALL RDCK
501 CONTINUE
    WRITE(6,810)ICD,IERR
810 FORMAT(I6,12H BLOCKS READ,I6,7H ERRORS)
750 CONTINUE
    WRITE(6,772)
772 FORMAT(///12H END OF TEST)
770 STOP
    END


    SUBROUTINE RDCK
C   READ BLOCK AND CHECK
    DIMENSION LIS(80),LSB(81)
    COMMON LSB,IBLK,ICD,IERR,NCOL
    DO 50 J=1,NCOL
 50 LIS(J)=IBLK
100 READ(4,200)(LIS(I),I=1,NCOL)
200 FORMAT(80A1)
    DO 300 J=1,NCOL
    IF(LSB(J).NE.LIS(J)) GO TO 997
300 CONTINUE
    GO TO 400
997 WRITE(6,998)ICD,(LSB(I),I=1,NCOL)
998 FORMAT(6H BLOCK,I6/10H SHOULD BE,2X,80A1)
    WRITE(6,888)(LIS(I),I=1,NCOL)
888 FORMAT(4H WAS,8X,80A1)
    IERR=IERR+1
400 RETURN
    END
```

Appendix 2

Serviceability Calculations for Complex Systems Using a Programmable Calculator

Chapter 12 showed a method of calculating serviceability of subsystems and systems, including those where standby units are available. The program described provides an easy method of carrying out the calculations and can embrace the weighting factor serviceability scheme. The program listing given is for a Texas SR52 calculator but a flow chart is also included so that the program can be converted to run on other programmable calculators.

BASIC THEORY

The Binomial distribution is used for calculating the serviceability of units in parallel:

$$(S + U)^N$$

where N is the number of units,
S is serviceability or probability of a unit working,
U is unserviceability or probability of a unit not working.

The probability of exactly Y units working or $N-Y$ not working is:

$$S(Y) = \frac{N!}{Y!(N - Y)!} \, S^Y U^{N-Y}$$

WEIGHTING FACTORS

Using a weighting factor scheme, rather than ignoring the down time, when units are out of service and work continues, but at a lower throughput rate, the down time is multiplied by the weighting factor W. So:

Down time $= $ Time $\times W$ and
Serviceable time $=$ Time $\times (1-W)$

For the serviceability predictions the effective serviceability is:

$$S(Y) \times (1-W)$$

OPERATION

The SR52 calculator has a number of user defined keys, seven of which are used in the program:

A	to enter data value for N	Step 1
B	to enter data value for S	Step 2
C	to enter data value for W (or 0)	Step 3A
D	to enter data value for Y	Step 4A or 3B
D'	to calculate $S(Y)$ single step operation*	Step 5A
E'	to display $S(N \to Y)$ total, full display	Step 6A or 5B
E	to calculate $S(N \to Y)$ total, looped calculation*	Step 4B

For single step calculations, without weighting factors, enter N and S (and $W = 0$ if W has been set to any other value). Then enter Y and calculate $S(Y)$ for each value $Y = N, N - 1, N - 2$ etc in turn. The total S can be displayed after each step, if required. For weighting factor calculations enter N and S. Then enter W and Y and calculate $S(Y)$ for each value of $Y = N, N - 1, N - 2$ etc in turn (also total S after each step, if required). For looped calculations enter N, S and Y then press key E to calculate $S(N) + S(N - 1) + S(N - 2) + \text{----} S(Y)$.

*These displays are of the form

NNYYS.SSSSS

or   NYYS.SSSSSS   where N is less than 10

or $\begin{cases} NNYY0 \\ NYY0 \end{cases}$ where S is a very low value

or $\begin{cases} NNYY1 \\ NYY1 \end{cases}$ where S is 1.0 or just under

The full 10 digits of $S(Y)$ can be obtained from register 12 and $S(N \to Y)$ total by pressing E'.

Weighting factor calculations can only be carried out in the single step mode and any calculated using a weighting factor of 1.0 are ignored. The value of $S(Y)$ when $W = 1$ can be obtained by using $W = 0$, but $S(N \to Y)$ total is then invalid.

TIMING

To calculate any 2 from 3 (or 9 out of 10 etc) in the looped mode takes about 4 seconds, 15 out of 30 takes 30 seconds and 25 out of 50 takes about 50 seconds. It should be noted that the latter calculation is the equivalent of over 1000 key depressions.

UNITS IN SERIES

The program uses 10 of the 20 registers available in the calculations (01–10 not used).

The spare registers can be used for storing the results and in other calculations for including recovery factors or for series network calculations.

FLOWCHART

Enter Data

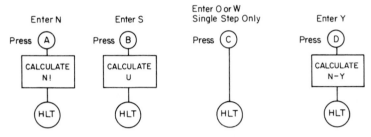

Single Step Calculations

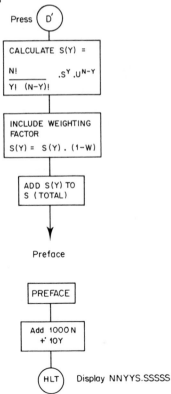

Display Total Serviceability

Press $\boxed{E'}$

$\boxed{HLT}$ Display S (N $\longrightarrow$ Y) total

Calculate S(N) $\rightarrow$ S(Y)

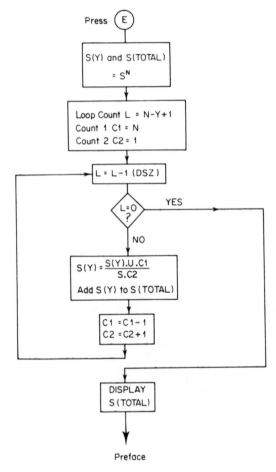

Press (E)

S(Y) and S(TOTAL)

$= S^N$

Loop Count L = N-Y+1
Count 1 C1 = N
Count 2 C2 = 1

L = L-1 (DSZ)

L=O
?

YES

NO

$S(Y) = \dfrac{S(Y).U.C1}{S.C2}$

Add S(Y) to S(TOTAL)

C1 = C1-1
C2 = C2+1

DISPLAY
S(TOTAL)

Preface

LISTING

Loc.	Code	Key	Comments	Loc.	Code	Key	Comments
000	46	LBL	Enter N	032	81	HLT	
	11	A			46	LBL	Enter Y
	42	STO			14	D	
	01	1		035	42	STO	
	09	9			01	1	
005	29	X!			04	4	
	42	STO			75	−	
	01	1			43	RCL	
	08	8		040	01	1	
	00	0			09	9	
010	42	STO			95	=	
	01	1			94	+/−	
	01	1			42	STO	
	81	HLT		045	01	1	
	46	LBL	Enter S		03	3	
015	12	B			81	HLT	
	42	STO			46	LBL	Calc.S(Y)
	01	1			19	D'	Single
	07	7		050	43	RCL	
	75	−			01	1	
020	01	1			08	8	
	95	=			55	÷	
	94	+/−			43	RCL	
	42	STO		055	01	1	
	01	1			04	4	
025	06	6			29	X!	
	81	HLT			55	÷	
	46	LBL	Enter W		43	RCL	
	13	C		060	01	1	
	42	STO			03	3	
030	01	1			29	X!	
	05	5			65	×	

Loc.	Code	Key	Comments	Loc.	Code	Key	Comments
	43	RCL		097	01	1	
065	01	1			46	LBL	Add
	07	7			16	A'	Preface
	45	Y^X		100	85	+	
	43	RCL			43	RCL	
	01	1			01	1	
070	04	4			09	9	
	65	×			65	×	
	43	RCL		105	01	1	
	01	1			00	0	
	06	6			00	0	
075	45	Y^X			00	0	
	43	RCL			85	+	
	01	1		110	43	RCL	
	03	3			01	1	
	95	=			04	4	
080	42	STO			65	×	
	01	1			01	1	
	02	2		115	00	0	
	65	×	Include		95	=	
	43	RCL	Weighting		81	HLT	
085	01	1	Factor		46	LBL	Display
	05	5			10	E'	Sum S
	95	=		120	43	RCL	
	22	INV			01	1	
	44	SUM			01	1	
090	01	1			81	HLT	
	02	2			46	LBL	Calc.Sum
	43	RCL		125	15	E	S Looped
	01	1			43	RCL	
	02	2			01	1	
095	44	SUM			07	7	
	01	1					

Loc.	Code	Key	Comments	Loc.	Code	Key	Comments
	45	X^Y		161	01	1	
130	43	RCL			03	3	
	01	1			46	LBL	
	09	9			88	2'	
	95	=		165	22	INV	
	42	STO			58	DSZ	
135	01	1			87	1'	
	02	2			43	RCL	
	42	STO			01	1	
	01	1		170	02	2	
	01	1			55	÷	
140	43	RCL			43	RCL	
	01	1			01	1	
	09	9			07	7	
	75	−		175	65	×	
	43	RCL			43	RCL	
145	01	1			01	1	
	04	4			06	6	
	85	+			65	×	
	01	1		180	43	RCL	
	95	=			01	1	
150	42	STO			04	4	
	00	0			55	÷	
	00	0			43	RCL	
	43	RCL		185	01	1	
	01	1			03	3	
155	09	9			95	=	
	42	STO			42	STO	
	01	1			01	1	
	04	4		190	02	2	
	01	1			44	SUM	
160	42	STO			01	1	

Loc.	Code	Key	Comments
193	01	1	
	01	1	
195	22	INV	
	44	SUM	
	01	1	
	04	4	
	44	SUM	
200	01	1	
	03	3	
	41	GTO	
	88	2′	
	46	LBL	
205	87	1′	
	43	RCL	
	01	1	
	01	1	
	16	A′	
210	81	HLT	

REGISTERS

00	LOOP COUNT
11	TOTAL S
12	S(Y)
13	N–Y
14	Y
15	W
16	U
17	S
18	N!
19	N

Appendix 3

Estimating Processor Speed

Various graphs in the book provide details of reliability relative to processor speed. Unfortunately, processor speed depends very much on the application and mix of instructions used, but the speeds given are intended to represent an average for business and scientific applications. For medium/large mainframes, the suppliers may provide a figure similar to those used with the actual examples of reliability but, in other cases, claimed speeds could lead to the wrong reliability figures being used.

On small, mini or micro processors, floating point hardware may not be provided so speed claims for business applications could indicate too low a level of reliability expectation: on the other hand, estimations including speeds using software based floating point operations could give far too low a speed in relation to processor construction and associated high levels of reliability expectations. Where difficulties are experienced, a reasonable estimate can be made by using the total time (T) in microseconds for the following instructions

No of instructions	Type
40	Fixed point add—store to accumulator or store to store, whichever is lower.
35	Branch on condition or state of accumulator.
20	Transfer 8 bytes using transfer, move or load and store instructions.
5	Floating point add—operation as fixed point add. Where floating point is carried out by software or is not available use 20 times the fixed point add.

The speed in kilo instructions per second (KIPS) is:

$$\frac{100,000}{T}$$

305

At the top end of the market, processors are being introduced with capabilities for vector and array processing, where the new techniques may not lead to an increase in component count relative to the speed achieved on these operations. In these cases, the scalar speed, that is for serial rather than parallel operations, should, be used multiplied in proportion to extra components provided.

Index

Accelerated testing, 39
Acceptance trials, 160
  alternatives, 176
  benchmarks, 166
  CCA procedures, 166
  compatibility testing, 166, 167
  configuration, 165
  contractor's responsibility, 165
  contractor's risks, 161
  contracts, 165
  criteria of success, 167, 168, 171, 177
  duration, 167, 168, 170, 177
  economics, 165
  effectiveness, 172
  engineering tests, 169
  facilities testing, 164
  factory, 167
  GSA procedures, 177
  performance measurement, 164, 166, 168
  records, 165, 172
  reliability considerations, 166
  results, 172
  software, 168
  speed testing, 164, 166, 168
  standard programs, 170, 238
  supervision, 166, 171
  system exercising, 169
  testing schedule, 172
  user programs, 168, 169
  user's responsibility, 165
  user's risks, 161
Accepted errors, software, 76
Acclimatization of media, 52, 53
Accommodation, 25, 44
Age, reliability effects, 1, 13, 182
Air conditioning, 44
  card punches, 53
  card readers, 53
  cost of, 66
  determining the need for, 62, 200
  disk packs, 52
  dust, 65
  equipment design specifications, 46
  exchangeable disks, 52
  filtration, 46, 65
  line printers, 53
  magnetic tape units, 52
  microprocessors, 47
  mini computers, 46, 47
  paper tape equipment, 53
  peripheral equipment, 48, 50
  processors, 47
  relative humidity effects, 20, 44, 64
  relative humidity specifications, 45
  room conditions, 45
  switched-off conditions, 45
  temperature effects, 20, 44, 58, 62
  temperature specifications, 45
  visual display units, 48
Air dehumidification, 65
Air filtration, 46
Air humidification, 64
Air pollution, 20
Alpha particles, 43
Alternate path retry, 154
Analysis of faults, 7, 41, 73
Architectural considerations, 185
Assembler faults, 103
Atmospheric pollution, 20
Attempts to repair, 7
Availability ratio, 119
  peripheral equipment, 210

Background heaters, 65
Backlog, software errors, 80
Bathtub curve, 1
Bedding-in, 1

Benchmarks, 166
Binomial distribution, 212, 297
Bit slicing, 145
Buffer store reconfiguration, 154
Burn-in, 1, 13, 182
  accelerated, 39

Cache reconfiguration, 154
Cannibalization, 22
Capacity effects, 196
Card punch,
  air conditioning requirements, 53
  down time per incident, 198
  error rate, 98
  fault symptoms, 102
  incident rate, 198
  investigation rate, 198
  investigation time, 198
  test program, 283
  undetected errors, 96
  utilization, 96
  waiting time, 198
Card reader,
  air conditioning
    requirements, 53
  availability, 210
  down time per incident, 198
  error rate, 98
  example of predictions, 220
  fault symptoms, 102
  heat dissipation, 60
  incident rate, 198
  investigation rate, 198
  investigation time, 198
  scheduled maintenance time, 118,
    210
  test program, 286
  undetected errors, 96
  utilization, 96
  waiting time, 198
CCA acceptance trials, 166
  advantages/disadvantages, 176
  criteria of success, 167, 168, 171
  cyclic testing, 169, 174
  demonstrations, 167, 174
  duration, 167, 168, 170
  extended testing, 177
  procedures, 166
  records, 172
  results, 172
  standard programs, 170, 238
  supervision, 171
  testing schedules, 172
CCA organization, 166

CCA standard contract, 166
Central processing unit,
  air conditioning requirements, 47
  cooling, 58
  down time per incident, 112, 192
  examples of predictions, 183, 188,
    200, 208, 217
  fault rate, 27, 58
  fault symptoms, 99
  heat dissipation, 54
  incident rate, 58, 190
  integrated circuit count, 186
  investigation rate, 180
  investigation time, 107, 188
  maintainability, 113, 138, 142, 144,
    149
  modifications, 32
  modifications, fitting time, 117
  modularity, 144
  number of integrated circuits, 186
  parity checking, 150
  practical predictions, 190
  reconfiguration, 154
  reliability, 27, 58, 190
  reliability prediction, 2, 179
  reliability testing, 162
  scheduled maintenance, 117
  serviceability, 217
  space requirements, 56
  speed calculations, 305
  speed testing, 164
  store prediction, 192
  system serviceability, 216
  test programs, 239, 241, 245, 247,
    249
  testing, 39, 134, 170, 238
  undetected errors, 92
  waiting time, 112, 191
  wrong results, 92
Channels,
  down time per incident, 191
  example of predictions, 217
  incident rate, 191
  investigation rate, 30
Circuit board,
  destruction, 143
  maintainability, 143
  repairs, 143
  serial numbers, 43
  testers, 142
  testing, 39
Clock margins, 149
Coding errors, 71
Collection of statistics, 41

Comfort of staff, 63
Commissioning, 19, 160
Communication processors, 30, 187
Communications subsystems, 229
Compatibility of peripherals, 141, 175
Compatibility test programs, 141
Compiler faults, 102
Complex system prediction, 211
Complexity, software, 72
Complexity factor, 2, 179
Component,
  count, 2
  design weaknesses, 147
  destruction, 64
  failures, 7
  loading, 26
  mtbf, 8, 120
  quality, 27
  selection, 26, 37
  sourcing, 37
Computer system,
  air conditioning requirements, 44
  down time, 115
  examples of predictions, 200, 216
  heat dissipation, 54, 60
  incident rate, 222
  reliability specification, 209
  serviceability calculations, 215
  space requirements, 54
  testing, 40, 160, 238
  undetected errors, 97
Condensation, 65
Confidence limits of,
  down time, 109
  incidents, 158, 163
  investigations, 158
  random faults, 162
  serviceability, 129
Configuration,
  minimum, 122
  representation, 222
Console facilities, 153
Constant failure rate, 1
Constructional effects, 21
Constructional modularity, 144
Contamination, 20
Contracts,
  acceptance trials, 165, 166
  CCA, 166
  maintenance, 155
  reliability specification, 209
  software services, 90
Cooling, 58
Core stores,

down time per incident, 192
error correction, 151, 192
examples of predictions, 200, 217
incident rate, 192
investigation rate, 183
investigation time, 189
maintainability, 144
modularity, 144
parity checking, 151
practical predictions, 192
test programs, 136, 241
utilization effects, 29
Corrective maintenance time, 107
Correctness of design, 71
Corrosion, 20
Corruption, data, 92
Cost of,
  air conditioning, 66
  maintenance, 24, 155
  spares, 90
Criteria for software reliability, 90
Criteria for testing, 41, 167, 168, 171, 177
Criteria for testing software, 79

Data buses, 30
Data corruption, 92
Dead on arrival, 39
Definition of,
  availability, 119
  down time, 105
  failures, 7
  maintainability, 133
  serviceability, 119
Dehumidification, 65
Delivery, 41
Design,
  automation, 34
  changes, 30, 117
  checks, 34
  correctness, 71
  defects, 6, 147, 182
  effects on reliability, 2, 15, 182
  errors, software, 71
  fault identification, 41
  freezing, 32
  improvement, 30
  procedures, 26
  qualification, 35
  qualification, software, 71
  specifications, 26, 31
  specifications, environmental, 46
  stabilization, 17
  tolerances, 26

Destruction of components, 64, 66
Destruction of modules, 143
Dew point, 65
Diagnosability, 133
Diagnosis, fault, 133
Diagnosis, remote, 156
Diagnostic processors, 142
Diagnostic test programs, 135
Diesel generator, 68
Direct memory access, 185
Disk,
  air conditioning requirements, 52
  availability 210
  compatibility, 141, 167
  controller, 30, 186
  down time per incident, 196
  error correction, 152
  error rate, 98
  example of prediction, 220
  fault symptoms, 99
  file directory, 155, 218
  hard failures, 100
  head crashes, 99
  heat dissipation, 54, 60
  incident rate, 194, 198
  investigation rate, 194, 198
  investigation time, 194, 198
  irrecoverable errors, 100
  packs, 52, 99
  recoverable errors, 100
  scheduled maintenance time, 118,
    210
  serviceability, 220
  soft failures, 100
  test programs, 137, 254, 259, 268,
    270
  testing, 170
  undetected errors, 95
  utilization, 95
  waiting time, 198
Disturbance effects, 20
Documentation changes, 34
Documentation errors, 76
Down time,
  distribution, 107
  effects on serviceability/availability,
    128
  hardware, 105
  per fault, 107
  per incident peripherals, 198
  per incident processors, 112, 192
  per incident software, 82, 115, 218
  per incident stores, 192
Drop shipment, 40

Drums, 198
Duration of testing, 37, 41, 167, 168,
  170, 177
  software, 78
Dust, 52, 65

Early failures, 1, 13, 182
  software, 85
Early production systems, 17
Earthing requirements, 69
ECL, 56
Effectiveness of,
  maintainability, 157
  scheduled maintenance, 20, 138
  testing, 35, 172, 175
  testing, software, 79
Electromagnetic radiation, 69
Engineering change order, 32
Engineering changes, 30, 147
  fitting procedures, 32
  fitting time, 117
Engineering test programs, 134
Enhancements, 24
Enquiry terminal, 234
Environment, 44
Environmental,
  chamber, 36
  effects, 2, 21, 58, 62, 179, 182
  requirements, 46
  testing, 36
Error,
  analysis, 92
  classifications, software, 72
  correction, 151, 192
  detection, 149
  log, 152
  log analysis, 42
  rates, lines, 229
  rates, peripherals, 98
  rates, software, 72, 78
  reports, software, 74
Estimation of processor speed, 305
Examples of predictions,
  air conditioning requirements, 200
  communications subsystems, 229
  complex systems, 211
  dual processor, 225
  hardware vs. software, 208
  mainframes, 200
  message switching system, 227
  microprocessor, 204
  mini computer, 200, 227
  multi-mini system, 227
  multiprocessor, 225

peripherals, 200, 220
processors, 183, 200, 208, 217
remote batch terminal, 233
serviceability, 216
software, 208
standby units, 22, 225
stores, 201, 217
systems, 216
terminals, 233
time sharing system, 235
transaction processing system, 234
units in parallel, 211
units in series, 212
Exchangeable disk unit,
air conditioning requirements, 52
availability, 210
compatibility, 141, 167
controller, 30, 186
down time per incident, 196
error correction, 152
error rate, 98
example of predictions, 220
fault symptoms, 99
hard failures, 100
head crashes, 99
heat dissipation, 54, 60
incident rate, 194, 198
investigation rate, 194, 198
investigation time, 194, 198
irrecoverable errors, 100
packs, 52, 99
recoverable errors, 100
scheduled maintenance time, 118,
   210
serviceability, 220
soft failures, 100
test programs, 137, 254, 259, 268,
   270
testing, 170
undetected errors, 95
utilization, 95
waiting time, 198
Exponential distribution, 9, 161
Extended investigations, 107

Facilities testing, 164
Factory tours, 35
Factory trials, 167
Failure,
analysis, 41
definition, 7
modes, 6
pattern, 136
rate, constant, 1

rate, integrated circuits, 5, 27
rate, theoretical, 2
trend analysis, 117
Failures,
random, 9
seen by the engineer, 7, 17, 107
seen by the user, 7, 18, 107, 189
system, 8
Fault,
analysis, 41
determination, software, 87
diagnosis, 133
not found, 7, 143
recording, 152
reproduction, 136
symptoms, 92
symptoms, software, 102
tolerance, 8, 133, 150
Faults,
intermittent, 7, 9, 95, 107, 134, 143,
   159, 175
solid, 7, 95, 107, 134, 143
transient, 7, 43, 134
Feedback, 41
Field change orders, 31, 117, 147
Field reliability, 180
File directories, 155, 218
File recovery time, 105
Floor resistance, 64
Floor space, 56
FORTRAN test programs, 238
Frequency tolerances, 66
Front-end processor, 187
Functional modularity, 144
Functional test programs, 135

General Services Administration trials,
   177
Goods inwards quality control, 38
Grounding, 69

Hard errors, 100
Hardware testers, 141
Hardware vs. software fault
   determination, 82, 99
Hardware vs. software reliability, 71, 87
Harmonic distortion, 66
Heat dissipation, 56
   maximum permissible, 62
High level language test programs, 238
History recording, 152
Humidification, 64

Incidents, 8
  per 1000 hours, peripherals, 194, 198
  per 1000 hours, processors, 190
  per 1000 hours, software, 206
  per 1000 hours, stores, 192
  per fault, 8, 58, 114, 151, 157
  per investigation, 113, 189
  short term effects, 157
Input/output processors, 185
Installation, 19, 160
  missing items, 41
  time, 160
Instruction retry, 150
Instructions,
  speed of operation, 305
  undetected error rate, 94
Integrated circuits,
  complexity, 28
  failure rate, 5, 27, 58
  heat dissipation, 56
  large scale integration, 43, 58, 147
  logic change rate, 31
  number in equipment, 27, 186
  plug-in, 148
  temperature range, 44
  testing, 38
  yield, 38
Integrity, 92, 133, 139, 150, 153
Interaction test programs, 138
Interactive system, 235
Intermittent faults, 7, 9, 95, 107, 134,
  143, 159, 175
  reproduction of, 152
Investigation rates,
  peripherals, 198
  processors, 7, 180
  stores, 183
Investigation times,
  distribution, 106
  peripherals, 112, 194, 198
  processors, 107, 188
  software, 82
  stores, 189
Investigations, short term effects, 158
Investigations per fault, 8, 109, 138,
  157

Kilo instructions per second assessment,
  305

Large scale integration, 43, 58, 147
Lifetime expectancy,
  electronics, 2, 20
  peripherals, 23

Limitations of testing, 6
Line printer,
  air conditioning requirements, 53
  availability, 210
  down time per incident, 198
  error rate, 97
  example of predictions, 220
  fault symptoms, 101
  heat dissipation, 60
  incident rate, 198
  investigation rate, 198
  investigation time, 198
  scheduled maintenance time, 118,
    210
  serviceability, 220
  test program, 275
  undetected errors, 97
  utilization, 97
  waiting time, 198
Line reliability, 229
Logical errors, 26, 71
Logic changes, 31, 34, 147
Lost time, 105
LSI, 43, 58, 147

Magnetic peripherals power supplies,
  66
Magnetic tape air conditioning
  specifications, 53
Magnetic tape unit,
  air conditioning requirements, 52
  availability, 210
  compatibility, 141, 167, 175
  controller, 186
  down time per incident, 198
  error rate, 98
  example of predictions, 220
  fault symptoms, 100
  hard failures, 101
  heat dissipation, 54, 60
  incident rate, 195, 198
  investigation rate, 195, 198
  investigation time, 195, 198
  irrecoverable errors, 100
  recoverable errors, 98
  scheduled maintenance time, 118,
    210
  serviceability, 220
  soft failures, 101
  tape wrecks, 100
  test programs, 137, 259, 268, 270
  testing, 170
  undetected errors, 95

utilization, 95
waiting time, 198
Main store,
down time per incident, 192
error correction, 151, 192
examples of predictions, 200, 217
incident rate, 192
investigation rate, 183
investigation time, 189
maintainability, 144
parity checking, 151
practical predictions, 192
reconfiguration, 154
test programs, 136, 241
testing, 39
utilization effects, 29
Mainframe,
reliability, 87
system serviceability, 216
vs. mini system, 227
Main supplies, 66
Maintainability, 133
down time, 107, 113
effects, 8, 181
effects, software, 205
measurement, 157
Maintainability of,
microprocessors, 147
mini computers, 144
modules, 143
peripheral equipment, 139
processors, 138, 142, 149
Maintenance,
contracts, 155
corrective, time, 107
costs, 24, 155
effectiveness, 20, 137
manpower levels, 156
manpower planning, 8, 159
on-call, 108
on-site, 107, 156
organization, 155
preventative, 117, 138, 210
resource planning, 8, 159
scheduled, 117, 138, 210
supplementary, 117
support, 113, 156
third party, 23
time, 105
Manufacturing, 38
defects, 13, 160
Margins, 148
clock, 149
temperature, 149

timing, 27, 149
voltage, 149
Mean down time per,
fault, 107
incident, 107, 189, 196
system failure, 115, 219
Mean investigation time, 107, 188, 198
Mean time between,
component failures, 7, 107
failures 2, 7
incidents, 7, 211
investigations, 7, 107
repeat incidents, 175
system failures, 7, 87, 107
Mean time to repair, 105
true, 107
Measurement of maintainability, 157
Measurement of reliability, 5
Mechanical changes, 34
Media acclimatization, 52, 53
Media problems, 44
Memory,
down time per incident, 192
error correction, 151, 192
examples of predictions, 200, 217
incident rate, 192
investigation rate, 183
investigation time, 189
maintainability, 144
parity checking, 151
practical predictions, 192
reconfiguration, 154
test programs, 136, 241
testing, 39
utilization effects, 29
Message switching systems, 227
Microprocessor,
air conditioning requirements, 47, 64,
181
board testing, 39
burn-in, 38
chip testing, 38
down time per incident, 190
example of predictions, 204
heat dissipation, 61
incident rate, 190
investigation rate, 181
investigation time, 189
maintainability, 147
number of integrated circuits, 28, 185
peripheral equipment, 56
practical predictions, 190
reliability, 28
software predictions, 205

space requirements, 61
testing, 39
waiting time, 189
Mil. handbook 217B, 2, 44, 179
Mini computer,
  air conditioning requirements, 46
  down time per incident, 191
  examples of predictions, 200, 227
  heat dissipation, 60
  incident rate, 190
  investigation rate, 180
  investigation time, 110, 188
  maintainability, 144
  modifications, 33
  modularity, 144
  number of integrated circuits, 28, 186
  parity checking, 93
  peripheral controllers, 187
  peripheral equipment, 56, 196, 197
  practical predictions, 190
  reliability, 28, 59
  reliability prediction, theoretical, 2
  reliability testing, 162
  scheduled maintenance, 117
  serviceability, 216
  software reliability, 206
  software sizes, 206
  space requirements, 61
  test programs, 136
  testing, 40
  undetected errors, 93
  vs. mainframe, 227
  waiting time, 113, 190
Minimum configuration, 122
Minimum room size, 54, 61
Modems, 232
Modifications, 30, 147
  fitting procedures, 32
  fitting time, 117
  rate, 31
  software, 72
  state, 24
Modularity, 144, 155
Module,
  destruction, 143
  maintainability, 143
  repairs, 143
  serial numbers, 43
  testers, 142
  testing, 39
Morning sickness, 69
MOS memories,
  down time per incident, 192
  error correction, 151, 192

incident rate, 29, 43, 192
investigation rate, 184
investigation time, 189
maintainability, 144
modularity, 144
practical predictions, 192
testing, 39
transient faults, 43, 152
utilization effects, 29
Motor alternators, 68
Motor generators, 68
Multi-mini system, 227
Multiprocessors, 154, 225
Multiprogramming, 121

New architecture, 32
New releases, software, 72, 78, 84, 86
New systems, 17
New technology, 21, 30, 43, 193
No break power supplies, 68
No fault found, 7, 143

On-call maintenance, 108
On-line test programs, 139
On-site maintenance, 107, 156
Operating system,
  acceptance trials, 164
  criteria for testing, 79
  data corruption, 103
  down time, 82, 115, 218
  duration of testing, 78
  early failures, 85
  effectiveness of testing, 79
  error reports, 74
  errors, short term effects, 159
  examples of predictions, 208, 218
  fault symptoms, 102
  hardware comparison, 87
  incident rate, 206
  investigation time, 82
  mean down time per system failure,
    116
  mean time between system failures,
    87
  new releases, 72, 78, 84, 86
  quality assurance, 71, 78
  quality effects, 207
  reliability criteria, 90
  reliability prediction, 204
  reloading time, 155
  serviceability, 81, 212, 218
  services contract, 90
  size, 206
  system down time, 82

system failures, 79, 82, 102, 206
testing, 71, 78, 168
unserviceability, 81
utilization effects, 86
variations with time, 83, 206
waiting time, 82
wrong results, 103
Operational down time, 106
Overhauls, 23, 117
Overheating, 44, 59, 62

Packaging, 41
Paper tape punch/reader,
air conditioning requirements, 53
down time per incident, 198
error rate, 98
fault symptoms, 102
heat dissipation, 60
incident rate, 198
investigation rate, 198
investigation time, 198
test programs, 291, 293
undetected errors, 96
utilization, 96
waiting time, 198
Parity checking, 150
Pattern sensitivity, 26, 29
Performance measurement, 164
Peripheral controller,
down time per incident, 191
example of predictions, 217
example of relative reliability, 188
incident rate, 190
investigation rate, 30, 187
investigation time, 189
number of integrated circuits, 186
Peripheral equipment,
air conditioning requirements, 52
availability, 210
compatibility, 141, 175
down time, 116
down time per incident, 198
error log, 153
error rate, 98
example of predictions, 220
exerciser, 141
fault symptoms, 99
heat dissipation, 60
incident rate, 198
investigation rate, 198
investigation time, 112, 198
life, 23
on-line testing, 139
reliability predictions, 5, 193, 198

scheduled maintenance, 118
serviceability, 220
spares, 23, 116
standby units, 115, 212
switches, 225
test programs, 137, 238
testing, 40, 137, 170
undetected errors, 95
utilization, 95
waiting time, 116, 196, 198
Peripheral multiplexor, 185, 190
Plug-in integrated circuits, 148
Poisson distribution, 10, 161
Pollution testing, 36
Population reliability, 16
Power fail safe, 68
Power supplies, 66
disconnections, 68
frequency specifications, 67
harmonic distortion, 67
reliability effects, 2, 68
transients, 67
voltage specifications, 67
Power supply unit,
heat dissipation, 57
modularity, 144
redundancy, 153
Practical calculations, 179, 211
Pre-delivery tests, 40, 167
Prediction of reliability, 2, 179, 211
Presentations by manufacturers, 35
Preventative maintenance,
effectiveness, 138
peripheral equipment, 210
time, 117
Printed circuit board,
destruction, 143
maintainability, 143
repairs, 143
serial numbers, 43
testers, 142
testing, 39
Printers, see Line printer, Typewriter
Priority, software errors, 80
Probability of failure, 9
Probability of working, 212
Problem analysis, 41
Problems identified, software, 76
Problems seen by the user, 7, 18, 107, 189
software, 74
Processor,
air conditioning requirements, 47
cooling, 58

down time per incident, 112, 192
examples of predictions, 183, 188,
   200, 208, 217
fault rate, 27, 58
fault symptoms, 99
heat dissipation, 54
incident rate, 58, 190
integrated circuit count, 186
investigation rate, 7, 180
investigation time, 107, 188
maintainability, 113, 138, 142, 144,
   149
modifications, 32
modifications, fitting time, 117
modularity, 144
number of integrated circuits, 186
parity checking, 150
practical predictions, 190
reconfiguration, 154
reliability, 27, 58, 190
reliability prediction, 2, 179
reliability testing, 162
scheduled maintenance, 117
serviceability, 217
space requirements, 56
speed calculations, 305
speed testing, 164
store prediction, 192
system serviceability, 216
test programs, 239, 241, 245, 247,
   249
testing, 39, 134, 170, 238
undetected errors, 92
waiting time, 112, 191
wrong results, 92
Program for serviceability calculations,
   297
Program restarts, 155
Programs, test, 134, 238
Prototype, 35
Punched cards,
  air conditioning requirements, 53
  problems, 64, 101

Quality, software, 71, 206
Quality assurance, 35
  software, 71, 78
Quality control, 15, 21, 35
Quality effects, 179, 181, 188
Quality of service, 209
Quality organization, 35, 43

Radar, 69
Radiation, 69

Radioactivity, 43
Random errors, 97
Random failures, 9
Reconfiguration, 133, 153
Recoverability, 155
Recovery factor, 213
Recovery time, 106
  software, 82
Redundancy, 115, 133, 153, 211
Relative humidity,
  effects, 20, 44
  specifications, 45
  variations, 64
Reliability as seen by the engineer, 7,
   17, 107
Reliability as seen by the user, 7, 18,
   107, 189
Reliability calculations on a
   programmable calculator, 297
Reliability effects,
  age, 1, 13, 182
  architecture, 185
  atmospheric pollution, 20
  availability, 126
  capacity, 196
  complexity, 179
  component selection, 21
  construction, 21, 144
  contamination, 20
  corrosion, 20
  design, 2, 15, 182
  disturbance, 20
  dust, 44, 65
  early failures, 1, 13, 182
  enhancements, 24
  environmental, 2, 21, 58, 62, 179,
   182
  error correction, 151, 192
  failure mode, 6
  fault tolerance features, 8, 151
  heat dissipation, 58
  intermittent faults, 7, 9, 95, 107, 134,
   143, 159, 175
  liquid cooling, 58
  location of modules, 43
  maintainability, 8, 12, 157, 181
  maintenance, 20
  multiple functional units, 28
  new architecture, 32
  new technology, 21, 30, 43, 193
  number of components, 27
  population of systems, 16
  power supplies, 2, 68
  quality, 179, 181, 188

quality control, 15, 21
radiation, 69
radioactivity, 43
relative humidity, 20, 44, 64
serviceability, 126
shock, 20
short term, 84, 129, 157, 210, 223
software on hardware, 82, 87
solid faults, 7, 95, 107, 134, 143
spares, 22, 39, 145
speed of operation, 196
static electricity, 44, 64
switching on and off, 68
temperature, 2, 20, 29, 44, 58, 62,
    179
transient faults, 7, 43, 134
user attitudes, 8, 89, 123, 229
utilization, 2, 5, 18, 24, 28, 69, 182,
    193
utilization, software, 86
vibration, 20
wear out, 1, 20
Reliability index, 27, 58
Reliability of,
  card punches, 96, 198
  card readers, 96, 198
  channels, 30, 191
  communication processors, 30, 187
  computer systems, 97, 216
  core stores, 29, 183, 192
  disks, 95, 98, 194, 198
  drums, 198
  integrated circuits, 5, 27, 58
  line printers, 97, 198
  lines, 229
  magnetic tape units, 95, 100, 195,
      198
  mainframes, 87, 190, 227
  microprocessors, 28, 190
  mini computers, 28, 59, 190
  modems, 232
  multi-processors, 154, 225
  operating systems, 83, 206
  paper tape punches/readers, 96, 198
  peripheral controllers, 30, 190
  peripheral equipment, 5, 198
  populations, 16
  processors, 7, 27, 28, 92, 190, 198
  remote batch terminals, 233
  semi-conductor memories, 29, 43,
      151, 192
  software, 71, 204
  stores, 29, 43, 151, 183, 192
  systems, 97, 216

  terminals, 233
  transaction processing systems, 234
  typewriters, 198
  visual display units, 198
Reliability measurement, 5
Reliability prediction, 2, 179, 189
  software, 5, 204
Reliability specification, 209
Reliability stabilization, 13
Reliability trial, 161
Reliability vs. speed of operation, 180
Remote diagnosis, 156
Remote batch terminal, 233
Repair attempts, 7
Repair of modules, 143
Repair time, 107
Reproduction of faults, 136
Re-run time, 105
Resilience, 133
Resource planning, 7, 156, 159
  software, 75
Response time, 112
  software, 80
Restarting programs, 155
Retry of instructions, 150
Room air conditioning requirements, 45
Room sizes, 54, 61
Running time of test programs, 135

Scheduled maintenance,
    effectiveness, 138
    peripheral equipment, 210
    time, 117
Screened room, 69
Self testers, 141
Semi-conductor memories,
    down time per incident, 192
    error correction, 151, 192
    incident rate, 29, 43, 192
    investigation rate, 184
    investigation time, 189
    maintainability, 144
    modularity, 144
    practical predictions, 192
    testing, 39
    transient faults, 43, 152
    utilization effects, 29
Serial numbers, 43
Serviceability of,
    card readers, 210, 220
    communication sub-systems, 229
    complex systems, 211
    disk units, 210, 220
    dual processors, 225

line printers, 210, 220
lines, 229
magnetic tape units, 210, 220
mainframe systems, 216
message switching systems, 227
mini computers, 216, 227
modems, 232
multiprocessors, 211, 225
operating systems, 218
peripheral equipment, 210, 220
processors, 120, 217
remote batch terminals, 233
software, 81, 218
stores, 217
systems, 124, 216
terminals, 233
time sharing systems, 235
transaction processing systems, 234
typewriters, 210, 220
units in parallel, 211
units in series, 211
visual display units, 210, 235
Serviceability ratio,
    calculation methods, 119, 212
    calculation program, 297
    comparison, 123
    confidence limits, 129
    definition, 119
    effects, of down time distribution, 128
    effects of varying periods of
        measurement, 127
    effects of varying reliability, 126
    engineering, 120
    example of predictions, 216
    minimum configuration, 122
    multiprogramming, 121
    recovery factor, 213
    short term effects, 129
    user observed, 120
    weighting factor, 121, 224
Serviceable time, 119
Shock effects, 20
Shock specifications, 70
Shock testing, 36, 38
Short term effects, 84, 129, 157, 210,
    223
Silver migration, 20
Single bit error correction, 151, 192
Single sourced components, 38
Soft errors, 100
Software,
    acceptance trials, 164
    accepted errors, 76
    assembler faults, 102

backlog, 80
coding errors, 71
commissioning, 160
compiler faults, 102
complexity, 72, 206
correctness, 71
criteria for testing, 79
data corruption, 103
design changes, 72
design qualification, 71
documentation errors, 76
down time, 82, 115, 218
duration of testing, 78
early failures, 85, 206
effectiveness of testing, 79
effects of hardware, 82, 87
error classifications, 72
error rate, 72, 78
error reports per problem, 77
error reports submitted, 74
errors, short term effects, 159
examples of predictions, 208, 218
fault determination, 152
fault diagnosis, 156
fault reporting, 42
fault symptoms, 102
hardware comparison, 71, 87
hardware fault determination, 82, 99
incident rate, 206
investigation time, 82
mean down time per system failure,
    116
mean time between system failures
    87
modifications, 72
new releases, 72, 78, 84, 86
priority of errors, 80
problems identified, 76
problems seen by the user, 74
quality assurance, 71, 78
quality effects, 207
reliability criteria, 90
reliability prediction, 5, 204
reloading time, 155
response time, 80
security breach, 103
serviceability, 81, 212, 218
services contract, 90
size, 206
support planning, 76
symptoms, 102
system down time, 82
system failures, 79, 82, 102, 206
testing, 71, 78, 168

testing criteria, 79
testing duration, 78
testing effectiveness, 79
undetected errors, 103
unserviceability, 81
utilization effects, 86
variations with time, 83, 206
waiting time, 82
wrong results, 103
Solid faults, 7, 95, 107, 134, 143
Spares,
    availability, 22
    costs, 156
    requirements, 145
    storage, 23
    testing, 39
    waiting time, 106, 110
Speed assessment, 305
Speed effects, 196
Spoilt work time, 105, 223
Stabilization, 13
Standby equipment, 115, 211, 225
Static electricity, 44, 64
Statistical analysis, 41
Storage of spares, 23
Store,
    down time per incident, 192
    error correction, 151, 192
    examples of predictions, 200, 217
    incident rate, 192
    investigation rate, 183
    investigation time, 189
    maintainability, 144
    parity checking, 151
    practical predictions, 192
    reconfiguration, 154
    test programs, 136, 241
    testing, 39
    utilization effects, 29
Stress factor, 2
Stuck at type faults, 134
Supervision of acceptance trials, 171
Supplementary maintenance, 117
Support, testing of, 164
Support planning, 7, 156, 159
    software, 76
Switched off air conditioning requirements, 45
Switching on and off, 68
Symptoms, 92
System,
    air conditioning requiremens, 44
    down time, 115
    examples of predictions, 200, 216

failures, 8, 222
failures, software, 79, 82, 87, 102, 206
heat dissipation, 54, 60
incident rate, 222
reliability specification, 209
serviceability calculations, 215
space requirements, 54
testing, 40, 160, 238
undetected errors, 97

Temperature,
    effects, 2, 20, 29, 44, 58, 62, 179
    margins, 149
    periods of excessive, 62
    specifications, 45
    testing, 38
Terminals, 233
Test programs, 134
    compatibility, 141
    control executive, 138
    diagnostic, 135
    exerciser, 136
    functional, 135
    high level language, 238
    interaction, 138
    on-line, 139
    peripheral equipment, 137, 238
    running time, 135, 175
    store, 136
    timing, 140
Testing,
    AC, 38
    acceptance, 160
    criteria, 41, 167, 168, 171, 177
    criteria, software, 79
    DC, 38
    duration, 37, 38, 39, 40
    duration, software, 78
    effectiveness, 35, 72
    effectiveness, software, 79
    effectiveness of support, 164
    environmental, 36
    integrated circuits, 38
    limitations, 6, 160
    microprocessors, 39
    mini computers, 40
    modules, 39
    MOS memories, 39
    new systems, 35
    organization, 35
    organization, software, 79
    peripheral equipment, 40, 170
    pollution, 36

processors, 39, 134, 170
reliability, 36, 161
shock, 36, 38
software, 71, 78
spares, 39
system, 40, 238
temperature, 38
time, 37, 38, 39, 40
time, software, 78
timing, 43
transportation, 36
unit, 39
using high level languages, 238
vibration, 36
Thermal effects, 20, 29, 44, 58, 62, 179
Third party maintenance, 23
Time,
burn-in, 13
commissioning, 19, 160
design stabilization, 17
design stabilization, software, 83
down, 82, 105
down, effects on serviceability, 128
file restoration, 105
investigation, 82, 106, 188, 198
maintenance, 105
modification fitting, 117
operating system down, 106
operational down, 106
preventative maintenance, 117
recovery, 106
reliability stabilization, 13
re-run, 105
response, 112
response, software, 80
scheduled maintenance, 117
serviceable, 119
software investigation, 82
software reloading, 155
software testing, 78
spares waiting, 106, 110
spoilt work, 105, 223
supplementary maintenance, 117
system down, 115
test program running, 135, 141, 175
testing, 37, 38, 39, 40
to repair, 107
up, 81, 119
user observed down, 112
waiting, 82, 106, 147, 191, 199
Timing, testing, 43
Timing margins, 27, 149
Timing test programs, 140
Transaction processing system, 234

Transient failures, 7, 43, 134
Transients, power supplies, 66
Transportation, 41
TTL, 56
Typewriter,
air conditioning requirements, 50
availability, 210
down time per incident, 198
example of predictions, 220
fault symptoms, 102
heat dissipation, 60
incident rate, 198
investigation rate, 198
investigation time, 198
scheduled maintenance time, 118, 210
serviceability, 220
waiting time, 198

Undetected errors, 92, 139
lines, 232
software, 103
Unit testing, 39
Units in parallel, 211
Units in series, 212
Unserviceability, ratio, 81, 132
computer system, 216
software, 82, 87
Up time, 81, 119
User attitudes, 8, 89, 123, 229
User observed down time, 112
User observed reliability, 7, 18, 107, 189
User programs, 165, 238
Utilization effects, 2, 5, 18, 24, 28, 69, 182, 193
software, 86, 206

Variations in reliability, 126
software, 83
Variations with time, 1, 13
Vibration, 20
Vibration specifications, 70
Vibration testing, 36
Visual display units,
air conditioning requirements, 48
availability, 210
down time per incident, 198
example of predictions, 235
incident rate, 198
investigation rate, 198
investigation time, 198
scheduled maintenance time, 118, 210

serviceability, 235
waiting time, 198
Voltage margins, 149
Voltage specifications, 66

Waiting time, 82, 106, 147, 191, 199
software, 82
Warranty, 160

Wear out, 1, 20
Weighting factors, 121, 224
Wire changes, 34
Worst case patterns, 29
Wrong results, 92, 139

Yield, integrated circuits, 38
Yield, modules, 39